My Unexpected Journey

THE AUTOBIOGRAPHY OF
GOVERNOR HARRY ROE HUGHES

To Melanie

Harry Hughes

Governor Harry Roe Hughes
with John W. Frece

Charleston   London

History
PRESS

Published by The History Press
Charleston, SC 29403
www.historypress.net

Cover Image: Courtesy of the Baltimore Sun.
Inside flap and frontispiece: Portrait of Governor Highes painted by Cedric B. Egeli that hangs
in the governor's living room in Denton. *Photo by Charles Planner.*

First published 2006

Manufactured in the United Kingdom

ISBN 1.59629.117.6

Library of Congress Cataloging-in-Publication Data

Hughes, Harry Roe, 1926-
  My unexpected journey : the autobiography of Governor Harry Roe Hughes /
Harry Roe Hughes with John W. Frece.
  p. cm.
  Includes index.
  ISBN 1-59629-117-6 (alk. paper)
  1. Hughes, Harry Roe, 1926- 2. Governors--Maryland--Biography. 3.
Legislators--Maryland--Biography. 4. Maryland. General Assembly--Biography.
5. Maryland. Dept. of Transportation--Officials and employees--Biography.
6. Maryland--Politics and government--1951- I. Frece, John W. II. Title.
  F186.35.H84A3 2006
  975.2'043092--dc22
  [B]
                            2006016763

Notice: The information in this book is true and complete to the best of our knowledge. It is
offered without guarantee on the part of the author or The History Press. The author and
The History Press disclaim all liability in connection with the use of this book.

To my grandson, Andrew.

Contents

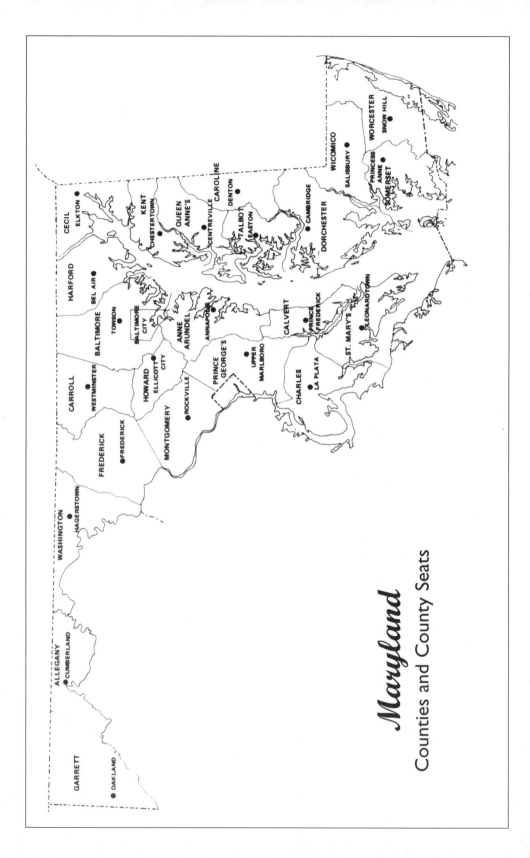

Maryland
Counties and County Seats

Acknowledgements

T HIS BOOK WOULD NOT HAVE been possible without the sustained and generous support of the Maryland State Archives and the personal support of both State Archivist Dr. Edward C. Papenfuse and Christopher N. Allan, Dr. Papenfuse's former deputy who now heads the Friends of the Maryland State Archives. Governor Hughes and I are indebted to both.

Nor would this project have happened without the steady help of Paul McCardell, librarian at the *Baltimore Sun*, who for nearly two years rummaged through old boxes of newspaper clips and reels of microfilm, searching for details about projects, programs, budgets, disputes, elections and various tales of political intrigue, some going back seventy years. Paul also helped harvest a huge array of photographs from the *Baltimore Sun* library for our selection, a number of which the *Sun*'s Jeff Bill helpfully compiled and scanned. The generous support for this project by the *Baltimore Sun* was made possible by my friend and former colleague, Sandra A. Banisky, now the newspaper's deputy managing editor.

Many others also contributed their time and attention to this project, for which we are most thankful. They include Rob Schoeberlein and Chris Kintzel at the Maryland State Archives, who helped search for and scan photographs and other images. They could have complained, but didn't.

A number of friends and former colleagues of Governor Hughes read, edited, commented upon the draft manuscript and generally helped recall some of the stories from their years of public service. Among them were Constance R. Beims, Verna Harrison Pelrine, John F.X. O'Brien, John R. Griffin, Michael F. Canning, Gerald Winegrad, Dr. Chuan Sheng Liu and Joseph M. Coale III. The chapter entitled "Lost Ball in High Grass" would not have been nearly as detailed were it not for Joe Coale's personal history and vivid memory of the 1978 campaign and election. Joe also supplied a number of the photographs and other images, including Mike Lane's terrific cartoons, which are part of Joe's private collection.

The governor and I are both indebted to U.S. Senator Paul Sarbanes for his kind introduction to the book and for the supporting work of his assistant, Judith Keenan.

Thanks also to my wife, Priscilla Cummings, an accomplished author in her own right who knows full well how much time it takes to complete a book. She and our children, William and Hannah, never—well, rarely!—complained when I would bury myself in tattered newspaper clips and old copies of the *Maryland Manual* while at the computer in our basement or spend many long weekends away from home meeting with Governor Hughes. This just proves once again that you can never do projects like this alone.

Finally, my lasting appreciation to Governor Hughes for giving me the opportunity to help share his story—the story of a life of honesty, integrity and lasting accomplishment—with what I hope will be generations of Marylanders to come.

John W. Frece
Annapolis, Maryland
May 1, 2006

Introduction

TOWARD THE END OF THIS extraordinary account of his lifetime in public
service, Governor Hughes sums it up as "a workmanlike career." This is,
in my view, a masterpiece of understatement. I have known Harry Hughes for
more than forty years. Early in our careers we served together in Maryland's
legislature, the General Assembly. Later, when Harry was Maryland's governor
and I was the state's junior U.S. senator, we had the opportunity to put our
combined efforts to work for our state and its people.

Whatever the substance of the issue at hand, Harry's approach was invariably
fair-minded and deliberative—qualities that have regrettably become all too rare in
our public discourse. He sought results, not credit or glory. He had a deep respect
for the delicate balance among institutions that democratic governance under our
Constitution requires. This did not change when he moved from the legislature
to an executive agency or on to the governor's mansion. As governor, Harry
considered the legislature to be a partner in working through policy matters, not an
adversary. This approach was a major factor in his success. Many of the reforms he
introduced remain bedrock policy today.

To appreciate fully the magnitude of Harry's accomplishments, it helps to have some
understanding of Maryland, where he was born, raised and lives to this day. Its people,
geography and history give the state its unique character. Maryland's topography is
extraordinarily variegated—hence the phrase, "America in miniature." East to west,
Maryland extends more than 325 miles, from the beaches of the Atlantic to the mountains
of Appalachia. Forty-second in area, Maryland ranks nineteenth in population, fifth in
population density and is home to about 5.6 million people. Numbers alone, however,
cannot reflect the diversity of the population. Many Maryland communities trace
their history back more than 350 years; at the same time Maryland has welcomed
generations of immigrants, each generation in turn welcoming the next.

The Eastern Shore has a culture and tradition all its own, since until the opening
of the Chesapeake Bay Bridge some fifty years ago, the Shore was cut off from the
rest of the state, accessible only by ferry across the Bay. The Bay, one of the nation's
richest and most magnificent natural resources, dominates the topography of the
state, reaching in some fashion into virtually every corner of the state.

In this regard it is of some interest that Harry Hughes and I both come from
small towns on the Eastern Shore. Harry grew up in Denton, in Caroline County,
where his family had a long history; one of his great-grandfathers had been a
member of the state Senate. I grew up in Salisbury, in Wicomico County, barely
forty miles away. My parents were newcomers to the community, who came as
immigrants from Greece and made Salisbury their home.

Harry grew up with dreams of playing professional baseball, and got as far as playing on semi-pro and even minor league teams. Only in law school did he conclude that he had reached the end of his baseball career, and for this telling reason:

> I had begun to get disillusioned by the way some of the young professional players played. There was very little teamwork—many were just out for themselves, out for self-advancement. I saw guys intentionally fail to catch fly balls because they were afraid of being charged with an error, or guys trying to get walks rather than swinging away because they were trying to protect their batting average. It just didn't appeal to me. As much as I loved to play, I just didn't want to play that way.

Harry was a team player who always believed in doing his best. When he left baseball he applied these principles to public service. He resisted the quick fix, instead seeking durable, systemic solutions that addressed the problems at hand. Harry's steady approach to public policy was a great asset in a period of social, economic and political transformation, and it equipped him to play a major role in guiding and shaping that transformation.

When Harry was elected to the House of Delegates in 1954, politics on the Eastern Shore were informal and personal, mostly a matter, as he says, of "getting into the car and driving up farm driveways and introducing myself and asking for their vote." His early mastery of the legislative process made him effective as a legislator from the very beginning and contributed significantly to what he was later able to accomplish as Maryland's secretary of transportation and then governor.

Born and raised in a segregated society, he met the civil rights issue head-on. When after years of failed attempts to desegregate public accommodations a bill was at last brought to a vote, Harry supported it for the most fundamental of all reasons: "It just seemed like the right thing to do. It was that simple."

It was typical of Harry that when he was asked to address the contentious question of teachers' salaries, he placed the issue in the broader context of funding for public education and developed a plan to overhaul Maryland's outdated system, thereby transforming "the public perception of education funding." Later, as chairman of the Senate Finance Committee and majority floor leader, Harry took on the daunting challenge of reforming Maryland's outdated and regressive tax system, a framework that remains in place today.

When Maryland's splintered system of government agencies was reorganized into a more coherent and efficient structure, it was Harry who led the effort in the General Assembly to establish a state Department of Transportation with a consolidated funding mechanism, the Transportation Trust Fund. In seven years he built the new department from the ground up, then proceeded to develop a comprehensive statewide, multi-mode transportation plan. Harry changed the way Marylanders thought about transportation, and more than earned the tribute the *Baltimore Sun* paid him when he ran for governor: "He took disparate agencies jealous of the autonomy they were losing and welded them into a department devoted to producing a balanced transportation system. He worked diligently to achieve that balance, watching out for the port, the city subway, Western Maryland roads and Eastern Shore railroads."

During Harry's eight years as Maryland's chief executive, we worked regularly together on the whole range of issues of concern to our state. Our joint efforts gave me an opportunity to observe at close range the qualities that I had always admired in him. He showed a deep respect for, and understanding of, the interplay of the executive and legislative branches in our system of democratic governance; it is on just this interplay that the proper functioning of our system depends. He carried out his responsibilities with an abiding integrity, decency and commitment to the public interest, which made it a privilege to have the opportunity to work with him.

Of Harry's accomplishments as governor, I would have to say that his resolute commitment to restore the Chesapeake Bay would be at the top of the list. Earlier than most he saw the need for a comprehensive and systemic approach, and he responded with a series of mutually reinforcing programs: to identify and address the numerous sources of pollution, to promote restoration of the Bay's traditional resources, to support public education and awareness (a key to long-term success) and to assure continuing monitoring and research. Interstate and federal-state cooperation were also essential, for although the main part of the Bay lies within Maryland's borders, the watershed extends far beyond them. The Chesapeake Executive Council, which was established as the formal framework for cooperation, functions today much as Harry first envisaged it. His determined and ambitious efforts to save the Bay's rockfish population proved successful, although initially it met strong opposition. In describing his efforts to save the rockfish toward the end of this wonderfully open account of his life in public service, Harry observes, "It takes years to see if your actions have had any effect."

That standard, which Harry Hughes applied to his efforts to save the rockfish, applies as well to his years in public office. As time has passed, we have experienced the positive effects of his actions. He changed fundamentally our perceptions of funding public education. He changed our approach to taxation, discarding antiquated and regressive practices and placing the tax system on a firmer and fairer foundation. He changed our thinking about transportation, bringing the different modes of transportation into a coherent package. He set high standards of integrity, commitment and discerning judgment to guide and inspire future generations of public servants. Governor Hughes's accomplishments have stood the test of time, and Maryland is much the better place for them.

U.S. Senator Paul S. Sarbanes
Washington, D.C.

Growing Up On the Shore

U NLIKE MOST KIDS, I KNEW from an early age exactly what I wanted to be when I grew up: a professional baseball player.

The first birthday gift I can remember receiving from my father, Jonathan Longfellow Hughes, was a baseball glove. That was in about 1932. I was a six-year-old boy growing up in the sleepy town of Denton, about halfway between the Chesapeake Bay and the Atlantic Ocean on Maryland's flat and then quite isolated Eastern Shore. Although it was the worst year of the Great Depression, my family was relatively comfortable, though not well-to-do.

My mother, Helen Roe Hughes, was a popular French and English teacher at Caroline High School, which was located just across the street behind our house. One of my grandfathers, Henry White Hughes, owned a lumber and coal company. My other grandfather, Harry A. Roe, ran a cannery.

My passion was baseball and by the time I was thirteen, I was playing my first organized ball for Caroline High School—a prelude to the university, semi-pro and professional teams I would play on as an older teenager and young man. I pitched and played the outfield. My desire was to be a big league player.

The other, subtler influence around my house was politics. My mother was not interested in politics and, as a youngster, neither was I. But my father was a dyed-in-the-wool Democrat. He was a big supporter of the local congressman, T. Alan Goldsborough, a Democrat who owned a big clapboard house on the town square in Denton and backed the New Deal programs of the country's new president, Franklin Delano Roosevelt.

Maybe the biggest thing that ever happened in Denton, at least during my childhood, was a visit by President Roosevelt on Labor Day 1938. As a twelve-year-old Boy Scout in uniform, I was stationed near the stage where the president spoke to a huge crowd gathered in front of the Caroline County Courthouse. Roosevelt had come to Denton to promote the candidacy of elderly Davy Lewis in the state's Democratic Primary against incumbent Maryland Senator Millard Tydings. Tydings had had the temerity to oppose the president's effort to pack the U.S. Supreme Court, so the president came to Denton to try to defeat him.

Before Roosevelt arrived, the Secret Service wanted to check out the building in back of the stage where the president would speak. It was called the Law Building and was owned by the Masonic Lodge. The Masons had left the key with J. Roland Chaffinch, who was president of the Denton National Bank and a strong

Republican. When the Secret Service approached Mr. Chaffinch and asked if for security purposes he would take them through the Law Building, he reached into his drawer and took out the keys and said, "Here. Here are the keys. You go look for yourself. I don't care if they shoot the sonuvabitch!"

Most of the Eastern Shore, however, was Democratic, so the president got a warm reception in Denton that day. Following his speech, the president was driven around to the other side of the courthouse green to have lunch at Congressman Goldsborough's house. Across a small yard on that side of the house was the county jail, which the Secret Service had somehow overlooked. All during the lunch, agents nervously paced back and forth on the porch in front of the wide window that exposed the president's back while he was seated at lunch.

Many years later, the Goldsborough house was converted to commercial use and became the offices of Everngam and Hughes, my first law practice. My chair and desk were right where Roosevelt sat when he had lunch that day. To make the most of our location between the county jail and the Episcopal Church, we had stationery printed up that described our office as: "Between Heaven and Hell on the Courthouse Green." As you might expect, it was a letterhead we used only with certain clients.

Next to the platform where the president spoke that day was a little building to the right of the Law Building, which was the office of a local lawyer named Bill Rickards. Rickards was a big Tydings supporter. So, before the president arrived, he had the biggest Tydings banner you can imagine stretched across the entire front of that little building. When they showed the president speaking in Denton on the *Movietone News*, which I used to see at the movie theaters before the main feature came on, you could see the Tydings banner just to the side of the president. The speech from little Denton, Maryland, was broadcast on radio to the rest of the nation. Despite the president's efforts, Senator Tydings was reelected and went on to represent Maryland in the U.S. Senate until 1951.

My grandfather Roe was also in politics, but he was from the other side of the aisle. While the Hughes side of my family was staunchly Democratic, the Roes were Republicans. My great-grandfather, Andrew B. Roe, had represented Caroline County as a Republican in the state Senate (from 1882 to 1886), and my Grandfather Roe later did the same (from 1902 to 1906). Unlike many career politicians today, my grandfather's interest in politics was only part-time. He might not have gotten into politics at all if the Republican candidate for the state Senate had not died shortly before an election and the local party leaders asked him to take the deceased candidate's place. He agreed to do it and won, but served only one term. In 1912, about six years after voluntarily leaving the legislature, Maryland Governor Phillips Lee Goldsborough, a Republican, appointed my grandfather as the state's second motor vehicle commissioner and then reappointed him for another two-year term in 1914. I suspect there probably weren't more than one hundred cars in the state at that time. Grandfather Roe was a fine gentleman and well respected by the entire community.

While I wasn't very interested in politics at that young age, I do recall a political argument I had with my Grandfather Roe. It was over Hoover versus Roosevelt. I was six and I was for Roosevelt. I have to say: my political views have been fairly consistent ever since.

Home Life

My mother was the central person in my life. She was a very nice and kind person and considered by many to be one of the school's best teachers. She also was extremely conscientious. I can still see her working late almost every night marking papers. And she was sensitive. If people had problems, she would empathize and be concerned about them. She frequently tutored or helped struggling schoolchildren in our home in the evenings, on weekends and in the summer. For most of this extra work, she neither asked for nor received any compensation.

Denton was such a small community that there was no avoiding your mother if she was a teacher at your school. My mother taught me English and was my homeroom teacher for four years. I am, of course, biased, but I would have to put her down as one of the best teachers I had. Mother tended to lean over backwards to show there was no favoritism. I didn't suffer because of that. She just wanted to make sure I was treated just like everybody else.

My father was entirely different. He wasn't very responsible. I guess he was quite a sport in his younger days and was somewhat spoiled by his parents. Mother went to the Baldwin School in Philadelphia and later to Goucher College in Baltimore, but my father never finished college. Through the efforts of Congressman Goldsborough, he got a job with Congress in Washington, which meant he came home only on weekends. My mother was the breadwinner. It was tough on her, but she managed. After she finished at Goucher, she did what I suppose was one of the most honorable things a woman in those days could do for work, which was to teach. The one thing she paid attention to was how you spoke. She corrected my English all the time.

I have one brother, Jonathan L. Hughes Jr., who is three years older and now lives in California. Buddy (as we all called him) and I got along fine growing up, but we were different. He smoked and I didn't; he drank a little and I didn't touch alcohol. He was just more daring than I was. He didn't go to college, and I always knew I was going to go to college.

Soon after high school, Buddy went to work for the DuPont Company's nylon manufacturing plant in Seaford, Delaware, and then enlisted in the navy early in World War II. After the war, he spent years as chief mechanic and copilot on Pepsi-Cola's executive aircraft.

Denton

Our family lived in a white clapboard house across the street from Grandfather Roe's house at the corner of Franklin and Third Street in Denton. My grandfather owned both houses, and we lived in the smaller of the two until he died in 1934. We then moved into the larger house with my grandmother, Sally Roe, whom we all called Nana.

It was a nice house: two stories plus a completed attic and a big porch around two sides. It had a big entry hall of dark wood, a parlor that was hardly ever used, a living room, dining room and big kitchen. Connected to the house were a row of buildings, a "summer kitchen," a coal bin and a shed. It was probably built around 1900 and I always heard it was the first house in town to have an inside bathroom. Out back was a barn we used as a garage for automobiles, but which had originally been built for horses and carriages. There was also a dirt floor chicken house, which after we quit raising chickens became my clubhouse. We also had a pretty big garden. Just beyond the backyard and across an unpaved street was the schoolyard for Caroline High School. It was so close that I can still remember waiting until the last minute to leave for school, running out of the house and jumping the fence to get to class just on time.

Denton in those days was small and quiet. The population was about sixteen hundred when I was growing up.[1] It was the county seat, so the courthouse was there and most of the county government offices. There were no big supermarkets in Denton back then, of course. There was a two-block area on Main Street that had two clothing stores for both men and women, three small grocery stores, a couple of banks, a drugstore, a tea room and a soda fountain on the corner near the courthouse where I started working at the age of twelve.

There was no hospital in Denton or in Caroline County, so both my brother and I were born in Memorial Hospital in Easton in neighboring Talbot County, Buddy on August 7, 1923, and I on November 13, 1926.

Some of the people who lived in Denton in those days owned farms, yet lived in town. Houses were not as spread out as they are today. Others who lived in town included insurance agents, storeowners and clerks, teachers, county and courthouse employees, lawyers, a couple of doctors, a dentist or two, filling station operators and mechanics. Some of the streets were paved, but many were not.

Tomatoes were a major crop around Denton and there were probably as many as sixteen canneries in Caroline County. Today, there are none. Local farmers also grew peas, beans, strawberries, cantaloupes and a lot of wheat and corn.

The Depression was hard on people in the area. Years later, after I became a lawyer, I could see from doing title searches that many Caroline County farmers lost their land during the Depression. Those hard times affected both of my grandfathers.

My grandfather Hughes had started off in life trading horses in Delaware, but later moved to a little community outside of Denton called Hobbs where he owned and

---

1. *Maryland Manual*, 1930.

operated a farm and opened a small country store. Then he started a lumberyard that became the Hughes Lumber and Coal Co. During the worst years of the Depression, however, he was forced to sell the lumber part of the business to a pair of brothers named Fred and Frank Nuttle. The Nuttle Lumber Co. is still in business today under that name. My grandfather kept the coal business and operated it until he was ninety-two years old with the help of his only employee, Mr. Trice, who was about eighty-seven and still delivered the coal by horse and wagon.

My grandfather Roe had been in the cannery business, but had gotten out. After World War I, however, his brother, Fred, who did very well with a tomato cannery in nearby Greensboro, convinced my grandfather to go back into the business. That was a mistake. After the war was over, the government released all the surplus canned goods and the market for new canned goods fell. My grandfather had already made contracts with farmers to pay them a certain amount per basket of tomatoes. He was an extremely honorable man, so even after the market was flooded with canned goods and prices fell, he stuck by his contracts. But it cost him dearly.

Grandfather Roe was a strong Methodist and refused to drink alcoholic beverages. But he loved to fish and hunt. To my grandmother's dismay, he frequently fished a pond down Tuckahoe Neck owned by a very well-known bootlegger.

I grew up listening to the radio. Almost every night after dinner, we would listen to the news from Lowell Thomas or Gabrielle Heater. I can recall Heater opening his show by saying, "Ah, there's good news tonight!" We also would listen to serials on the radio, like *The Shadow*, cowboys like *Tom Mix* and *The Lone Ranger*, and comedians like Fred Allen, Eddie Cantor and Burns and Allen.

My childhood friends were all boys and we used to play pick-up games: baseball, football, touch football and we used to ride bicycles all around. In the winter, sledding was a big deal because you could sled right down Main Street in Denton, down what we called Denton Hill, and sometimes all the way to the Choptank River Bridge. We would also sled down by the jail, to the back of the jail and down the hill onto the ice on the Choptank River.

Some of my friends hunted, but I rarely did. I went squirrel hunting once, but didn't like it. First, you had to get up too early. And then you just sat there and waited for some squirrel to appear up in the tree. And I didn't particularly like shooting them.

I went rabbit hunting once with an older farmer friend and never went again. Rabbits double-back. We were out in the woods in the Tuckahoe Neck area. The dogs jumped a rabbit and you could hear them going through the woods. My friend George said, "You stay here and I'll go the other way," because he said the rabbit would double-back to where we were standing. I could hear the dogs coming closer and I stayed perfectly still. This rabbit came up to me just a couple feet away and just sat. I couldn't shoot him. I said, "Move! Move rabbit!" He ran off and I shot and missed him. So, we were leaving the woods and out of the corner of my eye I saw something in a hole in the tree stump and I fired. I guess it was that same rabbit and I killed it. I felt so awful I never went again.

One friend from my childhood was a boy named Sherman W. Tribbitt, who was four years older than I and lived about a block away on Franklin Street. Sherman was quite an athlete who played a lot of soccer and baseball for Caroline High and town teams.

But what was most interesting about Sherman was not his childhood, but the parallel paths our lives took in later years. After he grew up, Sherman left Denton and moved to Delaware, where he became a businessman. Two years after I was elected to the Maryland House of Delegates, Sherman was elected to the Delaware House of Representatives. Sherman went on to become Speaker of the House, lieutenant governor and, in 1972, governor of Delaware—six years before I became governor of Maryland.

I can say without reservation that as boys growing up in rural Denton, Maryland, neither one of us would have predicted that either of us would eventually become a governor, much less both of us.

In a 1988 "oral history"[2] about his life, Tribbitt recalled his favorite teacher while growing up in Denton: "Now, I always liked Mrs. Helen Hughes," he wrote. "She was the nicest lady. She taught English. I thought as much of Mrs. Hughes as I did anybody else. I'm not saying that other teachers were not also great instructors, but Mrs. Hughes stuck out in my mind."

School

There were two schools in town: Denton Primary School, which my mother had also attended years before, and Caroline High School. In those days, you only went to the primary school for three years and then moved to the high school building. All public schools in Maryland at that time stopped after the eleventh grade.

In first grade, I had a nice teacher named Mrs. Brooks, but after a few weeks they switched classes around and put me in Mrs. Morgan's class. She was so tough she was known as "Iron Pants." I can remember the first year I was in school my friend Jimmy Merriken and I were talking out of turn and Mrs. Morgan came over and slapped us both in the face. I mean, she was tough.

In about 1927 or so, my Grandfather Roe donated the land that became Caroline High School. Denton Primary School is still standing, but no longer used as a school. Old Caroline High, where my mother taught for thirty or forty years, is gone. Shortly after I became governor in 1979, someone on my staff said to me, "Did you know they're tearing down your old high school?" And they did, replacing it with a district court and government multi-service center. Toward the

2. Roger Martin, Sherman W. Tribbitt, (Delaware Heritage Commission, Oral History Series, no. 2, 1998), 12.

end of my tenure as governor, Earl Seboda, then my secretary of general services, suggested the new multi-service center be named after me, but I felt that would be inappropriate while I was still serving in office.

I guess I missed my chance because the building was subsequently named after my friend John R. Hargreaves, a Caroline County businessman and legislator who rose to become the influential chairman of the House Appropriations Committee.

Ferries and Dirt Roads

Caroline County is the only landlocked county on the Eastern Shore. It borders Delaware to the east. The biggest city in the other direction is Baltimore, northwest of Caroline County and all the way across the Chesapeake Bay. It is hard to overstate how rural, quiet and isolated the Eastern Shore was in those days. To get to Baltimore from Denton in the 1930s, you either had to take one of the slow ferries across the Chesapeake or you had to drive north and loop around the top of the Bay. That is the way we would go most of the time, driving north up into Cecil County and around the top of the Bay and then south to Baltimore. Most of the state roads in those days were paved, but if you got off onto a side road maintained by the county, it was likely to be dirt. It took at least two-and-a-half hours to drive from Denton to Baltimore, but you would save having to pay a couple dollars or so for a ferry that would only shorten the trip by about an hour.

Some roads, particularly over in Delaware, had only one lane that was paved—what we used to call "nine-foot roads." They were done this way as a means for the state or county to save money on road construction. The road from Denton to Bridgeville, Delaware, was that way. As a kid, we used to drive to Bridgeville to the movies on Sunday nights. We had a theater in Denton, but it was closed because of Sunday blue laws in Maryland, so the only way to see a movie on Sunday nights was to drive to Bridgeville. But if you were riding on the paved side and that was on the left side of the road, you had to get off onto the dirt side if you met a car coming the other direction.

This was about two decades before the first Chesapeake Bay Bridge was built near Annapolis. Until then, the only way across the bay was by ferry. There were at least three different ferries from the middle Shore. One went from Claiborne down in Talbot County across Eastern Bay to Romancoke on the southern part of Kent Island. From there, you would drive to Matapeake and take a second ferry four miles across the Bay and right into a dock in Annapolis by the Naval Academy. (Years later, the terminus was moved to Sandy Point State Park, next to where the Chesapeake Bay Bridges now meet the Bay's western shore.)

The third and longest ferry—called *Smokey Joe*—went from Love Point, which is the northern tip of Kent Island, across the Bay to Baltimore. The trip took a couple of hours. Once passengers coming to the Shore from Baltimore arrived at Love Point, they could take a train through Denton and all the way to Ocean

City. I can remember hearing stories about how people on that train would stop in Denton, go to the Double Dip ice cream store and get a huge, double-dip cone for five cents. The Double Dip continued in business long after the train service was discontinued.

Townsend's

The first paying job I can remember is cutting lawns for neighbors with my friend, Bill Greenly, who was a year behind me in school. After all these years, Bill is still a very good friend. He and I used to cut the grass for a man named Mr. Willy on Saturdays and we got paid thirty cents for the job, so we made fifteen cents each. But that was enough to get us into the movies Saturday night to see the serial plus the double feature.

When I was about twelve, I started working at Townsend's, which over the years has had different names, most recently The Corner Restaurant and later the Market Street Cafe. It was right on the corner of Main Street, catty-corner from the courthouse and owned by a man named Everett Townsend. I worked from seven o'clock until eleven two or three nights a week for seventy-five cents a night. By the time I was in eleventh grade, I was up to one dollar and twenty-five cents a night. I did everything: I waited on tables, I made sandwiches (hot dogs, grilled cheese, grilled ham and cheese, grilled tuna fish), I made soda fountain Cokes, chocolate sundaes and milk shakes. A grilled cheese was ten cents. A grilled ham and cheese was fifteen.

I even made Bromo Seltzer with soda water for people with headaches. There were a couple of older men who would come into Townsend's and as soon as I saw them coming in the door, I'd start making them a Bromo Seltzer. Sometimes, they would ask me to put a shot of ammonia in their Bromo.

You had to chip ice for the Cokes from a hand-operated ice machine. I washed dishes and I swept the floor every night before leaving. Several of my friends, including Bill Greenly, also worked there.

World War II started about the time I entered high school. During those summers, from about 1941 through 1943, I worked at both a sawmill and cannery owned by a well-known local farmer named Harry Nuttle. The cannery didn't operate everyday. He only canned tomatoes and even during the height of tomato season, the cannery often operated only three days a week. He would open it up when he had enough tomatoes to run for a full day. The sawmill was close by, so if the cannery wasn't open, I'd often work in the sawmill.

My job at the sawmill was called "off bearing." There was just one big saw and Mr. Nuttle would feed the log in. As the log ran through, it would cut off a slab that you would have to take somewhere and stack. Some were heavier than others, but they were all long and unwieldy. That was really tough work, particularly on a hot day.

At the cannery, I did everything. When a farmer would come in with a truckload of tomatoes, I'd take the baskets off and stack them under the shed of the cannery. Or I would stack cases of canned tomatoes at the other end of the cannery. That's pretty heavy, hot work. Some days, I'd drive a truck out and get some farmer's tomatoes or haul the rotten tomatoes off and deposit them in a field somewhere. So, I did everything but pick 'em.

Mr. Nuttle had two other men who worked for him; one was a black fellow named Slim Baynard and the other was a white guy named Woody Lord. Every now and then, Mr. Nuttle would ask Slim and me to drive his two old International trucks up to Sudlersville to pick up logs to bring back to the sawmill.

Slim would drive one truck and I'd drive the other one and we'd race back to the sawmill. I was about sixteen at the time and had just gotten my driver's license. We were racing back one day and I decided to take a shortcut and get ahead of him around Marydel. I was really pushing that truck hard when, all of a sudden, she got hot and stopped and wouldn't move. I had to get somebody to come pull the truck back to the sawmill.

To his credit, Mr. Nuttle was very nice about it. I told him the truck just overheated. I didn't mention the racing part.

In my last year at the cannery, I opened a little lunch counter. I'd buy buns and cookies and other food and beverages and resell them. I sold those big buns for a nickel and the guys at the cannery loved them. I sold Nehi soft drinks and R.C. Colas, also for a nickel. Ham and cheese sandwiches were ten cents. There was a local soft drink bottler over in Ridgley called Marvel and a lot of people drank Marvels: orange, grape, chocolate.

Mr. Nuttle was a fine man. He was on the Board of Regents at the University of Maryland for many, many years. At one time, he was head of the Farm Bureau of Maryland and at that time the Board of Regents had a seat reserved for a Farm Bureau representative. He would come home from a meeting in Baltimore, put his old clothes on and go to the cannery and work. In no time, he'd be dirty and have tomato juice all over him.

2

Baseball, War and More Baseball

I WAS JUST A THIRTEEN-YEAR-OLD FRESHMAN when I started playing organized ball, pitching and playing the outfield for Caroline High School. By fifteen, I was the youngest guy playing for the Denton town team, but events overseas would interfere with my baseball career.

By the summer of 1943, when I graduated from high school, America was engulfed in war in both Europe and the Pacific. D-Day was still a year away, although we didn't know that, of course, so there was no telling how long the war might last. I decided the best way I could help out was to get into the U.S. Naval Academy.

In those days, high school in Caroline County only went through the eleventh grade. To have any chance of getting into the Naval Academy, I needed a twelfth year of high school. Even though my mother could barely afford it, she enrolled me in a private prep school in Pennsylvania called Mercersburg Academy, where I received a partial scholarship because she was a teacher. Meanwhile, my father and others in our family made efforts to get me an appointment to the Academy, but the process turned out to be more political than I expected.

The way it worked was that the State Democratic Central Committee made recommendations to the local congressman about who should be appointed. I visited with each member of the Central Committee that fall. But about the time I was midway into my first semester at Mercersburg, I learned that Jack Everngam, a friend who had gone through school with me, had received the appointment. Jack's parents clearly had more clout than mine. Had Congressman Goldsborough still been in office, my father might have had some influence and it might have turned out differently. But, just like that, my plans to go to the Naval Academy disappeared.

That November, I turned seventeen. Aware that the Naval Academy was no longer an option, I left Mercersburg and headed down to the Richmond Market Street Armory in Baltimore and took the test for the Naval Air Corps. I can still see the billboard in front of the Post Office: "Fly Off a Carrier in 15 Months." Only two of us took the test that day and the other guy's name was also Hughes. I didn't know him from Adam. I passed the test, but he flunked, and I always wondered if they got the results mixed up.

It was not a hard decision to join the navy. I knew my parents didn't have the money to afford to keep me at Mercersburg and with the country deep in the war, it seemed like the patriotic thing to do.

My actual induction date was set for March 1944, so while I was waiting I returned home to Denton, where I made some spending money playing trumpet in a local dance band. I had learned the trumpet while playing in the high school orchestra. I could read music, although not like a real professional. There was a teacher from Denton named Irving Smith—we called him "Pop" Smith—and he taught music and had a dance band that mostly played swing music. His wife played the piano. I took one lesson from Pop Smith, but don't think I learned that much. We would play two or three nights a week in dives and local dance halls. I made eight dollars a night, which was the most money I had ever made for a single day's (or night's) work.

When I finally entered the navy's V-12 officer training program, I was sent to Mount St. Mary's College in Emmitsburg, Maryland, about twenty minutes from Gettysburg, Pennsylvania. Many of the kids joining the military at that time were like me, right out of high school. The idea was to send us off to Mount St. Mary's for about four months of training to give us an opportunity to mature a little bit and get attuned to military life. As it turned out, we ended up staying there a full year rather than four months. Two reasons were given: One was that the navy had not lost as many pilots as had been anticipated. The other, which was probably the real reason, was that someone had made a clerical error in Washington.

While I was there, I continued my baseball career, pitching the 1944 season for the Mount St. Mary's team. By the end of that year, it became clear that the war was going our way and would probably be over within a year or two. As a result, the navy gave all of us aptitude tests to see what, if anything, we might want to do in the navy other than be a pilot. Our counterparts in the Army Air Corps were not so lucky. The army just washed out their flight-training program and shipped them to Europe. Many of those eighteen-year-old kids got caught in the Battle of the Bulge with only a few weeks training and paid an awful price.

When we finally finished at Mount St. Mary's in the spring of 1945, we were shipped down to the Patuxent Naval Air Station in southern Maryland. We were called "tarmacs" and I think I know why: tarmac is the part of the airstrip that everything runs over. We did everything, including washing down the planes.

Next it was off to the University of North Carolina (UNC) in Chapel Hill for pre-flight training. We did a lot of hard physical training in pre-flight school, but they had worked us pretty hard at Mount St. Mary's as well. Instructors at the Mount used to run us three miles through the snow and up and down the sides of mountains until our knees burned. At pre-flight school, we had classes in navigation and identification of aircraft and ships and things like that, but then we had two hours of wrestling or rope climbing or swimming and then we had two more hours of competitive sports.

A lot of our navy coaches had been professional players or coaches before the war. "Weenie" Wilson, a navy chief specialist and one-time Green Bay Packer, was a physical fitness instructor at Mount St. Mary's when I was there. One of the football coaches at flight school in North Carolina was Paul "Bear" Bryant, who went on to become a sports legend by leading the University of Alabama to six national championships, twenty-five winning seasons and twenty-four bowl games.

The food at pre-flight school was unbelievable: good and plentiful. They said we got about five thousand calories a day and they had German POWs waiting on us.

The plan was that after pre-flight school, they would send us to Memphis for flight basic training and then on to Pensacola, Florida, for advanced training. But the war ended before we could get out of North Carolina. On May 7, 1945, less than a month after President Roosevelt died, Germany surrendered. By the middle of August, Japan also surrendered. World War II was over. There was a big victory celebration at UNC and afterwards I can remember there was toilet paper hanging from just about every tree on campus.

After the war ended, the navy gave each of us a choice: we could stay in for four more years and go on to earn our wings, or we could go on inactive duty. That was a no-brainer for me. I had found that I didn't like navy life.

University of Maryland

I headed home to Denton and applied for admission to the University of Maryland. I was too late for the fall semester, but was admitted in January 1946 as a sophomore with a year's credit for my time at Mount St. Mary's.

I still find it interesting—though not particularly surprising—that the University was unable to admit me until the winter semester, but somehow managed to push through the paperwork to bring Bear Bryant and his entire navy pre-flight school football team to Maryland in time to begin the 1945 fall semester. Bryant's small but quick team went 6-2-1 that season, but it turned out to be his one and only year at Maryland. A tough disciplinarian, Bryant suspended one of his players for breaking training rules, but the college president reinstated him without consulting Bryant. Infuriated, Bryant left, moving on in a college coaching career that would take him to Kentucky, Texas A&M and, finally, back to his alma mater, Alabama.

At Maryland, I worked on a degree in business and public administration. A career in baseball, however, was still my dream. I was a pretty good pitcher. I had a good fastball, good control and a pretty good curve. I played for the University of Maryland team in 1946 and 1947 and I guess the high point was a game I pitched against George Washington University in old Griffith Stadium, then the home of the Washington Senators, and won, 3-2, in ten innings. But playing for Maryland is also when my prospects for a baseball career began to turn sour.

The Maryland baseball coach was a man named Burton Shipley. He became sort of a legend at Maryland and they later named the baseball field after him. But he would do a lot of crazy stuff. In one game against Duke, Shipley became upset with the umpire and moved his chair out in front of the dugout and sat there and cursed at the umpire the entire game. Another time when we were in Richmond, he pulled the whole team off the field in a tight game. In spring practice one year, we were doing calisthenics in Ritchie Coliseum before the basketball team came in to practice and Shipley ordered everyone off the floor. When one of the players didn't move fast enough, Shipley threw a hammer at him, but it almost hit me. I was bent over doing the calisthenics and when I came up, this hammer went by.

I think Shipley and his coaches really screwed up my pitching mechanics, as they did to a number of ballplayers. Shipley had a guy working with me named Doc White, who had once been a pitcher for the White Sox. White was a little lefthander, but I was a tall righthander. What worked for him didn't work for me. He completely messed up my pitching motion and I don't think I ever got it all the way back to where it had been.

During the summers while I was at Maryland and later at law school, I returned home to Denton and played for various teams—Denton, Centreville and Kent Island—in what was then known as the MarDel League. In 1946 or '47, I was the starting pitcher for the Maryland All-Stars in the MarDel League All-Star Game in Dover, Delaware. It was one of the best outings of my career. In three innings, I struck out seven of nine batters and the other two popped up and grounded out to me.

A month after graduating from Maryland in January 1949, I headed to Florida to find out once and for all if I could make baseball a career. In the 1940s, there was an Eastern Shore League of minor league clubs affiliated with various big league teams. The Dodgers had a team in Cambridge, the Cardinals had one in Salisbury, the Red Sox in Milford, the Phillies in Dover and the Yankees in Easton. Because Denton was centrally located, many of the umpires lived there during the season. I got to know one named Roman Benz, who during the off-season was an instructor in a baseball school in Ocala, Florida, run by longtime American League umpire Bill McGowan. Benz encouraged me to go down there when I finished college, so as soon as I had my degree, that's where I headed.

But I only stayed at McGowan's school for a couple of weeks before going to Orlando with a former Major League pitcher named Pete Appleton to see if the two of us could hook on with the Washington Senators. Appleton had been one of McGowan's instructors and hoped to become a coach for Washington; I wanted to get on the team's minor league pitching staff. We stayed about a week. I made just enough money at the dog races at night to keep me going. But nothing happened with the Senators, either, so Appleton headed back to Texas to play triple-A ball and, dejected, I headed home to Maryland.

While trying to figure out what I should do next, I began playing on a semi-pro team in Denton. A scout from the New York Yankees became interested in me and signed me to the Yankee farm team in Easton. I was paid $150 a month and $1 a day for meals, but was not given a signing bonus. That was a mistake. I later realized that the players who received bonuses were more likely to play because the teams felt they had an investment in them. I wasn't with the Yankee farm team long before they released me. I began playing for a team over in Federalsburg that was in the same league, but the end of my baseball career was fast approaching.

Most of our games were at night even though the field lights were so bad that a high fly ball often soared out of sight into the darkness above the lights. During the days, I worked in a General Electric store in Denton that sold appliances. They sent me on the road to try to sell refrigerators or other appliances, but I cannot remember selling a thing. That experience taught me a lesson, however. I realized I did not like working for others.

A couple years later, when I was in law school, I was playing for the Kent Island team and slid into third base and seriously sprained my ankle. I was right in the middle of law school exams and suddenly found myself on crutches. That was the last straw. I decided the risk of playing anymore was too great and I hung up my spikes for good.

It was time. I had begun to get disillusioned by the way some of the young professional players played. There was very little teamwork—many were just out for themselves, out for self-advancement. I saw guys intentionally fail to catch fly balls because they were afraid of being charged with an error, or guys trying to get walks rather than swinging away because they were trying to protect their batting average. It just didn't appeal to me. As much as I loved to play, I just didn't want to play that way.

Baseball had been my dream my whole life, but suddenly at age twenty-four it was over. I saw players who had tried for years to make it to the big leagues, but failed. I saw them on their way down, facing life without any occupation or career ahead of them. That sort of disturbed me and I knew I didn't want that to happen to me.

Pat

About three summers before I went to law school, I met a young woman in the living room of our house who my mother was tutoring in French. Her name was Patricia Donoho. I liked her, but she went off to the National Cathedral School in Washington that fall and I didn't really see her much until the fall of 1948 when she invited me up for a dance at Bryn Mawr College near Philadelphia, where she had entered as a freshman. That was our first date. By the summer of 1949, we were dating regularly.

That summer, Pat encouraged me to apply to law school. Other than that, I cannot really explain why I wanted to go to law school. There were no lawyers in my family and I only knew one lawyer in town very well. But, with Pat's encouragement, I applied to and was accepted at both George Washington University in Washington, D.C., and the University of Pennsylvania Law School. I decided to go to GW because I felt I'd have an easier time getting a job in

Washington. I had enough credit left from the GI Bill to get me through the first year of law school, but after that I would have to pay my own way. I moved to Washington and got a job for the Census Bureau for about $2,600 a year. I was there just a few weeks before moving to another job for the Department of General Services, which had offices along the Potomac not far from the Lincoln Memorial.

I lived in a rooming house up off Florida Avenue for five dollars a week and roomed with a guy from Jersey City named Murray Kivitz. Murray was a Jewish boy and smart as the devil. He used to bring back Jewish salamis to the room. They were really good, but our room just reeked of garlic.

My job location was nice, but my job was mind numbing. Congress had become concerned that different agencies were paying different prices for the same materials. The navy, for example, might pay fifteen dollars for a blanket, but the army was paying thirty-five dollars. To standardize prices, Congress directed General Services to develop a central catalogue from which all agencies would purchase goods. My job was to write the descriptions for thousands of catalogued items. I wrote about such weighty topics as whether nuts and bolts had round heads or hexagonal heads. Once a section was done, we had to circulate it among the various agencies until everyone approved, but it always seemed like the military agencies could never agree. Ultimately, Congress tired of the inter-agency bickering and cut off the funding, but that came a month after I left and the job got me through law school.

A 1937 Ford

During those law school years, I used to drive up to see Pat in Pennsylvania in a 1937 Ford V-8. I bought the car from my brother Buddy for twenty-five dollars after he got it from somebody who had won it at a carnival on a twenty-five-cent chance. I would drive up to see Pat on Friday afternoons and head back on Sunday nights. But in cold weather, I couldn't have the lights, heater and radio on all at the same time because the battery would die, so I had a lot of cold trips.

Once I drove the '37 Ford to Rehoboth to pick up Pat and her mother, but was stopped for speeding by a pair of Delaware state troopers. One of them asked to try out my car, which had mechanical brakes instead of hydraulic brakes and no power steering. We watched as the policeman drove back and I could see him trying to slow down. He was pushing hard on the brakes, but the car went right on by us and finally stopped. He said, "Your brakes are in pretty bad shape, aren't they?" I said, "Well, they're not too good." He said the lights were also a little dim, too, and asked, "What about the horn? Does it work?" I said, "Always has." So, he goes over and pushes the horn and not a sound—not a sound!

He said, "Your windshield is cloudy. Bad brakes. Your horn doesn't work. We're going to have to go see 'the Man.'" I said, "'The man'? Who's 'the man'?" He said,

"The justice of the peace." I said, "Is that really necessary? Look, I've just come from Washington. I'm working because my GI Bill ran out and I'm going to law school at night and I promise you I'll take this car in tomorrow and have all of this fixed." Finally, he said, "All right, if you promise." The next day I took it in and got everything fixed.

I had one other memorable experience after driving that '37 Ford to Bryn Mawr. During the middle of the night, I suddenly got a sharp pain in my stomach. I started vomiting and felt really sick, then it would go away and I'd feel fine. Then, in a half hour or so, I would go through the same thing again. I was staying at a rooming house right off the campus run by an elderly couple, one of whom was practically blind and the other was deaf. When I got sick, I pulled out a phonebook and looked up the nearest medical center and a doctor came to see me in the middle of the night. He was a nice guy. I remember him sitting on the side of the bed with his cold hands pushing on my stomach. He said, "I think you've got appendicitis. We'd better get you to the hospital."

They took me to Bryn Mawr Hospital and they were going to operate the following morning. But suddenly, I felt fine again and said if I was going to be operated on, I'd rather have it done at home. But when I got home, I felt fine and didn't have the surgery.

I had suffered a similar attack when I was about sixteen while working a summer job as a driver for a company that was searching for oil beneath the Eastern Shore. We were driving to Church Hill and I remember throwing up and then, about two or three hours later, feeling fine.

A number of years later, after I was married, I suffered several attacks and finally told Pat to take me to the hospital. When hospital employees started asking questions, "What's your parents' name? What's your grandparents' name?" I said, "You can get all of that later. I want someone to stick a knife in me." I got up and walked out of the room and sat in a wheelchair and said, "Take me somewhere so they can do something to me." They operated the next morning and found that I had a ruptured appendix. I was in the hospital for about twelve days. They said the appendix was marked, which indicated I had had attacks before. When they asked if I remembered having attacks, I said, "Yes, I did."

Marriage

In 1951, the year before I graduated from GW, Pat and I got engaged. Her family lived in Ridgely, about seven miles from Denton, and I drove over to ask her father for her hand. I met Dorsey Donoho in their living room—while Pat and her mother, Blanche, were eavesdropping from the kitchen—and I can still remember his reaction when I told him I wanted to marry his daughter: he groaned. After all, I didn't seem to have much of a future. My long shot bid for a career in baseball was essentially over; my unimpressive work resume included stints in a cannery, a lumberyard, a soda fountain and as a writer of descriptions of nuts and bolts and other items for the federal government. Even though by then I was attending law school at night, my prospects as Pat's future husband probably looked pretty bleak.

One of the rituals I had to go through was to meet with the matriarch of Pat's family, a great-aunt named Mina Robinson who lived over in Seaford, Delaware. In the course of our conversation, she said to me, "Are you a Democrat?" I said, "Yes." And she said, "That's good." Then she said, "Are you an Episcopalian?" I said, "No." She said, "Well, you will be." And she was right. We've been members of the Episcopal Church right on the town square in Denton ever since our marriage.

We were married in the Episcopal Church in Seaford on June 30, 1951. Pat's father had originally been from Seaford and her mother from Laurel, Delaware.

For our honeymoon I borrowed my dad's Studebaker rather than trusting the old '37 Ford. Our friends hid the Studebaker from us during the wedding and when they brought it out afterwards, it was plastered with all kinds of stuff. Pat and I ran to the car as they threw rice, but just as I opened the door I hit my front tooth and broke it. When I tried to start the car, it began to shake because someone had disconnected some of the spark plug wires.

One of the ushers was my friend and fellow Maryland graduate Bill Adkins, whose father was a local dentist. Once we got the car running correctly, the first stop on our honeymoon was at Bill's father's dentist office in nearby Milford, Delaware. He smoothed down the tooth and we were on our way, first to the Hotel DuPont in Wilmington that night, then on to Cape Cod for a few days and then to Maine for the wedding of a classmate friend of Pat's.

When we returned home, Pat parlayed her major in French into a job with what was then known as Armed Forces Security, a secret government agency that predated the National Security Agency. We moved into an apartment complex in the Fairlington section of Arlington County, Virginia, while I finished law school.

That Christmas we came home for a party in Denton, where I ran into a local lawyer named Tom Everngam, who said, "If you want to come back and come into practice with me, I'd be delighted to have you." I didn't have any other place to go, so when I finished law school in June 1952, Pat and I returned to Denton and I began the practice of law. I shall always be grateful to Tom Everngam for taking me into his office.

3

The Delegate from Caroline County

AFTER I GRADUATED FROM LAW school in June 1952, I went to Baltimore to prepare for the Maryland bar exam and Pat enrolled in a teaching course at Towson State Teachers' College. Before taking the exam that July, I took a ten-day refresher course and stayed in a room at the YMCA. The night before the exam it was really hot and there was no air conditioning at the Y. The next morning, I awoke sick as a dog. I guess it was partly from the stress or nerves. I went back to bed thinking there was no way I could get through the exam. But then I decided I had come this far, I should try to get up and see it through.

I had always heard stories about how difficult it was to pass the Maryland bar exam if you didn't go to a Maryland law school and GW, of course, was in Washington. When you take the bar exam these days, they assign participants numbers so that whoever grades the exam does not know who the participant is or where he or she went to law school. But when I took the exam, the first thing they asked was for me to put down my name and where I went to law school. I thought, "Oh, boy, I am sunk. I am sunk!" I jotted down my name and George Washington Law School and struggled through the test, drinking ginger ale for lunch. I didn't get the results until sometime in September, but if they had flunked me, I would never have raised a question about it. I had no idea how I did on that exam—I was so sick I barely remember taking it.

That summer, we returned home. Pat began teaching fourth grade at Ridgley Elementary School and I began practicing law—even before I knew if I had passed the bar exam.

I didn't have much choice. Right after I moved into Tom Everngam's office, Tom left for a month-long vacation to California. Even though we both knew I had not heard whether I had passed the bar, Tom put me in charge of the office in his absence because there was no one else. In November, I finally learned I had passed the bar.

Our first office was in the rear of the Law Building on the ground floor, about a half-block from the courthouse. You entered the office directly from an alley. Tom liked this location because he felt clients preferred not to be seen entering a law office. Most of my work early on involved letter writing, searching titles, drafting deeds and mortgages and holding property settlements. Trial work came much later.

I remember one case where a guy came in who said he was a canner. He had received a letter from a Boston woman who contended she got very sick after eating tomatoes he had canned. She complained about finding a piece of metal in the bottom of the can.

In tomato canneries in those days, women hired to peel the tomatoes would sit surrounding a merry-go-round. Every time they peeled a bucket of tomatoes, they would place it on the merry-go-round and someone would take it off and pour them into the cooker. Each bucket had a number on it that was used to identify the peeler and each time the bucket was emptied, a supervisor would plunk in a metal token. Before filling the bucket again, the peeler would pull out the token and set it aside. At the end of the day, the peeler would turn in all of her tokens and that would determine how many buckets she had peeled and how much she was to be paid. One of those tokens apparently got into the can of tomatoes that the woman in Boston said made her so sick.

The canner told me he had already written the woman back a letter that said, "You are one of the fortunate ones. Out of every ten thousand cases of tomatoes, we put one of these tokens in a can. You have won twenty-five dollars and I am enclosing a check herewith."

I looked at the canner and said simply, "You don't need me." I never heard another word about the case.

Jack Logan and a Vacancy in the House

We returned to Denton in 1952, the year President Harry Truman attended the dedication of Friendship Airport, a new regional airport owned by Baltimore City but built in neighboring Anne Arundel County. The first span of the Chesapeake Bay Bridge opened for traffic that summer, ending the era of Chesapeake Bay ferries and the relative isolation of the Delmarva Peninsula. By the end of the year, war hero Dwight D. Eisenhower succeeded Truman, becoming the nation's first Republican president since Herbert Hoover.

A year earlier, Republicans also had taken over the governorship in Annapolis for the first time in twelve years with the election of former Baltimore Mayor Theodore R. McKeldin. McKeldin defeated an incumbent Democrat, William Preston Lane Jr., who had instituted Maryland's first sales tax and was subsequently vilified—first by his Democratic Primary opponent, George P. Mahoney, and then by McKeldin in the general election—with the campaign slogan, "Pennies for Lane." But Democrats still retained control of the state legislature in Annapolis and much of that control was exercised by the Democratic senators and delegates from Maryland's Eastern Shore.

At that time, there was one state senator from each of Maryland's twenty-three counties and six from Baltimore City. That alone gave the nine Eastern Shore counties a powerful bloc of votes in each house. In the 29-member Senate, there were 18 Democrats and 11 Republicans, and half of the Democrats were from the Eastern Shore. The Democratic majority in the House of Delegates was even more lopsided, with 88 Democrats and only 35 Republicans. The Eastern Shore delegation accounted for 26 votes in the 123-member House.

This was the first post-World War II legislature and many of the members had served in the war in Europe or the Pacific and had only recently returned to civilian life. More than half of them (seventeen of the senators and sixty-eight of the delegates) were elected for the first time in 1950, including both of the delegates who represented Caroline County.

One was Orland B. Blades, a fifty-year-old feed and farm machinery dealer who was somewhat overshadowed by his two successful brothers: Dallas Blades was a partner of Sisk and Sons, a canning broker in Preston and one of the largest on the East Coast; A.T. Blades, the other brother, who was nicknamed "Snooks," started the Preston Trucking Company and ran it for more than forty years.

The other delegate from Caroline County was forty-year-old John Wood Logan. Jack Logan was born in Rockport, Massachusetts, but after serving in the U.S. Army Signal Corps during the war, married Ann Green, a girl from Denton, and moved to Caroline County. He became a canner, farmer and real estate agent and, in 1950, a member of the Maryland House of Delegates.

When he arrived in Annapolis, Logan quickly realized how powerful the Eastern Shore delegation could be if it stuck together and voted as a bloc. He helped engineer a solid vote by the Eastern Shore caucus for House Speaker John C. Luber of Baltimore, for which he was rewarded in 1953 with the chairmanship of the House Ways and Means Committee. Until then, that post had been held by Baltimore County's powerful A. Gordon Boone.

Jack's fortunes were quickly on the rise. Midway through his first term, he had flexed the Eastern Shore's muscle, knocked off Boone and claimed one of the General Assembly's most important leadership posts. As Ways and Means chairman, Logan automatically became the House's majority floor leader, making him the second most powerful man in the House.

In July 1953, Governor McKeldin offered to appoint Logan to the State Tax Commission. Jack took the job, but I think he regretted the decision the rest of his life. Despite Logan's departure, the Eastern Shore retained its clout for the remainder of the term as Aubrey Thompson, a delegate from Cambridge, replaced him as chairman of Ways and Means and floor leader. The Eastern Shore delegation continued to control most of the committee chairmanships and vice chairmanships, but in 1954, Thompson did not return to the legislature. With the position vacant and in deference to the well-respected Boone, the Eastern Shore delegation helped Boone regain the chairmanship and floor leader position.

Logan's unexpected departure in 1953 suddenly created a vacancy in the House of Delegates from Caroline County. Jack Logan later became my best friend and closest political confidant, but at the time he left the legislature, I did not know him at all.

Vacancies were filled by the governor based on recommendations from the State Central Committee. At that time, the State Central Committee in Caroline County had six members and having an even number turned out to be a problem. They were split, three-and-three, over whom to recommend. One faction was aligned with Logan, the other with Layman J. Redden, the state senator from Caroline County. Redden was born in Denton and had served as the Caroline County state's attorney. He and Logan did not get along. Layman saw Logan as an interloper from Massachusetts and, with his sudden successful advancement in the House, as a political threat.

The Central Committee remained split for months. Every time somebody would suggest another name, there would be three votes against him. So Tom Everngam said to me, "Why don't you throw your hat in the ring? You aren't associated with any faction. You haven't been involved in politics at all."

In those days, lawyers were prohibited from advertising. What a lot of young lawyers in rural areas did to get their law practices known was to run for state's attorney, which is the job of local prosecutor. I had no desire to be state's attorney, but thought applying for Logan's vacant seat might be another way for me to get my name around the county. So I decided to submit my name as a candidate for the vacant House seat.

Bill Orme, an older friend I had known all my life, was a Democrat who served as county treasurer. Bill said he'd take me around and introduce me to the State Central Committee members, which he did, and I got a very warm reception from everybody. They then held another meeting, my name was proposed and there were three votes against me. The Logan faction was for me; the Redden faction against.

This dragged on for weeks until finally the Central Committee met, stayed up half the night, drank a lot and finally picked a guy they knew neither faction wanted: Calvert Merriken, a local lawyer who had previously served in the House of Delegates in the late 1940s. I was angry at the way it happened, but it got me interested in politics and I decided to run for the House seat when it came up again in 1954. Everngam gave me the time off to campaign all over the county and I won, finishing first, with Blades retaining the second seat and Merriken finishing third and out of the running.

Until Tom Everngam suggested I run for Jack Logan's vacant seat, I had never considered becoming involved in politics. I had been president of the student council for one year at Caroline High School, but other than that had never thought about going into politics—not in high school, not in college and not in law school.

"Hi, I'm Harry Hughes"

Campaigning for state delegate from Caroline County in 1954 was about as basic as it gets. It was door-to-door. There were no debates, no joint appearances, no formal speeches and certainly no TV ads. It was getting into the car and driving up farm driveways and introducing myself and asking for their vote. I think in that whole campaign, I spent something like $156 plus gas and wear and tear on my car.

I was nervous about it at first and reluctant to go up and introduce myself. I was a little bit shy. I felt I might get some mean reaction, but what I actually found was that about 95 percent of the time people were pleasant to me. That didn't mean they were going to vote for me, but they were pleasant. Every once in a while I'd run into someone who'd say, "Oh, you're just another politician wasting my time," but that didn't happen very much. I was fortunate that some people in Caroline County still recognized me from my baseball playing days.

I'd just say, "Hi, I'm Harry Hughes. I'm running for the House of Delegates and if you'd support me, I'd appreciate it." But I started to notice a reaction to my simple introduction that would be repeated throughout my political career. After I would say, "Hi, I'm Harry Hughes," a lot of the people would quickly reply, "Fine, how are you?" I finally realized that "Harry Hughes" sounded like I was asking, "How are you?"

As for issues, there really weren't many. In the middle of my campaign that summer of 1954, the U.S. Supreme Court issued its landmark *Brown v. Board of Education* ruling ending racial segregation of schools. I remember thinking this was really going to be controversial, especially throughout the strictly segregated Eastern Shore. But the ruling took a while to sink in and didn't really become much of an issue in my first campaign.

My campaign literature, such as it was, amounted to cards that listed the Baltimore Colts's football schedule for the coming season with my name across the top. I also handed out blotters. This was before the advent of ballpoint pens, so people used blotters to keep their ink from smearing. My blotters were cardboard and had a picture of me with some catchy line like, "Vote for me." They were good because people would keep the blotters on their desks.

The campaign was about getting around to see as many people as you could and getting them to campaign for you, primarily on Election Day. I had people in the different small towns in the county who supported me. There was a man named Jesse Porter in Greensboro and another named Martin Sutton in Ridgley. They had their people in their area working for me on Election Day. I can remember meeting with one of Fletcher Sisk's men in the Preston area, but he sort of supported me *sub rosa*. I'd meet him at night at his home back in a field near Preston. He had lists of names that he would contact on Election Day.

I often wondered why Porter or others who worked for me did this. They never asked for anything. I guess it was just a feeling of power. Even after the election, they never came to me to ask for anything. As a matter of fact, this even held true after I became governor. I do not remember anybody coming back and saying, "I helped you, now help me." I really don't.

Redden Vies for Senate President

When I arrived to take my seat in the legislature in 1955, Annapolis was a sleepy watermen's town. Its population of just over ten thousand was about 1 percent the size of Baltimore, a quarter the size of Cumberland, and not even a third the size of Hagerstown. Annapolis had fewer people than Hyattsville, Takoma Park or Cambridge.[3]

Even though the Republican McKeldin had been reelected over Harry C. Byrd in 1954, the new General Assembly was more Democratic than ever. In the Senate, 21 of the 29 members were Democrats (a gain of three) and in the House, 98 of the 123 delegates were Democrats (a gain of ten).

The Senate had its offices in the basement and first floor of the Court of Appeals Building, which then stood across the street from the State House between Government House (the governor's residence) and a Methodist church. The Court of Appeals, the state's highest appellate court, occupied the second floor. (Years later, both the Court of Appeals and the Methodist Church were torn down to make way for a legislative staff building separated from Government House by a small public plaza. A new church and a new courthouse were built about a half-mile from the State House on Rowe Boulevard, the main entry road into Annapolis.)

Each senator had one secretary, who frequently was the senator's wife, a practice that became criticized. I remember from my later years in the legislature Senator Harry Phoebus's wife, Vera, a nice little old lady. Phoebus was never bothered by criticism about employing his wife. "I'm a poor man," I can recall him saying. "I can't afford to have my wife living up here in a hotel. We need the income."

The House of Delegates occupied the entire second floor of the State House except for a small portion reserved for the governor and his immediate staff. Those offices have since been completely taken over by the governor's greatly expanded staff and now the House of Delegates and Senate each have their own buildings.

When I arrived in Annapolis, the delegates from Caroline County shared a small caucus room on the second floor of the State House with their colleagues from Talbot and Dorchester counties. There was no secretary and only one telephone. The House committee hearing rooms were in the basement of the State House, where there was also a pool of three or four secretaries who served the entire House. When the House was in session, I sat in the last seat on the back row, all the way in the right-hand corner of the chamber—right where a freshman should be: a back bencher.

As a delegate, I was paid $1,800 a year for sessions that lasted ninety days in odd-numbered years and only thirty days in even-numbered years.

I used to eat quite often at the Naval Academy Officer's Club, where we had been given permission to dine. I often went there with two Republicans from

3. *Maryland Manual*, 1956.

Allegany County who quickly became good friends, George R. Hughes Jr. of Cumberland and Noel Speir Cook of Frostburg. In those days, the Republicans in the legislature were far more liberal than the Republicans a half a century later and the partisanship that is so commonplace now was almost nonexistent.

When my first General Assembly session finally convened, the first order of business was the election of presiding officers. The two incumbents were House Speaker Luber and Senate President George W. Della, both of Baltimore. Della was in trouble, however, for a racist remark he made before a crowd of seven hundred at an October 1954 rally for gubernatorial candidate Dr. Harry C. Byrd. Reacting to the Supreme Court decision ordering the desegregation of public schools, Della exhorted Marylanders to elect a Democratic governor and a Democratic legislature "so that we may come back and have white supremacy again in our schools."[4] News reports said the crowd "lustily applauded,"[5] but Byrd remained silent.[6]

As my first session opened, Caroline County Senator Layman J. Redden was vying for Della's former position as Senate president and Prince George's County Delegate Perry O. Wilkinson was trying to replace Luber. This two-part coup had been the behind-the-scenes handiwork of a political power broker from Prince George's County named Lansdale G. Sasscer. Sasscer, then sixty-two, had been a member of the state Senate for fifteen years, including two as Senate president, and had served seven terms in the U.S. House of Representatives. He was out of political office only because he had failed in his attempt to be elected to the U.S. Senate in 1952.

Sasscer's plan was to get the southern Maryland delegation to support Redden for Senate president and, in exchange, he expected the Eastern Shore delegation to support Wilkinson for House speaker. But Luber, an old-style, cigar smoking Baltimore pol who was employed by the then powerful B&O Railroad, made the rounds, buttonholing individual legislators to ask for their support, including me. I was so new I was simply ignorant of the backroom machinations of the legislature. I didn't know anything about Mr. Sasscer's deal or what was going on at the time other than I understood that Layman Redden was to be the next Senate president. That was not unusual because I hadn't been involved in politics—I wasn't paying attention to politics. I had been busy going to law school. And Layman never said a word to me—he never said, "I'd appreciate your support for Wilkinson in the House because that's going to help me become president of the Senate."

The night before the session started, the Eastern Shore delegation caucused and voted overwhelmingly to support Luber for speaker. Luber ultimately was reelected. There were about five of us out of the twenty-nine Eastern Shore legislators

4. Charles G. Whiteford, "Della Asks Election on Race Issue," *Baltimore Sun*, October 23, 1954.
5. Ibid.
6. Byrd supported "home rule," or the concept of letting each jurisdiction decide how it should respond to the Supreme Court ruling. McKeldin, his Republican opponent, however, said he would uphold the Supreme Court decision.

that night who voted for Wilkinson. I don't think Redden ever believed I voted for Wilkinson, but I did, solely because I finally understood that was part of the arrangement for Layman to become president of the Senate.

When Sasscer and his cohorts heard what had happened, that the Eastern Shore had supported Luber, they ditched Redden and picked one of their own from southern Maryland to become Senate president. In the middle of the night they called up Louis L. Goldstein from Calvert County, at that point the chairman of the Senate Finance Committee, and said, "Would you like to be president of the Senate?" Of course, you know what Goldstein said.

That's how Louis Goldstein became president of the Senate and how Layman Redden lost it. I do not think Goldstein ever would have become Senate president otherwise. Redden had been so confident of his election to Senate president that he held a big party the night before the session, to which many of his constituents came. For him, the loss was a big, big shock. Redden never said anything to me, but I always had a feeling he probably thought I voted the way Jack Logan wanted me to vote. Jack was on the tax court by then, but he was still active and he supported Luber, but I voted for Wilkinson.

Two senators from the Eastern Shore, Frederick C. Malkus Jr. from Dorchester County and Ralph Mason from Worcester County, abandoned Redden in favor of Goldstein. Malkus had a pretty good reason for supporting Goldstein: they had roomed together in law school. The new Senate president rewarded his Eastern Shore supporter by making him chairman of the Senate Judicial Proceedings Committee. He appointed Mason vice-chairman of the Senate Finance Committee.

Goldstein went on to become one of the most famous names in Maryland politics and he and Malkus became two of the longest serving elected officials in Maryland history. Their careers and mine would often clash as they became inextricably intertwined over the next quarter century.

The House Judiciary Committee

The committee structure of the House was much different than it is today. There were more standing committees and more members on them than there are today. Members also were allowed to serve on more than one major standing committee at a time, which is not the practice today. There were sixteen House committees when I arrived in Annapolis, the biggest and most influential of which were Agriculture and Natural Resources; Alcoholic Beverages; Banking, Insurance and Social Security; Chesapeake Bay and Tributaries; Education; Judiciary; and Ways and Means. Five of the chairmen of these seven committees, and two of the vice-chairmen, were from the Eastern Shore.

That first term, I served on three major committees: Banking, Education and Judiciary, although the bulk of my time and attention was with the thirty-two-member Judiciary Committee. It was chaired by Lloyd L. Simpkins, a lawyer from

Somerset County whose nickname was "Hot Dog." He was a funny guy. He always told people that his nickname was his father's maiden name. He could really tell stories. But he was a good chairman. He didn't get too much involved in the depth of the discussion, but he ran the committee really well. He worked at it hard and was fair. Everybody had a chance to speak.

It was a very good committee. A lot of these guys came out of World War II and weren't what you'd call the old-time kind of politicians. I never remember politics playing any part in our deliberations—I really don't. And I don't remember anybody ever feeling there would be recriminations because of the way you voted. When I later got into the Senate, it was different. But that committee was as non-political as you can imagine and really decided things on the substance of the matter.

Little did we know back then that big things were in store for many of the members of that committee. Two—Daniel B. Brewster and Joseph D. Tydings—would go on to become United States senators. Four—Ridgely P. Melvin Jr., "Hot Dog" Simpkins, Edgar P. Silver and John N. Maguire—went on to become Maryland Circuit Court judges and, in Melvin's case, later a judge on the Maryland Court of Special Appeals. George Hughes became the Senate Minority Leader and the father-in-law of Governor Parris N. Glendening; Carlton R. Sickles, a fine lawyer from Prince George's County, became Maryland's congressman at-large and nearly became the Democratic gubernatorial nominee in 1966; and I, of course, did become governor.

One member of the House Judiciary Committee was a blind delegate from Frederick County named C. Clifton Virts. He was really sharp. Cliff and John Maguire had gone to University of Maryland Law School together and Maguire had helped Cliff get through by reading law cases aloud to him.

But Cliff Virts wasn't the only blind legislator in Annapolis in those days. Charles M. See was a blind senator from Allegany County. Except for their disability, these two could not have been more unalike. Virts was a Democrat; See was a Republican. They had different personalities and did not get along, nor did their seeing eye dogs. They were different breeds and always barked at each other and often had to be held apart. I guess they sort of mirrored their masters.

A lot of funny things were said on the floor of the House and Senate over the years, but one of my favorites came from the mouth of a Prince George's delegate who complained during an exchange over the mundane issue of parking spaces on State Circle, "Mr. Speaker, this debate has degenerated into a matter of principle!" Another time, Senator Louis Phipps from Anne Arundel County left everyone speechless by declaring, "I may be wrong, but if I'm right, correct me."

In the middle of my four-year term as delegate, someone suggested I become more involved with the General Assembly leadership. In those days, a committee composed of ten delegates and ten senators met to deal with fiscal and other matters during the interim between legislative sessions. These days, standing and special committees meet almost year round, but then only this twenty-member leadership group, called the Legislative Council, met between sessions.

The representative on the Legislative Council from the Eastern Shore was E. Homer White Jr. of Salisbury. Some of my colleagues thought I could do a better job, so I campaigned among the Shore delegation and in my third year knocked White off the Legislative Council. He never forgave me. But my move to the Legislative Council broadened my understanding of the legislative process and was perhaps a window into my potential role in the legislative world.

4

The Next Step Up

WHEN I WAS A YOUNG man, Fifth Avenue was the nicest street in Denton. My friend Jack Logan lived there and I spent many an evening sitting on his porch, drinking bourbon and talking politics.

It was there on Jack's front porch that we first started talking about whether I should challenge Layman Redden in the Democratic primary for his seat in the state Senate. By then, Pat and I had purchased our first house on the south side of Denton for $17,500 and I had made a friendly separation from Tom Everngam and set up my own law practice. It was 1958. I had a wife, a young family (Ann had been born October 6, 1953, and Beth on April 13, 1956), a new home, a mortgage, my own business and I could see a move to the state Senate as my next step up.

Layman Redden had been born and raised in Denton. In high school, he was taught by, among others, my mother. He was a graduate of the Wharton School at the University of Pennsylvania and the University of Maryland Law School. He had never lost an election. In 1934, when I was only eight, Redden ran for state's attorney while still in law school and won. He was twice reelected and remained the county's chief prosecutor for twelve years. During World War II, he headed the local Selective Service Board. He was elected to the Maryland Senate in 1950 and then was reelected the year I went to the House—the year he almost became president of the Senate.

By the end of my first term, however, Jack and I felt Redden was vulnerable for several reasons. We believed he had really neglected the people in his district and that he also was rather aloof. But the incident that may have hurt Redden the most was his involvement in the widening of Route 404, the major east-west road through Caroline County.

The State Roads Commission had decided to improve Route 404 and purchase rights-of-way for a future dual-lane road. For that, they needed local attorneys to represent the state to handle the title work and settlements with property owners. The more lucrative job, of course, was representing the property owners against the state. In those days, the assistant attorney general assigned to the State Roads Commission would pick the attorneys needed to do title work for such projects. Layman Redden was both a lawyer and the local state senator, so he got all of that work. Wherever he could represent the property owners along Route 404, he did, and when he didn't, he represented the state.

Word of Redden representing both the state and the property owners on this road project began to spread around the county. Encouraged by Jack Logan, I started to campaign against him, but never mentioned the Route 404 arrangements. I didn't have to. This became more of a door-to-door campaign than anything I had ever done before. I would campaign during the day, and often Jack and I would sit together to discuss political strategy at night.

I saved Denton until last, going door-to-door in my hometown where almost everyone knew me. It wasn't until then, I think, that Layman got really concerned, but by then it was much too late and I beat him, 2,022 to 1,324.[7] I guess no one figured Redden would lose, because after winning the Democratic primary, I was unopposed in the general election. Another Eastern Shore native, J. Millard Tawes of Crisfield, also was elected that November as Maryland's governor.

To his credit, Layman Redden never said a mean word to me the rest of the time I knew him. I also was a good friend of his son, Roger, who became a prominent Baltimore attorney in his own right. Roger, who became a partner in the firm of Piper and Marbury, never showed anything but kindness toward me. He contributed to my campaigns and never, ever held it against me that I beat his father.

Life in the Senate

When I moved to the other side of the State House in January 1959, I soon learned that life in the Senate was considerably different than life in the House of Delegates. My four years in the House had been rather quiet. In the House in those days, you did what you wanted to do and you never thought about whether there might be retaliation for your failure to support one of your colleague's bills. But because of the much smaller number of members in the Senate, you had to begin worrying about such things.

In the Senate, I really started to grow as a legislator. I established a very good relationship with William S. James, a Democratic senator from Harford County. Billy was a dozen years older than I and had been in the legislature since 1947. He and I became very good friends and served together in different capacities through the end of my second term as governor. I had great admiration for Bill because he was such a student of government and a fine person.

Another big change for me in the Senate came when I was appointed to the Finance Committee. In the House, much of the legislative action had taken place in the Ways and Means Committee because that was where state budget issues were decided. The same was true of the Finance Committee in the Senate. I also was given a role on the Taxation and Fiscal Affairs Committee, which was an interim committee that dealt with fiscal matters between legislative sessions. I started to become more active in the fiscal affairs of the state—lessons that would serve me well for the rest of my Senate career, as a Cabinet secretary and later as governor.

When I joined the Finance Committee, it was chaired by Edward S. Northrop of Montgomery County, whom I admired and who also became a good friend. The

---

7. "Hughes Beats Redden in Caroline," *Baltimore Sun*, May 22, 1958.

committee's jurisdiction was broad, varied and important: First and foremost, it exercised oversight of the annual state budget; but it also dealt with capital construction projects, transportation investments, education issues and all fiscal matters.

Teacher Salaries

Teacher salaries were a perennial issue. At that time, minimum teacher salaries were set in state law and served as a basis for state aid for education. Counties were permitted to pay more than the minimum level set by the state, but in order to provide for a general increase in teacher salaries, the state minimum had to be changed. Every year, hundreds of teachers would converge on Annapolis, filling the legislative balconies and pushing for increases in the minimum.

One year, we decided to have a joint hearing with the House and held it in the House chamber. The balconies were full of teachers, some of whom hung long banners from the railing proclaiming their need for a salary increase. I was sitting next to Bill James when W. Dale Hess, a somewhat unpolished delegate from Harford County, rose to his feet and proclaimed to the crowded chamber, "I want you to know that Bill James and I have *did* [*sic*] more for education than anyone in the state of Maryland." I thought Bill would melt with embarrassment.

On the final night of the 1963 legislative session, there was a bill to revise the school aid formula by shifting it from being based on teacher salaries to one based on per pupil costs. I supported the concept, but I and others—including the Tawes administration—opposed other provisions in the $14.2 million bill and ultimately defeated it.

What ultimately killed that bill was that the legislature simply ran out of time. Facing a midnight deadline to adjourn and unable to agree on the education bill, the Senate repeatedly turned the hands of the Senate clock back to prolong the session by pretending twelve o'clock had not been reached. This was not the first time this legislative trick had been played. The chaotic final hours included ten roll call votes, including four to adjourn, which we finally did at what was really 4:18 a.m.

In the middle of the debate over the school aid bill, the Senate approved a measure proposed by Senator Robert P. Dean, a Democrat from Queen Anne's County, to insert in the Senate's official journal a notation that the bills were being acted upon at 1:45 a.m. on April 2: an hour and forty-five minutes after the General Assembly should have adjourned at midnight, April 1.[8] That spelled the end of the practice of "turning back the clock" because it meant that, from then on, any bill passed after midnight on a session's final night could be challenged as unconstitutional. Once the journal entry showed that midnight had come and gone, it made no sense to pass the education bill because it clearly would have been considered unconstitutional.

8. Stephen E. Nordlinger, "Assembly Kills School Aid Bill," *Baltimore Sun*, April 3, 1963.

In the aftermath, Milson C. Raver, the well-respected director of the Maryland State Teachers' Association, became angry with me because we defeated the bill. By then I was chairman of a commission established to review the teacher salary issue and I told Milson that I felt there were problems with the way the bill was drafted. "We'll come back next year with a good bill," I promised.

In 1964, my commission did. With the support of the teachers' union, we introduced and passed a proposal that completely overhauled the way public education in Maryland is financed, shifting it from teacher salary levels set by the legislature to a formula distribution based on enrollment. This shift in school funding also addressed the fiscal disparities among counties.

That was a big change. It essentially ended the annual onslaught of teachers coming to Annapolis begging for pay raises. More importantly, it changed the public perception of education funding. To many Marylanders, it was unseemly for hordes of teachers to be crowding into Annapolis each legislative session to demand higher salaries. It was also demeaning for teachers to be put in such a position. By changing the focus to a system of state aid based on enrollment and each jurisdiction's relative ability to pay, people began talking about "aid to education" rather than whether to "raise teachers' salaries." This change made it possible for the legislature to better address the serious educational needs of some of the state's poorest jurisdictions, such as Baltimore City. The public began to focus on the effect their tax dollars would have on educating students, not on whether teachers were overpaid or not paid enough.

Tuckahoe State Park

During that first term in the Senate, a state park ranger came to Robert P. Dean and me to suggest a plan to create a new recreation area on the Tuckahoe River in Caroline County. He said if the state were to build a dam on the Tuckahoe River near Hillsboro in Queen Anne's County, just north of the Route 404 bridge, it could back up a lake probably as large as twelve hundred acres. The ranger predicted it would become a great new recreational attraction for the state. He added that the dam would be relatively easy to build because the river at that point was fairly narrow and the banks were high.

Bob Dean and I were excited about the idea and convinced Governor Tawes to put some money in the capital budget to start the land acquisition for what would become Tuckahoe State Park. Plans for a park as large as four thousand acres generated immediate public support in the two counties and, in August 1961, the state's Board of Public Works—consisting of Governor Tawes, Comptroller Goldstein and state Treasurer Hooper Steele Miles— authorized a survey and dam feasibility study. At the time, there were only about six hundred acres of state-owned park and recreational facilities on the Eastern Shore.

The project moved ahead, but slowly. At first the problem was a lack of funds. In May 1967, two of my old friends from the House Judiciary Committee, Danny Brewster and Joe Tydings, who by then were Maryland's two U.S. senators, announced a $142,478 federal grant to Maryland to help the state acquire 3,634 acres.

Soon, however, plans for Tuckahoe and its twelve hundred-acre lake became ensnared in the environmental movement that was beginning to take root in the United States in the early 1970s. At first, environmentalists opposed the proposed lake because they said it would destroy wetlands and wildlife habitat and the state's Department of Natural Resources (DNR) agreed. In October 1971, nearly two years after I had left the General Assembly, Robert E. Bauman, by then the state senator for Middle Shore counties, complained in a letter to then-Governor Marvin Mandel that badly needed economic help for Caroline County was being blocked by the ecological objections of DNR.

Finally, in 1973, the state's Water Resources Administration approved plans for a lake in Tuckahoe State Park, but the size was whittled down by environmental concerns to 380 acres. Then, in May 1973, a tree blocked the way. The American Forestry Association announced that a great swamp white oak in the wetlands that would be inundated by the proposed lake had officially been declared "the national champion of its species." The tree was 116-feet tall, its branches spread 118 feet, the trunk was 21 feet and 5 inches in diameter and its age was estimated at 200 years. This was a tree big enough to block a lake.

To spare the tree, the lake plans were revised again in that summer, its size reduced to 120 acres. Finally, in 1974, development of the lake began, but by then what was once envisioned to be 1,200 acres had been cut in size to 60 acres.

The interesting thing is that the originally proposed dam was never built. And the irony of it was that the tree died anyway. Nonetheless, the 3,800-acre Tuckahoe State Park remains a great recreation area for the Eastern Shore and I think of it with pride as a legacy of my years of public service.

They now have a very successful arboretum at the park, built with a $1 million donation left following the death of an elderly man named Leon Andrus. The arboretum is named after my friend, Bill Adkins, whom I later appointed to the Court of Appeals and who had been Mr. Andrus's lawyer and friend.

My family had another unusual connection with Mr. Andrus. He used to play a lot of golf at the Caroline County Country Club and so did my daughter, Beth, who was only about ten then. I was practicing law in Denton and often would just take Beth over to the golf course and drop her off. She would either practice or find someone to play and I'd pick her up around five o'clock in the afternoon. Often, she would play with Mr. Andrus. They would bet a dollar a round and Beth would usually win.

Beth became quite a good golfer and was the Maryland Junior Miss Champ for five years in a row.

Condemnation Laws

While public service sometimes brings you glory or notoriety, sometimes you work on issues of importance that never show up on campaign literature and barely, if ever, make the news. Such was an issue I became deeply involved with during my first term in the Senate. I was asked to chair a committee to revise the condemnation laws of Maryland. It marked the first time in fifty years that the state's laws concerning condemnation of private property by public agencies had been revised.

The committee was made up of representatives from the legislature and the Maryland Bar Association. The group included some of the best legal minds in Maryland, including Wilson K. Barnes who later served for a decade on Maryland's Court of Appeals; Melvin Sykes, one of the smartest lawyers I ever met; and Perry Bowen, who led the committee's staff and later became a Circuit Court judge in Calvert County.

The committee worked on this dry and thankless issue for two years before our recommendations were finally enacted by the General Assembly in February 1963. The goal was to make sure that owners whose property was condemned for roads, schools, urban redevelopment or other public uses are justly compensated. The revision, for example, allowed property owners to show evidence that their property value actually declined simply as a result of the announcement of plans for a project that may have occurred long before a condemnation process could actually take place. The legislation also liberalized allowances for owners forced to move from condemned lands.

I am certain that Marylanders whose land was condemned in later years to make way for public projects never knew about the work of this obscure commission, but I am confident they were treated more fairly than they would have been had we not modernized this fundamental power of government.

Chesapeake Community College

Later in my Senate years, another idea was hatched in my office that has improved the lives of thousands of young people from the Middle Shore. Legislation had been passed that for the first time allowed counties to get together to form a local community college.[9] I brought in Bob Dean and we originally envisioned a college serving only Queen Anne's and Caroline. Later, however, I called together our colleagues from other Middle Shore counties and said we ought to get one going in our region. And we did.

9. Two bills were enacted in 1965, Senate Bills 419 and 420. One authorized the state to pay 75 percent of the cost of land and buildings for a regional community college, provided two or more counties joined together and agreed to pay the remaining 25 percent. The other provided the initial bond funds for the buildings and land, the bonds to be repaid by the state and participating counties at the same 75/25 ratio. These bills were passed by the Finance Committee, which I chaired.

The first and most contentious issue was to decide in which of our five counties—Caroline, Kent, Talbot, Queen Anne's and Dorchester—the new community college would be located. Before the process moved along very far, Dorchester dropped out (only to rejoin the effort somewhat later). Talbot and Kent Counties agreed to a site in Queen Anne's County and, finally, in December 1965, John W. Eveland, president of the Caroline County board of commissioners, went along, but only after receiving a strongly worded letter from me. By the end of the year, the State Board of Education had authorized establishment of the new community college. In early 1966, each board of county commissioners put up the enormous sum of $500 to cover start-up expenses! I suppose you could say that the college's first budget was all of $2,000![10]

By May 1966, we had selected the college's first president, Dr. George Silver, and a name, Chesapeake College, but still no site. In time, we would agree to build the new campus along U.S. Route 50 at Wye Mills. By the time of the groundbreaking in spring of 1967, we already had 50 students signed up for classes for the first fall semester. Eventually, there were 265 students in Chesapeake Community College's first class, which convened in September 1967 in temporary quarters in Queen Anne's High School. The college's first buildings opened for business the following year.[11] Initially, the Board of Trustees consisted of three members of the board of education from each of the four counties, but in 1970 I sponsored legislation that allowed the college to create its own separate board.

Chesapeake College has been a marvelous success story. This community college provides affordable educational opportunities for Shore residents of all ages (the average student age is twenty-eight), including those who are interested in going on to a four-year college, those who are satisfied with a community college education and those who just want training in job-related tasks, such as driving tractor trailer rigs, working as a therapeutic masseur or as a hotel manager. The creation of this community college is one of the most important things that ever happened to the Middle Shore area of the state.

10. Harry R. Hughes (Commencement Address, Chesapeake College, Wye Mills, MD, May 25, 2005).

11. Total enrollment by the fall 2004 semester was 2,557, which included 789 (31 percent) full-time students and 1,768 (69 percent) part-time students. 70 percent were female and about three-quarters were from Queen Anne's, Talbot or Caroline Counties. About a quarter were enrolled with plans to move on to a four-year college and nearly half were in programs designed to help them enter the job market, improve skills for current employment or make a career change. The two-year school offered sixty-four academic programs leading to various associate degrees in arts, science, applied science, teaching and nursing. The college commemorated its fortieth anniversary in May 2005. *http://www.chesapeake.edu/generalinfo/fact_book.asp*

"Little Vegas"

One of the most contentious issues in all my years in the General Assembly involved the abolition of slot machine gambling that from 1943 to 1949 had been gradually legalized in the southern Maryland counties of Anne Arundel, Charles, Calvert and St. Mary's.[12]

There were several things wrong with it. It was only legal in four of Maryland's twenty-three counties. There were five places in the United States where gambling was legal: the state of Nevada and the four counties of southern Maryland, which quickly earned the nickname "Little Vegas." And the slot machines were all over those counties. They were in every drug store, barbershop and filling station. They were even in restaurants on piers extending from the shore of Virginia into the Maryland waters of the Potomac River. They were everywhere. You rode down U.S. Route 301 in those days and you just saw one sign after another: "Slots, Slots, Slots."

There also were all sorts of stories of bad actors from Chicago being involved in the Maryland gambling operations. The slot machine operations were essentially a self-reporting system and the stories you kept hearing were that the operators would just skim everything off the top, that the money would go into bags and that there was a private plane that would fly the cash directly to Chicago. I don't know that anyone was ever convicted, but those were the stories. Under federal law at the time, it was illegal to transport slot machines across state lines. As a result, a big slot machine building and repair business flourished in Anne Arundel County.

What really bothered me were the sad stories of workmen blowing all of their pay on Friday night and having to borrow money to feed their families. The movement to get rid of the slot machines really began in Millard Tawes's second campaign for governor in 1962. He was opposed in the Democratic primary by a state delegate from Hagerstown named David Hume, who ran a single-issue campaign to abolish slots. He started harping on it, how we had to get rid of these slot machines and talking about all the terrible things they were doing. When the little-known Hume garnered 101,319 votes, Tawes had little choice but to pick it up. In September 1962, Tawes vowed that slots were "no longer a local issue" and thus "should be abolished."[13] I don't think he would have done it otherwise; it wasn't in his nature. Tawes had to make a commitment to do it. And he carried out his commitment to put the legislation in and, I can tell you, it was hard fought. Lobbyists for the slot machine interests were everywhere and there were allegations of attempts to bribe state legislators to change their votes.

The legislation, however, passed in the same hectic 1963 session at which Maryland's first public accommodations law was enacted. It called for phasing out the slot machines over a five-year period. But every year up until the time they were finally gone, supporters would go to the legislature to fight the phase-out.

---

12. Stephen Janis, "Little Vegas," *The City Paper*, December 1, 2004.
13. Ibid.

Paul Bailey was a senator and colorful trial lawyer from down in St. Mary's County and he fought for the slots. Supporting the ban, of course, were all the churches. In the Senate with me was J. Frank Raley, also from St. Mary's and a good friend and fine legislator. He favored the ban, but his position cost him his reelection.

But I think Raley was right. He said the economy was on a terrible basis down in southern Maryland. The social problems were just terrible. And you're seeing the same kind of problems today in some of the states that have legalized slots in recent years. Once they got rid of the slots in southern Maryland, the economy got on a healthier footing.

In 1968, the year the gambling in southern Maryland was scheduled to end, state Senator George E. Snyder said a man came into his Hagerstown office and offered him $10,000 if he would vote to extend the deadline. Rather than accepting the bribe, Snyder told Senate President Billy James and me what had happened. We were appalled, although I suppose we weren't surprised. When the bill came up on the Senate floor, where I was the majority floor leader, I reported the bribe offer to my colleagues and the revelation had a dramatic effect. Snyder later said my speech helped "turn the corner" on what had been expected to be a very close vote. That put an end to the efforts to extend the phase-out deadline.

I voted against the slots back in the 1960s and I would do so again today if I were still in the legislature. I certainly don't agree with those who think we should legalize slots at the racetracks and let the track owners reap millions out of it. I think that if the state is going to legalize slot machines again, then the state should own and operate them like they do the lottery. I always opposed the lottery when I was in the legislature. It finally passed after I was out of office and by the time I was governor, it had become the state's third largest source of revenue. At that point, there was little I could do about it. To try to abolish the lottery at that stage would have been politically impossible. I couldn't have gotten it done anyway, because we would have had to raise other taxes to replace the revenues lost by abolishing the lottery.

The only good thing about the state-run lottery was that it apparently replaced the illegal numbers racket. There used to be newspaper stories all the time about the numbers racket in Baltimore City. But you never read stories anymore about the numbers racket after the state lottery began.

Carvel Hall and the Blind Leading the Blind

It wasn't until I arrived in Annapolis that I really got to know newspaper reporters. In my early years in the General Assembly, the press corps consisted primarily of the *Associated Press*, three newspapers from Baltimore (the *Sun*, the *Evening Sun* and the Hearst-owned *News-American*) and two from Washington (the *Post* and the *Star*). There were a few radio reporters, mostly from Baltimore, but not much in the way of TV.

In those days, reporters and legislators seemed to get along. I don't remember any of us being afraid that anything we said or did might show up in print the next day. During the session, reporters sometimes lived in the same hotel as legislators and would often party with legislators after hours.

A number of legislators lived in a large hotel, since demolished, which had been built at the back of the historic Paca House, over what are now the beautiful Paca House gardens. It was called Carvel Hall and catered not only to legislators and reporters, but also to visitors to the nearby U.S. Naval Academy.

On one side of Carvel Hall was an annex known grimly as "the Death House." I don't know why they called it that other than it burned one night and some of the legislators were lucky to get out. Gabby Bowen, then the *AP* reporter, shared an apartment there with Lloyd "Hot Dog" Simpkins, the Judiciary Committee chairman, and Homer White, a delegate from Wicomico County. You wouldn't see a reporter or a legislator doing that today, but they did then.

On the ground floor of Carvel Hall there was a taproom and café with a piano, a favorite watering hole during the legislative session. In back of the piano was a hallway to another section that would lead you to some suites called A, B and C, where some of the reporters stayed. Reporters and legislators alike often partied together back in A, B and C.

At the time, there was a well-liked delegate from Somerset County named J. Ellis Tawes, whose nickname was Dido. He was a World War I veteran with a crew cut, a big round face and a heart as big as his face. At the time, there were three delegates from Somerset County: Dido, Hot Dog Simpkins and E. Layton Riggin, a big guy from Crisfield. Every time the Speaker would call on the chairman of the Somerset County delegation, all three of them would stand up.

Dido had a finger or two missing from one hand, but he still used to play piano in the taproom and I remember one of his favorite pieces was "Mississippi Mud." One night, Dido was playing and out from the corridor behind the piano came Cliff Virts, the blind delegate from Frederick, with his seeing eye dog leading the way. Cliff had clearly had a little too much to drink. But staggering in behind Cliff was another delegate who had perfect eyesight, but who had his hand on Cliff's shoulder being led through. These days, that incident might have ended up in the newspapers, but back then we all just laughed and that was that.

One night, the target of the pranksters in the Carvel Hall taproom was Earl Bennett, an older delegate from Cambridge. At the time, the Dorchester, Talbot and Caroline County delegates shared an office with a single telephone. Earl used to get up early in the morning and head into the office and start calling constituents in Dorchester County, saying, "I'm up here looking after your interests. Is there anything I can do for you?" At Carvel Hall, the trashcans were right outside Earl's window, so when the trash men rattled the cans in the morning, he knew it was time to get up. One evening the guys stayed up late in the taproom, having a few drinks, and decided to go outside about 2:00 a.m. and rattle the trashcans outside Earl's window. Poor Earl heard the racket, got up, shaved and dressed and went downstairs only to find the breakfast room closed. When he complained, the night clerk had to tell him, "Well, it's only 2:30 in the morning, Mr. Bennett."

Despite these pranks, there always were lots of discussions going on after hours that did have an effect on legislation. Some people used to joke that more business was done after hours in Carvel Hall or in the Maryland Inn than in the State House.

Suds in the State House

The most prominent lobbyists in my early years represented utilities and unions: the Baltimore Gas & Electric Co., the C&P Telephone Co., the B&O Railroad, the Maryland State Teachers' Association and the Maryland Classified Employees Association (the union of state workers). Labor was represented by a guy named Charlie Della, a quiet fellow who always seemed to be smoking a cigar. Charlie would give many of us a bottle of I.W. Harper at the end of every session.

I guess businesses didn't have many lobbyists back then. Today, so many businesses think they have to have someone down there representing them. It always amazes me. I remember a couple years ago a newspaper story that reported that Annapolis lobbyist Bruce Bereano had sixty-some clients. I'm amazed at how naïve the business community could be because there is no way he could represent sixty-some clients during a ninety-day session and do a good job for all of them.

One lobbyist who really rose to prominence during the Tawes administration was George H. Hocker, who represented the beer industry. In those days there were more beer breweries in Maryland than there are today: Gunther and National Bohemian in Baltimore, Queen City in Cumberland and others. Hocker had gotten to know the governor when Tawes had been the state comptroller and responsible for taxation on alcoholic beverages. They were friends and their wives were friends.

One issue that demonstrated Hocker's power arose over a proposal to extend bonuses to World War II veterans. The revenue to pay for these bonuses was to come from an increase in the tax on beer. There was a big fight on the House floor, led by William L. "Bip" Hodges, a restaurant owner from Baltimore. Hodges had served in the U.S. Navy in 1944 and '45 and was active in the Veterans of Foreign Wars. I can see him now standing on the House floor with his VFW hat on, yelling and screaming in support of the bonuses. But Bip never got it. While we were debating the bill, the House unexpectedly adjourned *sine die*, without telling the Senate and the bill died. The real power behind that move would have been the beer lobby and George Hocker.

One of the ways the beer lobby influenced legislation—something that would be unheard of today—was by providing cases of beer in each of the committee rooms and the pressroom, which were located in the State House basement. One night, a delegate from Bethesda named Warren Browning pressed for an increase in the beer tax, saying it hadn't been raised in more than two decades, and placing the blame on beer lobbyists. He said suds were flowing all over the basement floor of the State House—beer everywhere! The next day, there wasn't a can of beer in any committee room, but there was still a big trashcan full of beer and ice in the pressroom.

5

Civil Rights

G AY STREET IN DENTON WAS as good a symbol as any you could find to illustrate the divide between the races when I was growing up.

The black residents of Denton lived on one side of Gay Street and the whites lived on the other. Where people in Denton lived or went to school, which restaurants they ate in or where they sat when they went to the movies, were, quite literally, issues of black and white. The races in Caroline County—and in all of Maryland, for that matter—lived mostly separate, parallel, but hardly equal lives. Denton, like every other community on the Eastern Shore, was no different.

In the 1930s, '40s and '50s—in fact, all the way up until the great federal civil rights laws were passed in the mid-1960s—Maryland was as racially segregated as many states in the Deep South. In 1931, nearly a thousand people watched as a mob of men lynched a twenty-three-year-old black man in Salisbury. Just two years later, a twenty-seven-year-old black laborer was lynched in front of the courthouse in the town of Princess Anne. I was just a little thing then, but I can still remember the National Guard trucks rolling through town.

As I was growing up, whites went to white schools and blacks—they were called Negroes or colored in those days, or worse—went exclusively to black schools. There were separate bathrooms for "whites" and "colored" on the ferries across the Chesapeake Bay and in various public buildings. Blacks were not served in white restaurants. At the movies, the blacks sat in the balconies and the whites sat on the ground floor.

Yet, it was not as if we had no contact with our black neighbors. We used to play with black kids, usually on our bikes. A lot of time we played a game we called "fox and dogs." One group would start off on the bikes and the other group would try to chase them and find them. It was usually the whites versus the blacks. It was friendly. I don't remember any altercations with the kids.

But they went to a different school, which in those days was called the Lockerman School. Decades later, after schools were integrated, Lockerman's name was changed to Riverside, but at the insistence of blacks in the community the name was recently changed back to Lockerman again.

Some white families in Denton, including ours, hired blacks as domestic workers. We had a black woman in our house named Martha Rich for most of my childhood. She cooked and cleaned for $4 a week. (To put this in perspective, at that time my mother, who was the sole support for our family, was making the grand sum of $700 a year as a teacher.) Martha was an awfully nice person. She couldn't read or write, but she was a pretty good cook. She cooked on a wood stove, which I supplied with wood, and she fried almost everything.

For a while, we raised chickens for home consumption and either Martha, my brother or I would be responsible for feeding them. I remember having to kill them, chopping their heads off. Martha did most of that, but I did it, too. It wasn't one of my happiest moments. Martha plucked them.

Although life in Denton was segregated, my parents and grandparents had a basic respect for people regardless of their color. Neither my mother nor my grandparents Roe would permit anybody to use the word "nigger," and there were not many households around then that did that. But the separation of people by race bothered me even as a young boy.

At Townsend's, the soda fountain downtown, when blacks would come in and order something they had to take it out. I always had a bad feeling about that, some tinge of conscience. I went to the movies frequently, and the blacks were always seated separately in the balcony. I don't remember seeing any signs requiring it; it was just understood.

I can recall going to Philadelphia with my mother to see a show when I was just a boy. There were a lot of blacks in the audience and, I guess because it was an entirely new experience for me, I felt very uncomfortable. My mother had no problem with it at all. I remember we talked about it afterwards and she said it hadn't bothered her and that I shouldn't let it bother me.

There were not many blacks in Denton that you would call "middle-class." There was one, Bill Pinkett, who started a bus service and he was successful. There was another fellow named Charlie Greenich, who was a shoemaker. He had his place of business up in the white section of town. He was well regarded and I think he did a pretty good business. But each evening, he'd walk back to "colored town" after he closed his shop.

Most were laborers. A lot of the black women worked for white families as domestics. We did not have a washing machine; our washing machine was Martha. She used a washboard and tub and would hang the clothes on a line out back.

In later years when I was in the navy, both at Mount St. Mary's and later in North Carolina, our units were 100 percent white. Even Bear Bryant's football team, which after the war moved with him to the University of Maryland, was all white.

Growing Demand for Civil Rights

The year I was elected to the Maryland House of Delegates was the same year the U.S. Supreme Court finally ruled that separate, segregated public schools were unconstitutional. It was a case argued by Thurgood Marshall, a black lawyer from Baltimore who represented the NAACP and who one day would become the first black to sit on the nation's highest court.

I knew the *Brown* decision would have a big impact on the Eastern Shore and on Maryland, but change was slow in coming. Nearly one hundred years after the Civil War, the fight for equal civil rights for black Americans was only beginning to develop momentum. Over the sixteen years I served in the General Assembly, the struggle over civil rights was one of the most difficult and emotional issues I faced. In retrospect, it is still hard to understand the hatred so many whites felt toward blacks or how the obvious unfairness of segregation could be justified. Even though I had grown up in the midst of segregation, it was obvious to me it was wrong. The fight for civil rights in the General Assembly in the 1960s helped shape my view of the world, but it also shaped my view of my own colleagues, for better and for worse.

The state legislature I joined in 1955 was almost all white and all male. There was one woman in the Senate, my good friend Mary Nock from Wicomico County, and four women in the House.[14] There were only three blacks among the 152 elected lawmakers: Harry A. Cole in the Senate and Emory R. Cole and Truly Hatchett in the House. Both Senator and Delegate Cole were Republicans; Hatchett was a Democrat. At that time, there were more than 386,000 blacks in Maryland. About 17 percent of the state's population was black, but less than 2 percent of the state legislature.[15] By the time I was elected to the Senate, the numbers of blacks in the legislature had not increased. J. Alvin Jones of Baltimore was the lone black in the Senate; Irma George Dixon and Verda F. Welcome, two women, were the only blacks in the House of Delegates.

The situation nationally was—and still is—not much different. Blacks were first elected to Congress during Reconstruction (beginning in 1869), yet as late as 1966 there were still only five blacks in the entire 435-member House of Representatives. By 2004, the number had risen to 65, still less than 13 percent of the total. In the U.S. Senate, the first black was not elected until 1966 and there has never been more than one black at a time in the 100-member Senate since then.

As I was getting into politics, blacks tended to be Republican, not Democrats as they mostly are today. It all stemmed from Abraham Lincoln and the Emancipation. I'm sure that was generally true around the state. When I went campaigning in those early days, I didn't go door-to-door in the black areas. I was a Democrat and most of them were Republicans.

In the succeeding years, of course, blacks became a mainstay of the Democratic Party and to this day are the most dependable bloc of Democratic voters. I can guess why it changed. The Democrats were certainly known for promoting civil rights in the '50s and '60s, not the Republicans. It was Harry Truman, for example, who in 1948 integrated the armed forces and the federal civil service. And it was John F. Kennedy and Lyndon Johnson who pushed through the major civil rights

---

14. Lottie R. Brinsfield of Dorchester County; Dorothy T. Jackson of Baltimore County; Myrtle A. Polk of Worcester County; and Margaret C. Schweinhaut of Montgomery County.
15. Maryland Department of Planning, Planning Data Services, based on 1950 U.S. Census figures.

laws of the 1960s. Once those kinds of things happen, those affiliations linger on for years, even if circumstances change.

Democrats, in fact, have become so identified with the causes of black Americans and civil rights that Democrats ultimately lost the solid South to the Republicans. It has been reported that even as he was signing the new civil rights legislation into law in the mid-1960s, President Johnson and other prominent Democrats of the time understood they were about to kill their party's ability to win the South for at least a generation. So far, with a few notable exceptions, such as Jimmy Carter and Bill Clinton, it seems they were right.

The slow, painful but steady effort to rid Maryland of its abhorrent segregation practices began shortly after World War II ended, even before I got to the legislature. One of the early efforts in Maryland was to repeal the law that required segregation of passengers on railroads, steamboats, ferries and trollies. I can still remember as a boy riding the ferries connecting the Eastern Shore with the Western Shore and seeing the separate restrooms clearly marked for blacks and whites. When repeal was first proposed in 1951, it failed 19-7, with all but one of the nine senators from the Eastern Shore voting against repeal.

Later the same year, blacks went to federal court to overturn a segregation policy that stipulated separate days for blacks and whites at the bathing beach at Fort Smallwood Park in northern Anne Arundel County. One-third of each summer month was reserved for blacks, called "colored weeks." By 1952, the beach was divided into separate black and white areas.[16] In Baltimore, a regulation by the city liquor board barring blacks from taverns or other places that sold alcoholic beverages was taken to court. Several months later, Governor McKeldin, to his credit, said the practice of forcing blacks to sit in the balcony of Baltimore's Ford Theater—a practice that had been in effect since 1871—must be stopped. The Lyric Theater in Baltimore had no restrictions on seating patrons, but would not allow Negroes on stage. When the theater refused to book the famous black singer Marian Anderson in November 1953, however, the subsequent outcry forced a change in policy. On January 8, 1954, Anderson became the first Negro to appear on the Lyric stage.[17]

Public Accommodations

By the time I got into public life, this cruel and unfair way of life was beginning to change, but change was often slow, piecemeal and only at the direction of the federal courts. The same year as the *Brown v. Board of Education* decision, the University of Maryland became the first state university south of the Mason-Dixon line to be integrated. Public housing in Baltimore was integrated the same year.

16. Barbara Mills, *Got My Mind Set on Freedom: Maryland's Story of Black and White Activism*, 1663–2000 (Bowie, MD: Heritage Books, 2002), 136.
17. Ibid., 144.

A year later, the U.S. Supreme Court ruled that the practice of having "separate but equal" publicly owned parks, playgrounds and pools was also unconstitutional. Governor McKeldin responded by immediately saying he would desegregate public parks, playgrounds and golf courses. He also ordered the desegregation of the Maryland National Guard.

In March of 1955, my first legislative session, Senator Harry Cole—who years later was to serve with distinction on Maryland's highest appellate court—brought a civil rights bill to the Senate floor, only to have it referred back to the Judicial Proceedings Committee on a 19-9 vote. Referring a bill back to committee is a legislative maneuver tantamount to killing the bill. But Cole called the nine votes the bill received a "moral victory." Among the nine were Bill James and Edward S. Northrop, both of whom would become close friends of mine, and Layman Redden, whom I would challenge and defeat three years later.

By the late '50s, the drive to end the pervasive practice of segregation was heating up all around the country. In state after state, lawyers for blacks and other civil rights activists pressed their cases in the courts. Segregationists, alarmed, began to fight back. In 1956, a group of U.S. senators from Southern states signed what they called the "Southern Manifesto" calling for resistance to court-ordered segregation. Rather than allow their children to attend integrated public schools, white parents in many states set up separate private, whites-only schools and withdrew their children from the public schools.

In March 1957, Senator Cole tried again, this time with four bills aimed at prohibiting racial segregation in places of public accommodation, such as inns and hotels, or at resorts, amusement parks or race tracks, or at roadside restaurants. The famous calypso singer Harry Belafonte had been refused accommodation in downtown Baltimore. One of Senator Cole's bills would have established a commission with the power to eliminate or prevent discrimination in employment based on race, creed or national origin.

A half-century later, it is almost hard to believe we lived in a way that such legislation would be necessary. I can remember that the House and Senate held joint hearings on Senator Cole's bills and that in her testimony the Baltimore lawyer Juanita Jackson Mitchell of the NAACP branded the practice of racism as "barbaric."

But none of this swayed the legislature. Supported by Maryland hotel owners, the operator of private bathing beaches in Anne Arundel County and a Harford County segregationist group called the Maryland Petition Committee, among others, the General Assembly easily defeated the legislation.

By the time I moved into the Senate, the fight for civil rights became more sustained and more heated. Again, the courts stepped in where the legislature refused to act. In 1960, after two black bacteriologists from the U.S. Army labs at Fort Detrick were consigned to the balcony of the Marva Theater in nearby Frederick, a federal judge declared the practice illegal. An all-white rule by the Maryland Bar Association, which had excluded blacks from membership for sixty-five years, was also challenged.

Activists, frustrated by the inability to effect change through the legislative process, gradually began to be more forceful, at first taking their grievances to white-owned businesses and later to the streets. In November 1960, the same month that John F. Kennedy narrowly beat Richard M. Nixon for the presidency, three black students were convicted of staging a sit-in demonstration in Upper Marlboro, the Prince George's County seat.

The demand for equal rights seemed to spread to every corner and institution of the state: to swimming pools in Hagerstown, the Glen Echo amusement park near Washington, to bowling alleys and hospitals and to the big Bethlehem Steel plant in Baltimore.

Pierre Salinger, JFK's press secretary, cancelled a visit to Ocean City because the hotel where he was to appear barred Negroes.

Segregationists React

The pressure to end segregation was met by an opposite and almost equal pressure to keep the races divided. Remember, the 1960s was an era when blatantly segregationist candidates became extremely popular. At the presidential level, of course, there was Alabama Governor George Wallace, who in May 1964 narrowly lost the Democratic presidential primary in Maryland to Daniel B. Brewster, who was serving as a stand-in for President Lyndon Johnson. Brewster won, 267,106 to 214,849, but carried only six counties and Baltimore City. Wallace won everywhere else, including all nine Eastern Shore counties, taking my home county of Caroline by a margin of 1,796 to 757. That was absolutely disgraceful.

Wallace's counterpart in Maryland politics was perennial candidate George P. Mahoney, a paving contractor whose thinly veiled segregationist message against "open housing" was embodied in the slogan, "A Man's Home is his Castle—Protect It." Before the decade was out, Mahoney's particular brand of racism would split the Democratic Party and put an underdog Republican named Spiro T. Agnew into the governor's chair.

In the Maryland Senate, one of the strongest voices against civil rights and one of the strongest proponents for the status quo was Frederick C. Malkus Jr., the senator from Dorchester County. Malkus, who was made chairman of the Judicial Proceedings Committee in exchange for his support of Louis Goldstein for Senate president in 1955, was in a pivotal position to affect the legislative challenges to racial segregation. All civil rights legislation had to pass through his committee. Then, as now, the power of a committee chairman to decide the fate of legislation was enormous.

Malkus was a tall, large man with a red tint to his skin that betrayed his fondness for drink. He had a wavy mane of gray hair that earned him the nickname "the Silver Fox," and when he spoke he had a way of tilting his head back so that his nose pointed upwards into the air. He was born in Baltimore, but raised in Dorchester County and served in the army during World War II. A peculiar blend of city and country, Malkus both practiced law in Cambridge and trapped muskrat in the tall grasses of the marshland that made up most of low-lying Dorchester County.

As the 1962 General Assembly opened, Malkus announced that he intended to oppose any effort to enact a public accommodations bill. "It is not a question of race or integration," he said, "but a question of taking a man's property rights away from him." Seemingly oblivious to the injustices long faced by blacks, I can remember Malkus arguing that "whites and Negroes" have always lived in peace on the Eastern Shore. About two days before he made those comments, a white civil rights demonstrator from Ohio had been beaten and stomped at a demonstration at the Choptank Inn, a restaurant on U.S. 50 just outside of Cambridge that became the site of several violent racial incidents. There would be many and more serious civil disturbances on the Eastern Shore before the legislature could finally be coaxed into action.

The "New Era ticket" and a Change in Leadership

In 1962, when Governor Tawes was running for reelection, Danny Brewster, then a member of Congress, decided to run for the U.S. Senate. Danny and I served together in the House of Delegates in the late '50s and became good friends. Danny and his wife, Carol, spent a weekend with us in Rehoboth Beach where Pat and I had rented a cottage, something we did each summer.

Danny was trying to get on Tawes's ticket, which consisted of Tom Finan for attorney general and Louis Goldstein for comptroller. But Danny was getting nowhere, particularly with George Hocker, the beer lobbyist who was Tawes's friend and principal political adviser. My friend, Jack Logan, and his wife, Ann, also spent that weekend with us. Of course we discussed politics most of the time, which culminated in all of us deciding that to put pressure on Tawes, Danny should announce that he was running for governor, I for attorney general and Jim Lacey, a popular former Loyola College star basketball player who was in the insurance business, for comptroller. The plan was for Danny to leak this to the press.

When he got back to Washington, the recipient of the leak was Charles G. Whiteford, then the dean of the *Baltimore Sun* political reporters. Whiteford began calling around the state, trying out what he termed the "New Era ticket," Brewster, Hughes and Lacey. The response Whiteford got convinced him that the ticket would win and he wrote an article saying as much.

Needless to say, Danny quickly got a phone call from the Tawes's camp inviting him to go on their ticket as a candidate for the U.S. Senate. Danny called me in Rehoboth, told me what was going on and I agreed he should take their offer. That was the whole idea: to put the pressure on Tawes to take Danny.

I must admit, we didn't expect the "New Era ticket" to be as popular as Whiteford discovered. The result, obviously, was that Danny was elected to the U.S. Senate.

I can recall sitting on the beach enjoying the thought I might become attorney general. But that only lasted one day. Also, I discovered that I was a few months shy of the required age for that position. Oh well, it was great fun for a few days!

Organizing the Senate

Rather than becoming attorney general, I was elected in 1962 to a second term in the Senate and Tawes was elected to a second term as governor. There were also several changes in the legislative leadership that would eventually have an important impact on the debate over civil rights, an issue that was not going to go away.

One big surprise was the defeat of Senate President George Della, who was beaten by Bip Hodges. Della had become a high potentate of the seven thousand-member Boumi Temple Shrine[18] and was going all over the country representing the Masons but, meanwhile, was accused of totally ignoring his Baltimore district. Bip went out and just worked the district hard and knocked him off. Della's loss set off a scramble for the suddenly vacant Senate presidency between James A. Pine of Baltimore County, H. Winship Wheatley Jr. of Prince George's County, my friend Billy James from Harford County and Malkus.

Up until that time, the legislative leadership was generally selected by whoever was governor. I called a meeting at the Tea Room in Centreville with two of my friends and fellow Eastern Shore senators, J. Albert Roney Jr. of Cecil County and Bob Dean of Queen Anne's, and we agreed the Senate, not the governor, should pick its own leaders. "The Senate ought to organize itself," I said, "Tawes shouldn't do this." They both agreed. Then I said, "Billy wants to be president of the Senate, and so does Win Wheatley." Win was a bright, funny guy—a good guy. I said, "Why don't we see if we can get Billy to be president and Win to be chairman of the Finance Committee and floor leader?" Again, they all agreed. So, I started calling around and the other senators all thought it was a good arrangement.

There had been pressure on Governor Tawes to use his influence to make Jim Pine president of the Senate, so I went up to see him and said, "Governor, the sentiment of the Senate is for Billy to become president and Win Wheatley to become chairman of Finance." He said, "Are you sure?" I said, "Yes, I'm sure." He said, "Well, if that's what they want, I'll go for it."

I went to the first floor of the State House and called Winnie and asked him if he would agree to Billy being president and he becoming chairman of the Finance Committee and floor leader. I told him the Senate members were in favor of this and he said, "Okay, that's fine. Okay with me." I went back to Governor Tawes and told him it was settled and agreed to. So we did it.

I'll never forget that on the first day of the session, Bradford Jacobs, a reporter at the *Sun*, called me aside and said, "I understand you had something to do with the

18. Ernest B. Furguson, "Senator Della's Firmness Brings Top Assembly Job," *Baltimore Sun*, January 10, 1959.

organization of the Senate." I said I had a little to do with it and that the Senate was organizing itself. "Not Tawes?" he asked, then added, "I don't believe that." To which I said: "Well, Brad, I know you don't believe that, but it is true."

An Issue That Was Not Going to Go Away

The changes in the Senate were significant because now both the Senate president, Billy James, and the majority floor leader, Win Wheatley, were supporters of efforts to end racial discrimination in the state. Moreover, by then the Democratic Party had pledged to end discrimination in public places, so Governor Tawes—who had been raised in the segregated rural fishing and oystering community of Crisfield on the Lower Eastern Shore—was, somewhat reluctantly, on board as well.

Had Fred Malkus become Senate president, I think the fight over civil rights would have undoubtedly taken much longer. The power of the presiding officer to influence the outcome of legislative issues is undisputed. Nor was George Della likely to support the desegregation legislation during his tenure as Senate president. He had inflamed emotions with his "white supremacy" talk in 1954. So, I think it represented a significant change from a civil rights perspective for Bill James—and not Malkus—to become president.

It was Malkus, in fact, who came to personify opposition to desegregation in the legislature. Malkus was just too conservative. It was incredible the way he fought civil rights. He acted like a crazy man. To my face, he was always friendly, but behind my back, he attacked me all the time.

In the Senate, the committee chairmen traditionally sit in the first row closest to the rostrum where the Senate president presides. So Wheatley, the chairman of the Finance Committee, sat on the front row just opposite Malkus, the chairman of Judicial Proceedings. Wheatley was a lawyer and a very interesting man. He was a chain-smoker and a little overweight, but had a great sense of humor and was very, very bright. Wheatley was the floor leader when we had the civil rights battles. Winnie was pushing the civil rights legislation and Malkus was opposing it and the fight got ugly. Malkus said mean, really bitter stuff to Wheatley—to someone who had been his friend. I'll never forget it: Malkus got so angry at one point that he threw his glasses down and broke them. It was just awful, terrible stuff.

After one of those vicious fights, I was in Winnie's office in the Senate Finance Committee and Malkus came in and said, "No hard feelings, old buddy." It was incredible, just incredible!

The biggest fight of all was over the proposals to desegregate public accommodations. It is almost hard to believe today that we could have fought so hard over the basic freedom of a black citizen to go into a restaurant or hotel of his or her choosing. Governor Tawes introduced his own package of civil rights legislation in 1963, as did others. These bills would have banned discrimination in hotels, motels and restaurants, at soda fountains, hospitals, movies, theaters, concert halls, parks, picnic grounds, skating rinks, sports arenas, bowling alleys, golf courses and swimming pools.

U.S. State Department officials even weighed in, urging passage of the public accommodations law after they said the country had been embarrassed when a group of African diplomats were refused service along U.S. Route 40 north of Baltimore.

The 1963 legislation marked the ninth year that public accommodations laws had been introduced in the Maryland General Assembly. For the first time, though, passage seemed possible, more so in the House of Delegates than in the Senate, which was still dominated by rural conservatives. It didn't take long, however, for rural lawmakers to find a way out: they would simply exempt their counties from the bill's provisions. By February, a dozen counties had tacked on amendments exempting themselves, leaving the legislation to apply only in Baltimore City and the counties of Allegany, Baltimore, Carroll, Cecil, Charles, Frederick, Harford, Howard, Montgomery, Prince George's and Washington. Even though the residents of these twelve jurisdictions represented 70 percent of the state's population, some civil rights proponents, such as Baltimore City Delegate Julian L. Lapides, complained that exempting the other counties made a mockery of the legislation.

The House finally passed the heavily amended bill, 81-34, the first time a public accommodations bill had ever been approved by either house of the Maryland legislature. In Senator Malkus's Judicial Proceedings Committee, however, more amendments were tacked on, including one exempting taverns and another putting the issue to voter referendum in Carroll County. Malkus poured his own cold water on the bill by proposing an amendment to provide criminal penalties for any person who claimed discrimination under the new law that was later found to be "maliciously made, wholly unfounded or dismissed."

When Governor Tawes signed the bill into law at the end of March, Clarence Mitchell Jr., the Baltimore lawyer who represented the NAACP in both Annapolis and before Congress, lampooned Maryland's nickname as "the Free State," calling it instead, "the Half-Free State." Even so, the legislation made Maryland the first state south of the Mason-Dixon line to ban discrimination in public accommodations.

While progress was being made, it wasn't being made fast enough for those who wanted to wipe the books clean of laws dictating segregation. Even before Governor Tawes signed the legislation into law, large-scale demonstrations were being planned for Malkus's hometown of Cambridge. By May, after several youths were arrested while trying to enter the Dorset Theater with tickets purchased by whites, forty more blacks were arrested for protesting the initial arrests. Picketers demonstrated outside of Malkus's Cambridge office. Gloria Richardson, who headed the Cambridge Non-Violent Action Committee that organized the demonstrations, appealed to U.S. Attorney General Robert F. Kennedy to intervene, but before he could do so, Cambridge erupted in a summer of rioting, shootings, rock throwing and arrests.[19]

19. Mills, *Got My Mind Set on Freedom*, 272–302.

Governor Tawes dispatched the entire five hundred-member battalion of the Maryland National Guard and two hundred State Police troopers to quell the violence. Liquor stores were closed, a 10:00 p.m. curfew was put into effect and soldiers with fixed bayonets patrolled the streets. Tawes later went on TV and radio to talk about the race problems in Cambridge. The situation was so tense and the peace so fragile that the last remnants of the National Guard did not leave Cambridge until July 1964, just two months after using tear gas to put down another riot sparked by a speech in Cambridge by Alabama Governor George Wallace at the Fireman's Arena, the site of previous protests. Violence also broke out in Princess Anne, where demonstrators hurled bricks at State Police with K-9 dogs, but even there it was never as serious as in Cambridge. For some reason, we never seemed to have those kinds of demonstrations in Caroline County.

Political Ramifications

Despite the shortcomings of the Maryland public accommodations bill, I strongly supported it, as I had all the other civil rights bills that came up during my tenure. Even though I grew up and still lived in a part of the state with a long segregationist history, I did not find it difficult to support civil rights. It just seemed like the right thing to do. It was that simple.

I only remember feeling like I voted the wrong way on a civil rights bill once. Among the laws then on the books was one that banned the practice of miscegenation, or mixed marriages. A bill was introduced to repeal the law, but I voted against it. Afterwards, my vote really bothered me. The next day, I went to Verda Welcome, the first black woman elected to the Maryland Senate and a wonderful person, and said, "Verda, I couldn't sleep last night." I told her the vote really bothered me and that if she could get the Senate to reconsider the original vote, I would vote for it the second time. And that is what I did. It passed, but on a very close vote.

I remember Bob Dean, a friend but very conservative senator from Queen Anne's County who sat right behind me, saying, "Harry, you just killed yourself [politically]. That was a big mistake. You just killed yourself." But I didn't.

At one point during all of this, Pat was at home with our two kids, who were very small. She got a phone call threatening to burn our house down because of my votes. We had to get the police and the sheriff to go around to our house and it was pretty bad for a while, but nothing ever came of the threat.

Over the next couple of years, the fight that had been playing out in federal courts and state legislatures for a decade or more was finally addressed by the United States Congress. On July 2, 1964, President Lyndon Johnson signed into law major federal civil rights legislation prohibiting segregation. A year later, he signed a new federal Voting Rights Act assuring blacks of an equal role in the election process. Blacks on the Shore immediately put the new 1964 federal law to a test, lining up to see the movie *The Carpetbaggers* at the Dorset Theater, bowling at Colony Lanes and eating at various restaurants that, until then, had been for "whites only."

Although racial issues would flare up again in later years, especially following the assassination of the Reverend Martin Luther King Jr., the major legislative fight over civil rights in Maryland was essentially over by the mid-'60s and most of us began to turn our attention to other legislative issues.

When I ran for reelection for a third term in the Senate in 1966, however, I discovered that others remembered my votes on civil rights quite clearly and held them against me. I recall, for example, campaigning in Easton and going into a Moose Lodge looking for votes. A couple guys were sitting in there playing cards, including a local undertaker who was pretty prominent in town. As I walked in, he said, "Well, here comes that nigger lover." It was not a very nice time.

In that year's primary, my opponent was a man named Sam Setta, who was originally from Baltimore but had moved to Talbot County and owned a liquor store on U.S. 50, the major throughway on the Eastern Shore. Setta put up signs outside his store and paid for large ads in the local newspapers that said things like, "Know the truth about Harry Hughes: He voted to integrate your swimming pools and barber shops," and so forth. It didn't cost me the election, but it sure didn't help.

Certainly, there were people who were opposed to the civil rights bills—no question about it. But I think what happened was that people may have disagreed with me on that, but still voted for me. I know I didn't pick up a whole lot of votes on the Shore because of my pro-civil rights stance and, in fact, I probably lost some. But I give people in the district credit for seeing through those kinds of tactics, because it didn't defeat me.

The nation's struggle over civil rights, of course, did not disappear due to the passage of legislation, state or federal. In 1965, Governor Wallace stood in the schoolhouse door to bar black students from entering the University of Alabama. In the summer of 1967, there were race riots in Newark, Detroit, Atlanta and 160 other American cities. H. Rap Brown, who had replaced Stokely Carmichael as head of the Student Non-Violent Coordinating Committee and was making the organization more militant, arrived in Cambridge July 24, 1967, for a forty-five-minute speech in which he urged blacks to arm themselves and be ready to die—to be ready to meet violence with violence. Ranting against whites, he said, "When you tear down his store, you hit his religion." That night, Cambridge again erupted in riots, Brown was wounded by gunfire and seventeen buildings were damaged by fire, in part because the all-white fire department, fearing for their lives, refused to enter the black section of town.[20] Governor Agnew again sent the National Guard to the county seat of Dorchester County.

Less than a year later, on April 4, 1968, the Reverend Martin Luther King Jr. was assassinated in Memphis, sparking more race riots in New York, Boston, Chicago, Detroit, Memphis and one hundred other cities, including Baltimore.

20. Theresa Humphrey, "The Night Cambridge Burned: Blacks Remember," *Associated Press*, January 4, 1988.

The Morgan State Budget

Even toward the end of my Senate years, racial tensions still ran high. I vividly recall one situation when, as chairman of the Finance Committee, we were considering the Morgan State College budget. By then, we had moved our committee offices and hearing room to a second-floor wing of the Senate Office Building that is now named after Bill James.

The morning of the hearing, we met in Governor Marvin Mandel's office and were told that a large number of students were coming down *en masse* in support of the proposed budget for Morgan, a historically black university in Baltimore. It was agreed that the State Police would be there to provide protection and make sure that the number of students let in was kept low enough so as not to violate fire codes. While we were over at the State House deciding what to do, we got a call from one of the police officers in the Senate building who said, "Comptroller Goldstein is down here and he's opened the door and told all these people to 'Come on in, come on in!' And we thought, damn, Louie!"

When I got back to the committee room and started the hearing on the Morgan State budget, I let students come in and sit on the floor during the hearing. I didn't realize it at the time, but as the hearing was about over, Dr. Martin Jenkins, who had been Morgan's president since 1948, had quietly slipped down the stairs and out a back entrance to the building. It seemed to me later that Dr. Jenkins must have sensed that trouble was brewing and he didn't want to be anywhere near it.

After the hearing, I went into my committee office when I heard some commotion and the secretaries came in and said, "There's a problem out here." The students had jammed the hall and they wouldn't let anyone out of that wing of the building. More troubling, many of them had smeared Vaseline on their faces as a protection against Mace.

I quickly got Senator Verda Welcome to come over and I said, "Verda, let's you and I go out and talk to them." That's what we did, but I can tell you, it was an awfully tense moment. State Police were standing in back of us, wearing riot masks with glass fronts. And the students refused to let anybody out.

Verda and I talked with them for a while when the bells that go off when senators are being called into session began to ring. Finally I said, "This is wrong. But I'll tell you what I'll do: You let these other senators out and I'll stay here. I won't go to the session. And you pick a few of your friends to be your representatives, and they can come into my office and we can discuss this matter." And they finally agreed to do that. I got hot dogs and Cokes for them and we sat around and had a good discussion.

That incident was very tense, but it ended peacefully. I thought the students might very well get violent. They wouldn't let anybody out of that end of the building. They were jammed in that hall and with Vaseline on their faces, which was an indication they were serious. I think Dr. Jenkins could have controlled it, but he just scooted out.

I was lucky to have Verda with me that day. She was a lovely person. She used to get confused once in awhile, but she was a genuinely nice person. She had some arduous battles to fight and she did so with dignity. She really did. I liked her very much.

6

One Man, One Vote

M Y SECOND TERM IN THE state Senate, from 1963 to 1967, was one of the most tumultuous periods of my life—and part of one of the most tumultuous decades our country has ever faced. It was the decade of civil rights, Vietnam and the assassinations of JFK, Robert F. Kennedy and Martin Luther King Jr. It was the era of the Beatles and Bob Dylan, of long hair, "black power" and "women's lib," of Lyndon Johnson and Richard Nixon.

In just the four years of my second Senate term, I participated in the landmark votes to expand civil rights in Maryland, ran for a seat in Congress but lost, became floor leader of the Senate and chairman of its influential Finance Committee, watched in dismay as the Eastern Shore lost its political clout to the "one man, one vote" rulings of the U.S. Supreme Court, helped design and push to passage one of the most far-reaching tax reform measures ever approved in Maryland and sadly saw a staunch segregationist become my party's gubernatorial nominee.

During those years, I also was approached for the first time by people who thought I might be a good candidate for governor.

In 1964, however, I wasn't thinking about being governor; I was thinking about becoming the congressman from Maryland's First District. History had shown that once a congressman got elected to Congress from the Eastern Shore, he tended to keep the seat for a long time. The incumbent in 1964 was Rogers C.B. Morton, a Republican just finishing his first term. Morton was a big guy, about six-foot-five, and rich. He had moved to Maryland from Kentucky and had bought a farm in Talbot County. After only a single two-year term, I thought he might be vulnerable. If you're going to do it, I thought, it is better to try to knock him off early in his service. I had lived on the Shore all my life and my legislative base had expanded from Caroline County to include other Middle Shore counties, so I thought I had a chance.

There was really no reason not to give it a try. It was what you would call "a free race" for me. I didn't have to give up my state legislative seat to run for Congress because it was in the middle of my Senate term. If I lost, I was still in the General Assembly.

I ran a hard campaign up and down the Shore, but with very little money. I tried to paint Morton as an outsider, a guy from Kentucky who had moved here to be the Eastern Shore's congressman. By contrast, I advertised myself as a "native Eastern Shoreman." I put out a tri-fold brochure that mentioned the "Eastern Shore" no fewer than seven times. On the cover, over a picture of Pat, Beth, Ann and me sitting on a big log in the woods, were the words: "Vote for Harry R. Hughes,

Democratic candidate for Congress, a true native son…an Eastern Shoreman."
On the back it proclaimed, "An Eastern Shoreman who understands Eastern Shore
problems." Upon reflection, that was a rather parochial thing to do, but I really did
believe that I knew more about the area, its people and its problems than he did.

Toward the end of the campaign, the Salisbury television station ran a poll
showing that Morton was going to beat me big. We didn't have enough money for
our own pollster, so we did our own polling by leafing through the phone book and
calling every fifth name or so. Our admittedly amateur poll also showed Morton
was going to win, but that it was going to be much closer than the Salisbury TV
station poll led viewers to believe. Our poll also showed that Lyndon Johnson was
going to carry the Eastern Shore, which turned out to be true. It was about the only
poll that showed that.

A guy who did advertising for my campaign named Wink Foster said he thought
there was something fishy about the Salisbury TV poll, so we met with the station's
manager. It turned out that the way he had done the poll was just to call a bunch of
his Republican friends on the Shore. It was really an awful thing. Foster urged me to
file a complaint with the Federal Communications Commission, because the results
of the poll had been broadcast as if it were a news item. He prepared the telegram
to the FCC, but told me that we may not prevail and, even if we did, the election
might be over by then. At least, he said, we might be able to point out that the poll
was erroneous. In the end, however, I decided not to file the complaint. I was afraid
it might be considered a dirty campaign tactic. I think now that I was wrong—I
should have done it. It might have made the difference in the election.

When the votes started to come in, I beat Morton in Cecil County by about nine
hundred votes and thought, "Boy, this is great!" But the more votes came in from
farther down the Shore, the worse it got for me. Morton rolled up big margins in
Wicomico, Worcester and his home county of Talbot. I won four of the district's
nine counties (Cecil, Queen Anne's, Somerset and my home county of Caroline)
and fell one vote short of winning Kent. But Morton's campaign had spent a lot of
money on the Lower Shore and his vote totals there showed it. In the end, I lost,
40,762 to 36,013.

Pat and I didn't mope about it long. I returned to the General Assembly in
January 1965 and later that summer, Pat, our two girls and I took a six-week cross-
country trip to Oregon and back, stopping at national parks and having a great
time. We couldn't have done that if I had been in Congress.

Rural Power

When I went to the Maryland Senate, rural areas like the one I represented enjoyed
exceptional power in state government. Each of the Eastern Shore's nine counties
had its own senator, as did every other county in the state regardless of population.
Sparsely populated counties such as Somerset, Kent or Caroline had the same

number of senators (one) as heavily populated urban counties such as Montgomery, Prince George's or Baltimore County. As a result, Eastern Shore senators chaired one-third of the Senate's twenty-one standing committees and Eastern Shore delegates chaired one-third of the House's eighteen standing committees. Rural lawmakers exercised extraordinary power over what laws were passed and how funds from the state budget were spent.

In 1960, a group of Maryland citizens representing the more urban jurisdictions filed a lawsuit in Anne Arundel County Circuit Court alleging that apportionment of the Maryland General Assembly based on political jurisdictions rather than on population was unfair. They argued that such a system discriminated against the residents and voters in the more populous areas of the state.

Thus began a legal struggle that was to stretch over a dozen years before it was finally settled. The fight over how Marylanders should be fairly represented in the General Assembly tied legislators in knots for years, moved from the circuit court up to the state's highest appellate court and back down several times, and ultimately made it all the way to the United States Supreme Court—not once, but twice.[21]

Maryland's system of legislative apportionment was hardly unique. As the United States became more urban following World War II, states that for years had rural majorities suddenly had rural minorities. Yet those rural minorities clung stubbornly to the political power they had long enjoyed. States such as Tennessee and Alabama were shown to have avoided redrawing their legislative boundaries for sixty years or more. As a result, the discrepancies between rural and urban districts were sometimes extreme. In Vermont in the early 1960s, for example, the most populous legislative district in the state had 33,000 residents and the least populous had 238. Yet each was represented by one delegate.

While the disparities in Maryland were not as extreme, they were large enough to attract the attention of the courts. By the time the decade was over, Maryland's era of rural control was over and a new era of urban dominance had begun.

In the spring of 1962, toward the end of my first term in the Senate, Maryland's Court of Appeals ruled on a 5-to-2 vote that the state's method of apportioning membership in the House of Delegates was unconstitutional. Interestingly, the court made no finding about the Senate.

At the end of May, Governor Tawes summoned the General Assembly into special session to come up with a new reapportionment plan, but we had difficulty agreeing on what to do. In the end, we simply passed a stopgap measure that added 19 more delegates to the 123 allowed under the existing plan and distributed the new delegates to the more populous counties. We hoped that would be the end of it, but it wasn't.

---

21. *Daily Record* (Baltimore), September 19, 1966. Maryland Court of Appeals decision, Rodowsky and Liebmann opposed by Thomas B. Finan (attorney general) and Robert F. Sweeney (assistant attorney general), argued by Alfred L. Scanlan of Bethesda, John B. Wright of Annapolis, Francis X. Gallagher of Baltimore, before Prescott, Hammond, Horney, Marbury, Oppenheimer, Barnes and McWilliams.

A few months later, the same group that filed the original suit asked the Court of Appeals to rule that the Senate apportionment plan was also unconstitutional. This time, however, the Court of Appeals refused, voting 4-3 to affirm a lower court ruling that concluded the Senate apportionment scheme was constitutional. In August 1963, the plaintiffs appealed the case to the U.S. Supreme Court.

By then, the Supreme Court had become active in reapportionment cases, an area of law that in prior years had been left to the states to decide. The cases arrived in Washington from Alabama, Colorado, Delaware, New York, Virginia and other states, including Maryland. The thrust of the Supreme Court's examination of these cases was whether apportionment plans violated citizens' rights under the U.S. Constitution's Equal Protection Clause.

Thomas B. Finan, Maryland's attorney general, opposed the idea of basing the state Senate's membership strictly on population and said that state legislatures should be allowed apportionment plans similar to the one used for the U.S. Congress, with one house apportioned by population and the other equal representation by jurisdiction. Arguing against Solicitor General Archibald Cox before the Supreme Court in November 1963, Finan said he feared an apportionment plan based completely on population would result in "the tyranny of the majority." Two years later, Finan would find himself on the opposite side of the same argument.

The Supreme Court finally dropped its apportionment bomb on June 15, 1964. In an opinion written by Chief Justice Earl Warren that would have ramifications throughout the country, the high court dismissed the suggested analogy between Congress and state legislatures as irrelevant. Instead, the Supreme Court declared that "one man, one vote" would be the rule for apportioning state legislative bodies nationwide.

"Legislators represent people, not trees or acres. Legislators are elected by voters, not farms or cities or economic interests," Warren wrote. "Logically, in a society ostensibly grounded on representative government, it would seem reasonable that a majority of the people of a State could elect a majority of that State's legislators."

Later in his opinion, he stated, "This is at the heart of Lincoln's vision of 'government of the people, by the people, for the people.' We hold that, as a basic constitutional standard, the Equal Protection Clause requires that the seats in both houses of a bicameral state legislature must be apportioned on a population basis."

The ruling hit the Maryland political world like a thunderbolt. My friend Paul D. Cooper, by then director of the legislature's Fiscal Research Bureau, immediately saw the ruling's practical effect, saying the state's small counties would be at the mercy of larger subdivisions.

By summer of the following year, a plan to reapportion the Senate based on the Supreme Court ruling was circulated that would provide for one senator to represent the four Upper Shore counties and two for the four Lower Shore counties—eight counties that had been represented by eight senators. Rural lawmakers worried not only about their own loss of power and representation, but about ceding control of the General Assembly to urban delegations often controlled by well-organized political machines.

Governor Tawes again summoned the General Assembly into special session in October 1965 to respond to the Supreme Court's ruling. Our response was to pass not one plan, but two. The first plan, embodied in Senate Bill 5 and sponsored by Senate President Bill James, apportioned membership of both houses based on population. It provided for forty-three senators (up from the existing twenty-nine), some of whom would represent more than one county. Under that bill, Caroline County would be grouped with Talbot, Queen Anne's, Kent and Cecil Counties in one senatorial district with two state senators. For those of us from the Eastern Shore and other rural counties, such a plan was unacceptable.

Talbot County Senator John-Clarence North and I cosponsored an alternative plan that provided for fifty-three senators and would guarantee that nineteen of Maryland's twenty-three counties would be represented by at least one senator. The balance would be allocated to the more populous counties and Baltimore City based on population. Our plan was based on the congressional model, in which the House of Representatives is apportioned by population, but the Senate has two members from each state. The bill we sponsored (known as Senate Bill 8) also contained a provision that said if it was determined to be constitutional, Senate Bill 5 "shall not become effective." Our bill had been developed about five weeks earlier by the Legislative Council, a group of ten delegates and ten senators (including me) that acted on behalf of the entire legislature when it was not in session. Our bill was clearly the legislature's preferred plan.

But Attorney General Finan, relying on the Supreme Court's one man, one vote ruling, issued a press release stating that "with great reluctance" he had advised Governor Tawes that he believed the bill Senator North and I cosponsored was unconstitutional.

After both bills were enacted in the special session, I wrote Governor Tawes a letter saying that "the majority of the members of both houses would prefer the provisions of Senate Bill 8, particularly that part which assures each county of having at least one senator."

Tawes said he agreed with Finan that Senate Bill 8 was probably unconstitutional, but nevertheless signed both bills into law and said he would let the courts decide. Within three months, Maryland's highest court decided Finan and Tawes were right: it struck down Senate Bill 8 as unconstitutional. This time, Senator North and I appealed to the U.S. Supreme Court.

I got Tawes to agree that we could hire a special counsel to argue for Senate Bill 8 and I lined up Lawrence F. Rodowsky for the job. Larry had been an assistant attorney general and was by then in private practice in Baltimore. Smart and meticulous, Larry would later help me in my race for governor and, after I became governor, I would appoint him to the Maryland Court of Appeals, where he served with distinction for twenty years. He remains a close friend.

But Larry was not successful in our appeal. The Supreme Court ruled that its one man, one vote standard applied to both houses of the legislature. It concluded that the argument we were making with "the little federal system" analogy was wrong. The high court said that in the original instance, the thirteen colonies had a choice either to go off and form thirteen separate nations or join together in a union, but to do so in a way that preserved a good part of their sovereignty. That is where the logic of our argument broke down. Unlike the thirteen original colonies, Maryland counties have no sovereignty; they are creatures of the legislature and can be changed or altered by act of the legislature. There is, therefore, no analogy to the federal legislature. I had argued that the federal system was working well, that it provided a sound check-and-balance, but to no avail.

The Aftermath

We were all pretty upset about that. It was such a drastic change. For some rural lawmakers, this signaled the end of their political careers. Of nine Eastern Shore senators elected in 1962, only four survived the one man, one vote decision: Bob Dean from Queen Anne's, Mary Nock from Wicomico, Fred Malkus from Dorchester and me. Dean and I were pushed into a new district representing five Upper Shore counties: Cecil, Kent, Queen Anne's, Caroline and Talbot. Nock and Malkus represented four on the Lower Shore: Dorchester, Wicomico, Worcester and Somerset. The twenty-seven members of the Eastern Shore House delegation elected in 1962 shrunk to eleven after 1966. Some were defeated and some just decided not to run again.

For others, the one man, one vote decision marked the end of their role as power brokers in Annapolis. None was hit harder than Fred Malkus, who in 1966 was deposed as chairman of the Senate Judicial Proceedings Committee. It was the direct result of an influx of new urban senators who strongly opposed Malkus's conservative views on civil rights and other issues. "I was a country boy and the city boys took over," he later explained.[22]

Before the newly elected legislature could be seated, some of those "city boys" asked Bill James and me to meet them at a restaurant near the State Office Building in Baltimore. They told us they were going to change the Senate organization and that they had the votes to do it. They said Malkus had to go.

In those days, there were three major committees in the Senate. Jim Pine was chairman of Economic Affairs, I was chairman of Finance and floor leader and Malkus was chairman of Judicial Proceedings. The newly elected senators said they wanted to replace both Malkus and Pine. Billy objected to this and they offered the Senate presidency to me. I said no, that I wanted Bill to stay on as president. I liked being floor leader because there was more action. So, I said, "Billy, you don't have a choice. Either Malkus goes or you're not going to be president of the Senate. It's that simple. They have the votes." He finally said, "Alright, alright, but I'm sticking with Pine."

22. Anne Hughes, "I Have Always Been the Happiest When the Battle Became the Hottest," *Cambridge Daily Banner*, April 22, 1993.

They let Pine stay, but Malkus lost his chairmanship and I think Fred always attributed that somewhat to me. J. Joseph Curran Jr., of Baltimore, a much more liberal and compassionate legislator, replaced him as chairman of Judicial Proceedings.

Even before that, Malkus and I had our run-ins. When I ran for Congress in 1964, Malkus opposed me. He threatened the teachers' union, which had held a fundraiser for me, telling teachers not to attend. I don't know what sparked it, whether it was jealousy or something else. To my face, Malkus was always friendly, but behind my back, he would frequently attack me.

Fred Malkus remained in the Senate for another twenty-eight years after losing his chairmanship, retiring in 1994 after forty-four years in the Senate and forty-eight in the legislature overall. But he never again exercised the authority he had before the one man, one vote decision. He became embittered by both the Eastern Shore's loss of power and by his own demotion. Even though he was later appointed to the largely ceremonial position of president pro tem, his later years were mostly spent railing against the urban and suburban majorities that had assumed control over the General Assembly.

It was not until 1972 that the issue of legislative reapportionment was finally put to rest. The General Assembly passed, and the citizens of Maryland ratified, an amendment to the state Constitution that divided the state into 47 legislative districts, each to be represented by one senator and three delegates—47 senators and 141 delegates. This amendment, which is still in force today, states that "each district must consist of adjoining territory, be compact in form, and of equal population."

When all of this happened, I think everybody thought that Baltimore City was going to control everything. In fact, Baltimore City had more control under the old system than under the one in place now. In 1950, the city had 6 out of 29 senators and 36 out of 123 delegates. They really had clout. Now, with apportionment based on population and the city population steadily declining for half a century (from nearly 1 million residents in 1950 to about 635,000 today), the Baltimore delegation consists of only 6 senators out of 47 and only 18 delegates out of 141.

It took awhile for the Eastern Shore and other rural areas to adjust, but it is interesting to note how well those rural areas have done in securing leadership roles in the aftermath of one man, one vote. I remained as chairman of the Senate Finance Committee and majority floor leader. Years later, others from the Eastern Shore moved into positions of power. Thomas Hunter Lowe of Talbot County became Speaker and a few years after that Clayton Mitchell Jr. of Kent County also became Speaker. John Hargreaves from Caroline County chaired the House Appropriations Committee, which oversees the state budget, and was succeeded some years later by Norm Conway from Wicomico County. John Hanson Briscoe, a lawyer from rural St. Mary's County, became Speaker, as did Cumberland tavern owner Casper R. Taylor Jr.

Even with the change in the legislature's makeup, people from rural counties seemed to move up the ladder depending on their abilities or their personality, not because of where they were from. That's a good thing.

Cooper-Hughes

THE 1960s WAS AN ERA of unexpected and sweeping change—change brought on by the judicial rulings, sit-in demonstrations and riots of the civil rights struggle; by the publication of Rachel Carson's *Silent Spring* and the rising interest in environmentalism; by the protest marches and enormous controversy over the conduct of the war in Vietnam; by political assassination; and by a national political swing from the liberalism of John F. Kennedy to the conservatism of Richard M. Nixon.

Maryland, too, was rapidly changing. Baltimore, Maryland's only major city, was in full-scale post-war retreat, with thousands of its inhabitants, most of them white, pulling up roots and moving to the fast-expanding suburbs. They left behind abandoned row houses, empty factories, increasingly failing schools and rising crime. One by one, the downtown department stores along Howard Street closed or moved to big new malls springing up in places like Towson and Glen Burnie. The city's once vibrant shopping district began to decay, shipping interests declined at the port and manufacturers hit hard times as the economy shifted to service jobs and the city's core tax base moved elsewhere.

Baltimore officials did their best to fight back, constructing the Charles Center office complex and the Morris Mechanic Theater and laying the foundation for what would become Baltimore's famous Inner Harbor. They rode a wave of fan support for Johnny Unitas and the Baltimore Colts, who won the National Football League championship in 1958 and '59, and Brooks Robinson and the Baltimore Orioles, who won the World Series in 1966.

The governor's office, meanwhile, swung from rural to suburban to urban. The decade began under the stewardship of J. Millard Tawes, a Democrat from the remote Lower Eastern Shore fishing community of Crisfield. But in 1966, the State House passed into the control of Republican Spiro T. Agnew, the county executive of suburban Baltimore County who seemed like a moderate next to the segregationist nominee of the Democratic Party, George P. Mahoney. The decade ended with Agnew becoming Nixon's vice-president and the General Assembly electing House Speaker Marvin Mandel, a Democrat from Baltimore, to replace him.

Against this frenetic backdrop, the size, strength and sophistication of state government grew and the legislature's professional staff steadily expanded. Senate President Bill James, Montgomery County Senator Blair Lee III and I went to California to look at their legislature in Sacramento. We met with A. Alan Post, the chief fiscal adviser to the legislature. He was quite an institution out there. As a result of this visit, we came back and expanded the Department of Fiscal Services in Maryland. We also transferred the state auditors' office from the executive branch to the legislature, where it could be more independent.

Fairly Balancing the Tax System

One of the thorniest issues facing the legislature was whether the state's tax structure was fairly balanced between state and county interests. Was the state doing its share to help local governments provide needed services? Were taxpayers being treated fairly?

Maryland counties were struggling because property taxes were their only major source of revenue. The counties were fully paying for the cost of school construction, and it was a big part of their budgets. One of the central issues we faced was whether the state could stop taxing property and leave that revenue source exclusively to the counties. The other problem was that Baltimore City was losing population, businesses and its tax base and many of us felt we needed to find a way to send more state revenue Baltimore's way. There was also just a general feeling then that the state tax system was regressive. The income of everyone in Maryland was taxed at the same flat rate, obviously hitting those at the lower end of the income scale proportionately harder than those with higher incomes. The state sales tax was also seen as regressive because it most harmed those least able to pay.

In February 1962, the Maryland County Commissioners' Association proposed legislation to create a Commission on State and County Finance. By summer, Governor Tawes named the ten-member commission to be headed by John S. VanBibber Shriver, director of the legislature's Fiscal Research Bureau. The commission was originally asked to make recommendations to the 1963 legislature, but as so often happens with controversial issues, its study took much longer than expected.

In the midst of this commission's work in April 1964, Shriver was hospitalized for a leg ailment and died following emergency surgery.[23] On my recommendation, a month later he was replaced as director of the Fiscal Research Bureau by Paul D. Cooper, then assistant state school superintendent for administration and finance. Cooper and Shriver had worked with the Committee on Taxation and Fiscal Matters, which I chaired, on school funding issues. After this appointment, Cooper became staff to the House Ways and Means Committee and the Senate Finance Committee and worked directly with me on devising the state's new formula for distributing education aid.[24] Cooper turned out to be one of the best staff appointments the General Assembly ever made.

I was on the Senate Finance Committee, chaired by Ed Northrop of Montgomery County. In January 1962, Northrop was appointed to the federal bench and

23. "J. S. VanBibber Shriver, State official," *Baltimore Sun*, April 10, 1964.
24. Stephen E. Nordlinger, "Cooper to Head Fiscal Bureau," *Baltimore Sun*, May 22, 1964.

replaced by James A. Pine. Born, raised and educated in West Virginia, Pine was a product of Baltimore County's then-powerful political machine. He had been vice-chairman under Northrop and was therefore the almost automatic choice for chairman. But Pine had difficulty explaining committee legislation on the Senate floor and the following year, right after the 1962 election, he was replaced by Winnie Wheatley and I became vice-chairman.[25]

During the 1963 and '64 sessions, Wheatley was floor leader through the Senate's most contentious civil rights battles. I always thought the strain took a toll on him. In early January 1965, Wheatley underwent lung surgery and I was asked to take over as Finance Committee chairman and floor leader on an "acting basis." But three days before the 1965 session was to convene, Wheatley unexpectedly died. Winnie and I were good friends and his passing was a big loss for the Senate and for me personally.

But the legislature, of course, had to move on and in the days that followed Winnie's death, I was officially appointed chairman of the Finance Committee and majority floor leader. I would hold those two powerful posts until I left the General Assembly for good six years later.

I had just become chairman when Cooper presented to Governor Tawes the commission's 140-page report entitled, "Guide Lines for Improving Maryland's Fiscal Structure." It recommended sweeping changes in state and local taxes and the fiscal relationship between state and local government. In a key chapter entitled, "The Roots of Our Financial Problems," the commission stated that "the net effect of all taxes in the state at present is decidedly regressive."

This politically explosive report was clearly going to be too much for us to deal with during the regular legislative session, so we passed a joint resolution calling for the appointment of a special legislative commission to study and evaluate the report and prepare implementing legislation for the 1966 Assembly to consider. Six senators and six delegates were appointed to the Commission and I was named chairman.[26]

At our first meeting on May 10, we decided to hold a series of public hearings on each of the different tax proposals contained in Cooper's report. These hearings were widely publicized, but lightly attended. As Cooper was later to report, "Testimony was typified by statements such as, 'We support the report in principle, but must see a more definite proposal before committing ourselves.'"

Two Skinny Pamphlets

We then decided to discontinue the hearings and examine each of the recommendations in detail and develop our own detailed proposal. There was

25. Pine later became chair of the Economic Affairs Committee, where he did a good job.
26. Other members included: Senators James Clark Jr.; George R. Hughes Jr.; Joseph V. Mach; Mary L. Nock; and J. Frank Raley Jr.; and Delegates William M. Houck, vice-chairman; C. Stanley Blair; J. Raymond Buffington Jr.; William B. Dulany; Irwin F. Hoffman; and Herbert H. Tyler.

no shortage of controversy. Almost before the ink had dried on Cooper's report, Hyman Pressman, the feisty comptroller for Baltimore City, publicly stated his opposition to the Cooper proposal. By summer, Janet Hoffman, Baltimore's fiscal director, said the Cooper Commission recommendations would not solve the city's fiscal problems. City Mayor (and former Governor) Theodore McKeldin suggested we address the Cooper Commission recommendations at a special legislative session being planned for October, but there was no way we could be ready that fast.

By late July our legislative commission gave tentative endorsement to the major tax reform measures recommended by the Cooper Commission, moving toward a graduated income tax, a broader sales tax, changes and increases in the corporate income tax and a greater degree of equalization in state spending on the education needs of local jurisdictions. The Commission agreed that property taxes should be reserved for local use.

From then until the late fall, we started holding hearings again all over the state. I think we held more than forty meetings in all. Governor Tawes said he supported the recommendations "in principle," but would go no further. Later, the absence of strong support from Tawes would prove pivotal. County Executive Agnew flatly opposed the plan, saying it would mean "real trouble for Baltimore County." (Later, as governor, he would change his tune.)

In September, the Commission held two days of meetings aboard the state yacht. By the time we stepped off the boat, we had reached agreement on most issues. In October we issued our preliminary report, a skinny little pamphlet entitled, "Let's Think First." It was intended to elicit public reaction before the Commission prepared its final report to the governor and the General Assembly.

It began with a succinct statement of three principles:

> Local governments provide the strength of our State and Nation, and, if they are to survive, they must have adequate resources to provide for the basic needs of the people they serve...The role of the State in the State-local fiscal partnership must be one of equalization.
>
> Taxation must be fair and equitable...To meet the test of equity, the overriding requirement is that tax burdens must bear a reasonable relationship to ability to pay.
>
> Favorable business climates redound to the benefit of all...All business should be treated alike, and taxes imposed should be related to ability to pay them.[27]

After stating these principles, the pamphlet outlined the "facts we have found" about taxation as it related to local governments, to the issue of equity and to the health of the state's businesses. That, in turn, was followed with a series of conclusions and

27. Special Legislative Commission on State and Local Taxation and Fiscal Relations, "Let's Think First," (preliminary report, October 1965).

recommendations, including precise tables showing how many millions of dollars would be raised or lost as a result of each recommended change. The pamphlet ended with a review of the projected "overall effects" if the recommendations should be implemented.

Cooper wrote this little masterpiece over the course of a single weekend while holed up in a cabin he owned in the Pennsylvania woods. We wanted to get the ideas out there, so after "Let's Think First" was published Paul and I took the pamphlet to all the newspaper editorial boards to lobby for their support.

In November, the Baltimore City Council endorsed our recommendations, as did Anne Arundel County Senator Joseph W. Alton Jr. and the Maryland Farm Bureau. Baltimore lawyer Clarence Miles, already a candidate for the Democratic nomination for governor in an election that was still a year away, urged approval of the Cooper-Hughes's recommendations. By year's end, Agnew also began sending signals that he might be able to support the recommendations.

Even Charles Della, the longtime lobbyist for the AFL-CIO, endorsed all of the recommendations but one: the proposed tripling of the beer tax from three cents a gallon to nine cents. Della said he "feared a price increase for the beer-drinking working man."

My counterpart in the House of Delegates at that time was Roy Staten, a Baltimore County legislator who was chairman of the Ways and Means Committee. Staten was no friend of the Commission's plan, but said he would not block its passage. He said he didn't have to—it would "die of its own weight."

On January 7, 1966, the Special Legislative Commission on State and Local Taxation and Financial Relations issued its final report. Addressed to Governor Tawes and members of the General Assembly, our second skinny pamphlet, entitled "Let's Take Firm Action," spelled out the Commission's "fundamental premises," the "facts we have found," our conclusions and, finally, a list of sixteen major recommendations. Among them: replacement of the flat rate income tax then in effect with a "mildly graduated" tax rate of 3 to 6 percent; elimination of the state property tax and reservation of this tax base for local governments; elimination of all state and local taxes on business personal property and, in their place, imposition of a uniform state tax on business personal property at a relatively low rate; increases in education aid, establishment of a "realistic" program of aid for school construction and equalization of other formulas used to divvy up state aid to local governments; creation of a program through which the state and local governments would share the cost of all health service costs on a basis related to need and ability to pay; and an increase in the excise tax on beer from three cents per gallon to six cents per gallon.

So that counties would not have to continue to rely solely on the property tax, we also recommended that they be required to impose a "piggyback income tax" equal to at least 20 percent of the state income tax with a local option to levy a piggyback tax as high as 50 percent of the state amount.[28]

28. This 50 percent cap on piggyback taxes has subsequently been increased to 60 percent.

These changes, we concluded, would be fairer to individual taxpayers, improve the state's business climate and would greatly strengthen local governments. A lot of what we were doing was trying to help the city of Baltimore. This omnibus tax proposal became known as "Cooper-Hughes," the product of Paul Cooper's original recommendations as modified by the legislative commission I chaired.

Viewed with the perspective of forty-some years, it is almost hard for me to imagine that so much change could have come from so little. The two skinny pamphlets we produced, one a mere seventeen pages and the other a barely more robust twenty-six, helped clear the way for the most sweeping single piece of tax and fiscal aid legislation in Maryland history.

Their simplicity in style and straightforward approach would be unheard of today. The covers of these two pamphlets, "Let's Think First" and "Let's Take Firm Action," were apparently the work of some amateurish bureaucrat rather than a professional graphic artist. These were not documents you would expect to sway the masses, but they were extraordinarily effective. The tax reform these two thin pamphlets spawned, the Cooper-Hughes plan, is the tax structure still in place in Maryland today.

In the Foreword section of the pamphlet, I wrote a brief statement thanking those who helped put the recommendations together, singling out Dr. Cooper and his staff for their ability, dedication and "boundless energy." Of the senators and delegates who made up our panel, I said: "No legislative committee ever worked harder or with more dedication to the task assigned to them…These elected officials approached the difficult problems involved in State and local finances and taxation with a maximum emphasis on fairness and with a minimum of political considerations." I described the Commission recommendations as "a balanced program for greater fairness in fiscal policy and taxation in Maryland."

Tough Going

Once the Commission's legislation hit the General Assembly, however, it was tough going. Whenever any tax is adjusted, some citizens benefit from the change and some are hurt or fear they will be hurt. In this case, we were suggesting an overhaul of virtually every major tax that state and local governments then levied, creating enormous cross-currents of groups and individuals both for and against all or some of the changes.

Governor Tawes, for example, asked for a last-minute change to raise more state revenue than the Commission had initially recommended. Republican John A. Cade, a young Anne Arundel County councilman, decried the Cooper-Hughes plan as "destructive of the principle of local self-determination." W. Dale Hess of Harford County, the majority floor leader in the House, said he was "shocked" at the effects the proposed income tax would have on wage earners.

At the same time, Cooper-Hughes enjoyed broad support, including from the influential Baltimore newspapers, which editorially labeled Hess and Staten as "obstructionists."

On February 9, 1966, I appeared before Staten and members of the Ways and Means Committee and was grilled for two hours about the details of our fifty-three-page bill. The proposal was so controversial and the potential impact of the recommendations so far-reaching that the hearing was held in the House chamber in the State House rather than in the much smaller Ways and Means Committee room. About half of the members of the House attended and Governor Tawes watched from the balcony for the first hour.

"This is not a tax increase," I told them, "but a shift of the tax burden from property to income." I described it as "the progressive, fair, equitable way of imposing taxes."

As inevitably happens with any major piece of legislation, the two presiding officers, Bill James in the Senate and Marvin Mandel in the House, made clear that Cooper-Hughes would have to be modified to stand any chance of passage.

Yet James, to his credit, understood that all the component parts of Cooper-Hughes were interdependent and any modification would be hard to balance. "It must pass as a package or fall with a tremendous crash," he said. "It's like a jigsaw puzzle—pull out one piece and you'll destroy its symmetry and validity." We would get Cooper-Hughes through the Senate; it was in the House where I knew we would run into the stiffest resistance.

In the Ways and Means Committee, Staten set up a special subcommittee to handle Cooper-Hughes when it came over from the Senate and appointed Hess to chair it. I think he expected the subcommittee to kill it, but just before the end of the session we managed to get the bill out and onto the floor of the House. That would not have happened had it not been for the work of Delegate William M. Houck, a Democrat from Frederick who was vice-chairman of my commission and also sat on the Ways and Means Committee.

We knew the vote would be close. One delegate from Baltimore was sick and wasn't there, so we temporarily lost his vote. Another whom we had counted on, J. Samuel Dillon Jr. of Hagerstown, got angry about some education bill we had defeated and said he was going to vote against Cooper-Hughes. But Dillon said if the bill failed, he would vote for it if it were brought up a second time on a motion for reconsideration. That meant we just barely had the votes to pass it.

When the bill finally came up on the final night of the 1966 session, it failed as expected by two votes. But Hess then filibustered it and we never got the bill back up for the reconsideration vote, which we were confident we could have won. It went right up until the last few minutes of the session. I was across the hall, sitting in the Senate, and I can remember somebody came in and told me the bill didn't make it.

Later that night, Bob Murphy, who then was a deputy attorney general (and years later would become the chief judge of the Court of Appeals), told me that failure of the bill had left the city of Baltimore with a fiscal problem and that Governor Tawes was going to call a special session the following day to address it. The governor, he said, would like me to be in his office early the next morning.

The next morning, however, I overslept. By the time I got to the governor's office, Staten, Jim Pine and other legislative leaders were there and it was obvious they had been discussing what to do. I thought the reason they wanted a special session was to run Cooper-Hughes through for another vote because we had lost it by such a narrow margin in the House and we really did have the votes to pass it.

Suddenly it dawned on me what they were talking about. It wasn't Cooper-Hughes at all. It was some kind of quickie fiscal fix to cover the revenue that Baltimore City had anticipated receiving from the Cooper-Hughes bill. When I realized they weren't talking about enacting the full Cooper-Hughes proposal, I said, "You guys have already made up your mind about what you are going to do," and I walked out.

In place of Cooper-Hughes, lawmakers returning for the one-day special session enacted legislation that gave Baltimore City and the twenty-three counties authority for only one year to enact an earnings' tax. The bill allowed the local jurisdictions to collect a local income tax that was not to exceed 1 percent and the tax could be applied to residents of the jurisdiction or to *non-residents* whose income was derived from or earned in the county or city. The authority to levy this commuter tax would become "void and of no further effect" on June 30, 1967.[29] The only subdivision that took advantage of this one-year tax was Baltimore.

Asked to speak at an event in Baltimore about two weeks later, I refused to bite my tongue about what had transpired, blaming the defeat on both the "obstructionists" in the House and the tepid support the bill received from Governor Tawes and his aides.

"In the last hours of Tuesday, March 29, 1966," I said, "the Maryland General Assembly came within two votes of responsible legislative action. It was clear to all that while the two additional votes were attainable, time had run out. The unconscionable delaying tactics of the opposition, coupled with faltering and uncertain top Administration leadership, had thwarted the will of the majority.

"The public image projected by the state legislature is generally poor, justifiably or not," I added. "The tax fiasco of the 1966 session illustrates the type of irresponsibility which creates this poor image."

A Gubernatorial Election Diversion

The fight over Cooper-Hughes was not over, but it lay dormant for most of the rest of 1966 as the state focused on what became one of the most divisive gubernatorial primary elections in Maryland history. Tawes could not run again, so it was an open seat.

---

29. The special session was held on March 30, 1966. The legislation to fix the fiscal problem created by the failure of the Cooper-Hughes act the day before was embodied in House Bill 3.

Eight Democrats jumped into the race, although only three had any realistic chance of winning: Attorney General Thomas B. Finan of Cumberland, who many considered the heir apparent to Tawes; Congressman Carlton R. Sickles from Prince George's County; and George P. Mahoney, the politically connected paving contractor from Owings Mills.[30] Five candidates filed for governor on the Republican side, but only one (Baltimore County Executive Spiro Theodore Agnew) had any name recognition.[31]

In retrospect, it may have been a fourth Democratic candidate (Baltimore lawyer Clarence W. Miles) who inadvertently shaped the outcome of the election and thrust Republican Agnew into the governor's chair.

Sickles was the liberal in the field. Finan was the moderate, but he was identified with Tawes, whose popularity after two terms in office had fallen, and that hurt him. Mahoney was the conservative, running under the transparent segregationist slogan, "A Man's Home is his Castle—Protect It." Things were still hot and he was eager to capitalize on the broad backlash to the civil rights laws that had just been enacted at both the state and federal levels. Mahoney seemed to run for governor or senator every two years. His fame, such as it was, came from his appointment to the State Racing Commission. He held that seat for a long time until I finally knocked him off after I became governor.

Sickles might have won had he campaigned harder, but he didn't. He gave the impression that the job needed the man, not that the man needed the job. At the time, he was congressman at-large, the only time Maryland has ever had a congressional seat elected at-large by the whole state. Carlton was a good guy, but he didn't wage a very good campaign. If he had really campaigned, he would have won that primary and, I'm sure, he would have won the general election, too.

Finan also might have won had it not been for Clarence Miles. Miles probably cost Finan the election because I think every vote Miles got probably would have gone to Finan. That would have been enough to nominate him. When the votes of the September 13, 1966, primary were tallied, Finan had finished third with 134,216 votes, Sickles second with 146,607 votes and Mahoney first with 148,446.

George P. Mahoney, a perennial candidate for public office who had never been elected to anything, had appealed to the baser instincts of voters who opposed civil rights and was suddenly, shockingly, the Democratic Party's nominee for governor.

Agnew, whose overwhelming victory in the GOP primary was never in doubt, suddenly appeared to be the moderate in the field—someone who even Democrats might support. He characterized Mahoney as a throwback to the Dark Ages, accused him of conducting a "yellow, skulking, slinky campaign," and of being tied to the Ku Klux Klan.[32]

---

30. The other candidates in the 1966 Democratic gubernatorial primary were: Morgan L. Amaimo of Baltimore; Andrew J. Easter of Baltimore; Charles J. Luthardt Sr. of Glen Burnie; Clarence W. Miles of Queenstown; and Ross Z. Pierpont of Baltimore.

31. The other candidates in the 1966 Republican gubernatorial primary were: Andrew John Groszer Jr. of Catonsville; John Joseph Harbaugh of Glen Burnie; Henry J. Laque Jr. of Baltimore; and Louis R. Milio of Baltimore.

32. Richard M. Cohen and Jules Witcover, *A Heartbeat Away: The Investigation & Resignation of Vice President Spiro T. Agnew* (Viking Press, 1974), 25.

Hyman A. Pressman, the irrepressible Baltimore city comptroller, joined the race as an Independent and siphoned away enough votes (90,899) from Mahoney to assure Agnew's 81,775-vote victory (455,318 votes to Mahoney's 373,543).[33] The only reason Agnew won was because Mahoney was so bad. When I look back on it, it is probably good that Agnew won because Mahoney would have stayed at least four years and Lord knows what would have happened then.

Reviving Cooper-Hughes

Shortly after he was elected, Agnew called me to ask if I would head up a group to revise and revive the Cooper-Hughes program. I said I would. Some of my Democratic friends thought I should not help the Republican governor, but I said I had worked long and hard on this program, that it was a good program and that I was going to do it.

Between Agnew's election in November 1966 and the legislative session in January 1967, we set up a new commission to look at Cooper-Hughes again. We made some modifications, but the basic program was not changed much. When the General Assembly convened, Cooper-Hughes was reintroduced as an initiative of the Agnew administration and became known as the Hughes-Agnew program.

To increase the amount of aid to local governments, the revised proposal included a new program through which the state would, for the first time, help counties pay for the cost of police protection. About the only other major change to the program occurred during the session. As we had originally done, a core component of Cooper-Hughes was to shift the state's flat income tax to a graduated tax. But what we proposed had a higher graduation than what was finally enacted. It was an amendment from my friend Blair Lee III, the wealthy scion of a famous Montgomery County family, that cut back the graduated income tax rate by 1 percent. That was about the only major change.

The Cooper-Hughes-Agnew program finally enacted by the 1967 General Assembly not only replaced the flat state income tax with a more progressive graduated tax, it also broadened the state sales tax and reduced the state's property tax. The measure also sharply increased state aid to Baltimore and the twenty-three counties (by $102,880,000 overall in the first year) including increases in state aid for school expenses and school and kindergarten construction. It allowed the counties for the first time to levy a piggyback income tax of up to 50 percent of the state income tax to augment revenues they received through property taxes. Finally, it authorized new programs to not only help local governments pay for police, but also to provide a property tax credit for those sixty-five years of age and older.[34] I think property taxes would have doubled or tripled had we not reformed the tax system.

33. Agnew became the fifth Republican governor in Maryland history.
34. House Bill 378, 1967 session of the Maryland General Assembly.

It did all of this in a single piece of legislation.[35] To make any one of those changes today would be difficult. To make them all at one time would be nearly impossible.

Strangely enough, there was an incredible amount of support for Cooper-Hughes—from labor, business and from the newspapers. It was good politics to be for that program. Can you imagine that today?

Much of the credit must go to Paul Cooper. He was the most resourceful man I ever met. Years later, after he retired, Paul got cancer. But he loved to travel, so he got one of those motor homes and a motorcycle that he tied on the back. When I was elected governor in 1978, Paul came out of retirement and worked for me full-time on the transition without pay. After he got sick, I remember going to visit him at his home in Baltimore County and I took him a bottle of his favorite bourbon, Old Grandad.

Paul died in 1981 at the age of sixty-seven. In an editorial, the *Baltimore Sun* said: "Paul D. Cooper was the quintessential public servant—that is, the best...Let the public know that there in the bureaucracy sit their servants, working away with skill, imagination and dedication to make the best of a government that is inevitable—to make it work as equitably and rationally as possible. This is what Paul Cooper did in the highest degree...He epitomized the public servant at his best."

I couldn't agree more.

Hughes for Governor?

One postscript to the Cooper-Hughes story: There was such an unusual combination of support for that tax reform program—and my involvement in it—that a group came to me while Cooper-Hughes was pending in the 1966 legislative session and asked me to run for governor.

The first contact came from state Senator Paul A. Dorf, a lawyer from Baltimore, who said he had been part of a group that had been in New York observing the campaign for mayor of liberal Republican John V. Lindsay. Comparing me with Lindsay, Dorf said the group figured I would make a good candidate.

There were a couple of meetings to discuss it. One was arranged by Bip Hodges in the old Emerson Hotel in Baltimore and my friend Jack Logan accompanied me. Some of those involved had interests in West Virginia racetracks and were angry at Tawes over a dispute involving the state's awarding of racing days at Maryland horse tracks. Their anger at Tawes spilled over to Attorney General Finan. They opposed Sickles because they felt he was too liberal. So they were looking around for another candidate they could back, and they found me.

---

35. The Cooper-Hughes-Agnew program was embodied within Senate Bill 263, 1967 session of the Maryland General Assembly, cosponsored by Senators Harry R. Hughes, J. Joseph Curran Jr., Meyer M. Emanuel Jr., Jervis S. Finney and John W. Steffey. The title of the bill alone takes up one-and-a-half pages in the Senate Journal.

One of the meetings was held at the offices of one of the Baltimore area paving contractors, and Jack Pollock, the head of a Baltimore political machine and Dorf's father-in-law, was there. They talked to me about running in the fall of '66 and said for me not to worry about Mahoney—they could convince him to get out of the race.

In the end, it just didn't feel right. They weren't my kind of people. They were all business people who had made their money by influencing government. Mahoney was a paving contractor who depended on government jobs. People said Pollock's success came from controlling the building inspectors in Baltimore, although nobody was ever able to pin anything on him. But the word on the street was that if you didn't get your performance bond from him on a construction job, you could expect to run into a lot of trouble with the inspectors.

I listened, but decided instead to seek reelection to the Senate.

8

From Spiro Agnew to Marvin Mandel to Home

S PIRO T. AGNEW WAS AN enigma. I was surprised when he asked me to revive Cooper-Hughes and thought that was an unexpectedly progressive thing for him to do. At the end of his first year in office, he also issued a comprehensive "Code of Fair Practice" that banned racial discrimination in virtually every phase of state government activity and expanded the enforcement powers of the state Commission on Human Relations—not what I had expected the new Republican governor to do. I got along well with him at first and he was publicly very complimentary to me. During his first year in office, he even asked me to become the State Insurance Commissioner, although I had no interest in the job and declined.

By his second year as governor, Agnew seemed to change. He was different. He told me once he didn't particularly like the job and I got the distinct impression he might not run for governor again. He implied he wanted to make some money.

As he began his second legislative session, he started criticizing the Democratic leadership, both in Annapolis and in Washington. We would meet him at Government House over breakfast and at one of these meetings he chastised us for not cooperating with him. I remember getting up and saying, "Governor, I don't know what you're talking about because I've had more communications with your office than with Governor Tawes's."

One afternoon following a particularly stormy morning meeting in his office, I received a telephone call from him as I was presiding over the Finance Committee. "Want to come over and play some pool?" Agnew asked. There was a pool table and ping-pong table in the basement of the mansion and, before that, we used to play pool and ping-pong a lot. His wife, Judy, was usually there. She was very nice. I said, "Well, Governor, I don't really have time. I'm down here working on your programs." As you might imagine, his reaction was a little cool. He always seemed a little cool—Agnew's eyes were like coal and no expression.

As we got deeper into 1968, a year of escalation in the Vietnam War, student protests on campuses and continued agitation over civil rights, Agnew's rhetoric turned more conservative. In March, President Johnson announced he would not be a candidate for reelection, throwing the race for the presidency wide open. On April 4, the Reverend Martin Luther King Jr. was assassinated in Memphis and blacks in more than one hundred cities, including Baltimore, rioted.

A few days after the assassination, with the legislature still in session, we had a meeting in Agnew's office to discuss the University of Maryland budget. Budget officials and the top people at the University were already gathered when Agnew walked in. To our surprise, he started off the meeting by saying, "I don't mind telling you all that it took a certain amount of gut-wrenching on my part to fly the Maryland flag at half staff for Martin Luther King." This is verbatim. I will never forget it because I remember repeating it many times right after it happened. That was exactly what he said. Everybody just looked at each other and wondered, "What's going on?"

On April 11, in the wake of the riots, Agnew invited a select group of about one hundred moderate black civil rights leaders to a meeting at the State Office Building in Baltimore. The contingent included a large number of ministers, educators, union representatives, state Delegate Troy Brailey of Baltimore and Parren J. Mitchell, head of the Baltimore Community Action Agency and later a U.S. congressman. Rather than extending an olive branch, however, the governor sternly lectured his black audience about giving in to militants like Rap Brown and Stokely Carmichael for fear of being called an "Uncle Tom." He said it was "no coincidence" that Carmichael appeared in Baltimore just three days before the riots began.

"It is deplorable and a sign of sickness in our society that the lunatic fringes of the black and white communities speak with wide publicity while we, the moderates, remain continuously mute. I cannot believe that the only alternative to white racism is black racism," he said.

"I am sure that these remarks come as somewhat of a surprise to you; that you expected nebulous promises and rationalizations,"[36] Agnew said later in his speech. But by then, many of the blacks who had expected the governor to listen to their grievances had already walked out. By the time the governor was through, only about thirty of the original one hundred remained.

As you might imagine, that speech subjected Agnew to a firestorm of criticism from civil rights leaders, but it also suddenly raised Agnew's visibility around the country. I know a lot of people think that speech is what helped Agnew get on Richard Nixon's ticket. Virtually unknown to the rest of the nation until then, Agnew was Nixon's surprise pick as a running mate at the GOP national convention held in Miami that August. There, Agnew said, "Racial discrimination, unfair and unequal education, and unequal job opportunities must be eliminated no matter whom it displeases," but added, "and quite compatibly, that anarchy, rioting or even the currently stylish civil disobedience has no part in a constitutional republic."[37]

I don't suppose I will ever know who the real Spiro Agnew was, the progressive of 1966 and '67 or the conservative of 1968 and beyond who became the attack dog of the Nixon administration. I think there is no doubt that he fooled a lot of people with his election as the more liberal of the candidates for governor.

36. Ibid.
37. "Agnew Acceptance Speech at GOP Convention in Miami Beach," *Baltimore Sun*, August 9, 1968.

Agnew Departs

I don't recall when I first heard that Agnew was a candidate to be Nixon's running mate. I had no inside information on that. My reaction was surprise. There has been a lot of speculation about why Agnew was picked. One theory is that Agnew would help the ticket because Maryland is a border state and he might help the Nixon ticket in the South. Others thought that Nixon liked Agnew's hard-line speech to blacks in Baltimore. This was a time of racial strife and it was thought that that speech sort of clinched it for him to be vice-president as both he and Nixon capitalized on the backlash against Democrats for their support of civil rights legislation.

At the time, Maryland had no office of lieutenant governor and no provision for succession for a governor leaving office in the middle of a term. This meant that once Agnew was elected vice-president in November 1968, it was up to the General Assembly to meet in joint session to choose a successor. The two presiding officers, House Speaker Mandel and Senate President Bill James, were the clear favorites. But several others were eager to seize this rare opportunity and got into the race as well, including Thomas Hunter Lowe, a Talbot County delegate who chaired the House Judiciary Committee, Dale Anderson, the Baltimore County executive, Baltimore lawyer Francis X. Gallagher, state Comptroller Louis L. Goldstein, Republican Congressman Rogers C.B. Morton and Congressman Carlton R. Sickles. Both Mahoney's victory in the 1966 Democratic primary and Agnew's election that year as governor proved to me that almost anything could happen in politics, so I threw my hat in the ring, too.

All of us, especially those of us on the Senate side, knew it was an uphill battle because the House had three times as many votes as the Senate. Marvin's election as governor looked like a foregone conclusion. But one thing I did was demand that we hold debates around the state so the public could see and hear the candidates before the legislature voted. I wanted citizens to have an opportunity to tell the legislature how they felt.

About a week before the General Assembly was to convene its joint session, the *Baltimore Sun* assessed the field of nine candidates and said, "We prefer Mr. Gallagher and Mr. Hughes. We believe either would make an outstanding Governor and that the Legislature would act wisely in selecting one of the two."[38]

A week later, the *Evening Sun* weighed in: "Senator Hughes is firmly established as Annapolis's finest fiscal mind. Both Governor Tawes and Governor Agnew hurried to him when the harshest governmental question of all arose, how to design a tax program fair to everyone."[39] The flattering descriptions were nice, but I suspected they would not be enough.

It finally came down to the day of the vote and it was pretty obvious to me that if anyone from the Senate was to have a chance, we had to field a single candidate. I

---

38. "Extraordinary Election—Governorship: Some Preferences," *Baltimore Sun*, December 29, 1968.
39. "They're Picking Our Governor," *Baltimore Evening Sun*, January 3, 1969.

went to Bill James that morning and said, "Bill, we both can't stay in this. If we both stay, we'll kill each other off. The only chance we have is if one of us gets out."

"Well," he said, "as president of the Senate, I think I'm the one who ought to stay in." We discussed it for a while and I finally said, "Okay, I'll withdraw."

So, I went out to withdraw and was being interviewed on television when the reporter told me, "President James has just announced that he is withdrawing." I was stunned. "What?" I asked. "Senator James just told me he was staying in this race." I got out of the television interview as quickly as I could and went into Bill's office again and said, "Bill, what in the world is going on?" He said, "Well, we haven't got a chance, so I thought I better get out." I said, "Bill, I thought we had an agreement. If I knew you were going to get out, I would have stayed in." A lot of the senators wanted the chance to vote for one of their own.

I summoned Blair Lee and the two of us finally convinced Bill to stay in the race. But of course, Mandel easily won. I don't think Billy had ever thought he would run for governor and, had Agnew not resigned, I doubt Mandel would have, either.

About two days after the election, Blair Lee called me to meet him for a drink at the Maryland Inn. During the conversation, he told me that Mandel had asked him to be secretary of state, a position appointed by the governor with an array of responsibilities, many of them related to election laws.[40] The position has frequently been filled by political operatives who are close to the governor. I was sort of taken aback. Blair had not been supportive of Mandel at all; in fact, just the opposite. He had strongly supported Bill James and me and wanted one of us to become governor. I said, "Well, Blair, you do what you have to do. I don't know if you're asking for my consent or my approbation, but you do what you have to do and I'll understand that." And, so he did.

Afterward, the speculation was that Marvin had told Blair that if he would become secretary of state, Marvin would do his best to have the position of lieutenant governor created and Lee could run on Mandel's reelection ticket in 1970. I'm sure that is what enticed Blair to do it because I don't think he really wanted to be secretary of state.

It turned out, of course, that the state Constitution was subsequently amended to create the office of lieutenant governor, that Blair did run on Mandel's ticket in 1970 and became Maryland's first lieutenant governor in modern times, and that he used his position as lieutenant governor and later as acting governor (when Mandel got into legal trouble) as the springboard for his own race for governor in 1978.

I'm sure Mandel thought that Blair would be a great help to him. They were

---

40. The Secretary of State, a position created in 1837, has many duties, including attesting to the signature of the governor on all public documents; custodian of the Great Seal of Maryland; certification of results of all referenda or constitutional amendments to be submitted to the electorate; keeper of the records of the State Board of Canvassers, of which he or she is a member; keeper of the records of all commissions and appointments made by the governor, as well as trademarks and service marks; preparation and distribution of election laws; receiving certification of candidacy for all statewide offices; and preparing all extraditions, pardons and commutations for the governor.

entirely different personalities and from entirely different backgrounds. Blair's lineage included the likes of Montgomery Blair, postmaster-general for Abraham Lincoln, and colonial patriot Richard Henry Lee, while Mandel was simply a pol from working-class Baltimore whose rise through the political ranks was championed by a west Baltimore furniture store owner and behind-the-scenes political power broker named Irv Kovens.

As it turned out, I think picking Blair was a great political move on Mandel's part because Blair helped the new governor with the budget, education funding and other issues. I generally do not think people vote for someone for governor based on who he has running with him for lieutenant governor. My race for governor in 1978 is a pretty good example of how that maxim is true. But I think Blair being on Mandel's ticket probably helped Mandel get elected.

The Bay Bridge and the Harbor Tunnel

The year Agnew was elected governor, I was reelected to a third term in the Senate. After Cooper-Hughes-Agnew was finally enacted, I found myself increasingly involved in transportation issues. This shift in focus from tax issues to transportation actually began in the 1966 session, when my committee handled legislation to authorize the construction of a second bridge across the Chesapeake Bay.

That year, the General Assembly authorized construction of a $73 million parallel span to the existing bay bridge near Annapolis, which had opened in 1952 linking Sandy Point with Kent Island. The bridge bill was enacted over the objections of legislators from Baltimore and Baltimore County on the one hand, and from the Lower Eastern Shore on the other. The two groups, respectively, wanted the new bridge to be built at locations either north or south of the existing bridge. Senator Paul Dorf headed the Baltimore group of opponents and Fred Malkus led delaying tactics by the Eastern Shore group.

After the '66 session ended, Clarence D. Long, then the congressman representing Baltimore County, petitioned the legislation to a statewide referendum and succeeded in convincing voters to repeal it, although voting on the issue was light and most of the opposition came from Baltimore County voters.[41] Undeterred, the General Assembly in 1967 introduced new legislation to authorize a second bay crossing, but because the new bill had to be different from the one defeated in the referendum, it authorized the state to select from among three separate locations: one from Miller Island in Baltimore County to Tolchester in Kent County; one parallel to the existing bridge at Sandy Point; and one from Bertha in Calvert County to Taylors Island in Dorchester County.[42]

41. Douglas Watson, "New Bridge Span Opens Over Bay," *Washington Post*, June 29, 1973. The vote was 289,418 against the bridge, 248,932 for it.
42. De Leuw, Cather & Co. (consulting engineers), "Traffic Evaluation Study for Proposed Chesapeake Bay Bridge at Three Alternative Locations" (Maryland State Roads Commission, Newark, NJ, January 17, 1966).

The bill was referred to my committee, as was a separate piece of legislation to authorize a new tunnel under Baltimore harbor.

Our committee and the Senate approved the new bay bridge legislation and sent it to the House, but held up the bill for the new harbor tunnel after we received testimony indicating a bridge across the harbor would be considerably less expensive than a tunnel. A couple members of my committee, especially Dorf and Bip Hodges, fought like mad to have the tunnel legislation approved as drafted and I began to sense something was wrong. At the same time, I found out that the speaker, Mandel, was holding up action on the bay bridge legislation in the House. They were doing that to leverage me into passing the harbor tunnel bill through the Senate.

I soon learned why. There was a tunnel construction company from New York that wanted the contract and had aligned itself with a politically influential Baltimore contracting firm called Baltimore Contractors, headed by a man named Victor Frenkil. This marked my first run-in with Frenkil and his allies, but neither my last nor my most serious. One of Frenkil's many supporters in Annapolis was J. Millard Tawes, the governor. Toward the end of the session, Jim Morton, a Tawes aide, came down to meet with me in the Senate lounge, the large, wood-paneled room located just behind the Senate chamber. "Well, the governor wants that tunnel bill," Morton said, pleading with me to pass it out of the Finance Committee. I countered by saying that I wanted "that parallel span bill to move" through the House.

Finally, I relented, but said, "Jim, I want you to know I know exactly what is going on. I will move the tunnel bill out, but I want the bay bridge bill to move." So, we passed them both.

Engineering consulting firms hired by the state[43] subsequently studied the three alternative bridge locations and recommended the parallel span at Sandy Point, just as we had originally suggested in 1966.

(The irony of this story is that years later, after I became Secretary of Transportation, I managed to get the state's Transportation Authority, which oversees toll facilities, to change that Baltimore harbor tunnel project into a bridge after all. We knew a bridge would be less costly to build and to maintain. The approaches to the tunnel had already been graded, but I got the project changed around and it became known as the Key Bridge.)

Reorganization of State Government

But I am getting ahead of myself. In 1966, when the bay bridge and harbor tunnel bills were under consideration, there was no such thing as a state Department of Transportation. Everything was handled separately. There was a State Roads

---

43. Ibid.; Coverdale & Colpitts (consulting engineers), "Report on a Proposed Second Crossing of the Chesapeake Bay" (New York, June 17, 1966).

Commission for highways and a Port Authority to oversee shipping into Baltimore harbor. The regional airport, Friendship, was owned by the city of Baltimore. In those days, state government was highly fragmented, with nearly 250 different offices, agencies and departments.

In July 1968, Governor Agnew appointed me to a commission that would change all of that—a commission that would change the fundamental structure of state government and, in doing so, change the direction of my life.

Chaired by Baltimore businessman John N. Curlett, the Committee on Executive Reorganization was to develop a comprehensive plan to reorganize the hundreds of separate agencies, departments and other fiefdoms and power centers that had developed piecemeal throughout state government.[44]

By the time the Committee on Executive Reorganization was ready to report its findings, Agnew had become vice-president and Mandel had replaced him as governor. Mandel, to his credit, implemented the recommendations of the committee, which had worked for years to develop a much improved reorganization of state government.

The Curlett Committee's report, presented to Mandel just after he took office in January 1969, identified what it called "an astonishing" 246 separate departments, boards, commissions and other agencies within the Executive Department, which it said varied widely in size, jurisdiction, organization and relationship to the governor or to other related agencies. Just to list them all took six pages of the commission's report. The system, the Curlett report said, was functionally fragmented and suffered from diffused responsibility.

The committee found that the heads of state agencies often were neither responsible nor responsive. As a result, we decided to make the heads of Cabinet agencies serve at the pleasure of the governor so you could really hold the governor responsible for their actions.

The report recommended that the Executive Department be reorganized into ten "functional areas": budget and fiscal planning; program evaluation and research; personnel and general services; natural resources; health and mental hygiene; public safety and correctional services; transportation; licensing and regulation; social and employment services; and economic and community development.[45]

Over time, Governor Mandel implemented most of these recommendations. While there have been changes since then in the names and precise jurisdiction of various departments from administration to administration, this set of functional areas of responsibility still represents the basic structure of state government in Maryland today.

44. The report of the Committee on Executive Reorganization was submitted to Governor Mandel on January 24, 1969. Other members of the Committee included: William S. James, Jervis S. Finney, C. Stanley Blair, Marvin Mandel, William M. Houck, John G. Lauber, James R. Miller, John S. McInerney, state Treasurer John A. Luetkemeyer and former Governor J. Millard Tawes.
45. Ibid.

Maryland Department of Transportation

One of the most controversial areas of proposed reorganization involved transportation. Mandel appointed Lieutenant Governor Blair Lee to oversee a work group charged with organizing Maryland's first consolidated Department of Transportation. I, again, was asked to serve on that group. As a consultant, we hired a well-known national expert on transportation issues named Lowell K. Bridwell, who had been the federal highway administrator.

Slowly, we worked through the issues and finally created a consolidated Department of Transportation funded by a single Transportation Trust Fund. This Trust Fund was central to the functioning of the new department. It consolidated all of the revenues and bonding authority that had previously flowed separately to the State Roads Commission, the Port Authority or other transportation units we brought into the fold. To do this, we had to end all of the existing bonds and create a new state transportation department bond. To this day, I do not know of any other state that has really done this—that has created an all-inclusive trust fund into which gas taxes, bus fares, vehicle registration fees and all other transportation revenues flow into one big fund. Maryland is the only state with a transportation department that is all-inclusive in the modes of transportation and with a single funding mechanism.

Even though the Port Authority opposed this consolidation, it really gave the Port Authority more financial ability than they had when they were issuing their own bonds. Mostly, this was a turf battle.

Time to Go Home

By the time we passed the legislation creating the Maryland Department of Transportation, it was 1970 and the last year of my third term in the Senate. I had been in the General Assembly for sixteen years, had run for election five times (including my race for Congress), had chaired the state Democratic Party for two years (from 1969 to 1970), had served on more commissions and task forces than I could count and had twice flirted with the idea of becoming governor. I decided I had had enough.

It was impossible to raise a family on a legislator's salary of $2,400 a year. You had to have outside employment, but I was spending so much time in Annapolis that it was hurting my law practice in Denton. Both of my girls were going to private school and I had tuitions to pay. I decided I would just spend my time practicing law and make enough money to send my children to school.

The idea of getting out of public life didn't bother me at all. I always felt when I was in public office that there was another life out there and that it was not a bad life, either. I think feeling that way gave me an advantage over legislators who did everything they could to stay in public office.

I was a sole practitioner in my law office and had been since Tom Everngam and I separated back in 1958. That had been a big gamble because it was the same year I ran for the Senate for the first time. But I eventually got to represent the Denton National Bank, which was a good and constant source of business.

When you're in a country law practice, there are two good sources of business: the undertaker and the bank. The undertaker is good because surviving family members are always very upset and the undertaker is always very nice and helps them out. Often they say they need somebody to help them with the estate and ask, "Who can we get?" The undertaker will say, "Well, I recommend so and so." That's how Tom Everngam got a lot of his business.

The same was true with the bank: every time they loaned money for a mortgage, somebody had to search the title and do all the deeds and other paperwork. The Denton National Bank picked me to be their representative after their regular attorney died. But it became obvious to the bank that my absence during legislative sessions prevented me from quickly responding to the bank's legal needs so they ultimately split the business between me and Marvin Smith, an accomplished lawyer from Federalsburg who later went on the Maryland Court of Appeals. I understood, but it made me realize I will never know how much business I lost that I never heard about.

In the final analysis, quitting the legislature was just a practical decision. I was forty-four years old and felt I couldn't afford to allow my law practice to languish any longer.

To some extent, I also had become tired of hearing the same testimony on the same types of bills year after year. I was getting a little bored with that. The Senate had also changed. When I arrived, there were only twenty-nine of us; now there were forty-seven. It was not as close a group as it had been. And a single senator from the Eastern Shore was no longer as powerful as when I first went to Annapolis.

Pat and I had built a house on a lot south of Denton in 1968 and we had decided it was simply time for me to go back home.

9

Taking Over at Transportation

O N THE FINAL NIGHT OF the 1970 General Assembly session, I announced that I would not seek reelection to the Senate in the fall and instead would head home. But when fall arrived, my life took another unexpected turn.

Governor Mandel approached me and asked if I would consider becoming secretary of the new Maryland Department of Transportation, the consolidated transportation agency I had labored so hard to create. Mandel later explained his offer by saying of me, "He said he didn't have the time any longer to serve in the legislature on a full-time basis. I thought it a great shame that this kind of talent and dedication and knowledge of state government should be lost."[46] In retrospect, I think I must have been recommended for the job by Blair Lee and Lowell Bridwell, with whom I had worked on the transportation consolidation legislation.

While I was considering whether to accept that offer, President Nixon announced his plan to appoint Rogers C.B. Morton, the Eastern Shore congressman I had unsuccessfully challenged in 1964, as secretary of the Interior. Suddenly there was to be a rare vacancy in my district's congressional seat and I was again tempted to stay in politics. I seriously considered running for the seat and a lot of people suggested I do so. But I had decided I was going to return to the practice of law.

When Mandel pressed for a decision, I told him I couldn't do it unless there was adequate compensation and he agreed to raise the salary. But it was still a hard choice because I knew that several lawyers from the Denton area had recently died and others had been appointed to the bench and there were suddenly ample opportunities for a lawyer to line up some solid business there.

The challenge of taking over the new transportation department, however, appealed to me and I agreed to take the job. The public announcement was made on January 4, 1971, before a crowd of five hundred people at a fifteen-dollar-a-plate testimonial dinner held in my honor at a banquet hall called Eastwind in Middle River. "We've got the best law in the country and a chance to build a balanced, integrated transportation system,"[47] I said that night.

---

46. Larry Carson, "Hughes Picks State Role," *Baltimore Evening Sun*, January 5, 1971.
47. Frederic B. Hill, "Hughes Due Transit Job, Upper Shore Senator Will Not Seek Seat Left by Morton," *Baltimore Sun*, January 5, 1971.

To honor my many years in the General Assembly, I was presented with the keys to a new car. They told me in advance that they were going to do this and told me to order a new car of my choice. I was flattered, so I went to L. Tayloe Lewis, a local car dealer and friend of mine in Denton, and ordered the biggest Plymouth station wagon they had.

After dinner that night, however, I found out the keys they had handed me were not the keys to a new car, but rather the keys to Senator Bill James's car. It turned out that they had only raised about one-third of the money needed to pay for the car that was to be my going-away present. I ended up paying for the other two-thirds! I never said anything about it, although I did tell some friends privately. This story never made it into the press.

First the Legislation, Then the People

Although my new job in the Mandel Cabinet was not to begin until April 1 and the new Department of Transportation would not officially open for business until July 1, 1971, there was an enormous amount of work to do and I began working on it immediately. I was about to take over a department that would combine agencies with a total of nine thousand employees and a budget in excess of $800 million.

We set up a small office on the second floor of a church-owned building located on the corner of Bladen Street and College Avenue in Annapolis, where the current House of Delegates' office building now stands. That session I presented the new department's budget to the legislature.

While we were in those temporary quarters, I hired Michael F. Canning to handle public relations for the new Department of Transportation. Mike had been doing similar work for the National Governors' Association, where he got to know Maryland Motor Vehicle Administrator Ejner J. Johnson, who recommended him to me. I also got Attorney General Francis "Bill" Burch to let me have Assistant Attorney General J. Michael McWilliams as legal counsel to the department. I had to convince Burch to do it because Burch didn't like McWilliams very much. Both Canning and McWilliams would later play key roles in my campaign for governor in 1978.

It was during that transitional period that we also found a building at BWI that could become the home of the newly consolidated department. The building was owned by Martin Marietta. We bought it for a little more than $900,000, which was a pretty good deal. It was a good building and I liked the location. We actually moved into the building before the department was officially operational.[48]

---

48. After I left the governor's office, the state renamed the building the Harry R. Hughes Transportation Building, which was the only building in the state named after me. In January 2003, the state demolished the building to make room for more airport parking garages and built a new transportation headquarters building on the outskirts of the BWI property. Now, the new headquarters building is named after me, but the building is so buried in the woods that I don't know how many people actually see it.

The most formidable task facing me, of course, was to make what had been separate and, in some cases, powerful and autonomous agencies function together effectively as a consolidated department. The legislation was in place, but now I had to deal with the people.

Joe Stanton was the port administrator and he opposed the consolidation, as did some members of the Port Authority. The same was true with the State Roads Commission, which under the legislation was to become the State Highway Administration. Dave Fisher was the chairman of the old State Roads Commission. He was a very competent, nice, low-key guy, easy to get along with. Joe Stanton was the same, but Joe was more assertive. It was tough because you end up with people who are running a department in an organization they don't like. It is just something they had to get used to, but I knew it would take time.

One of the ways I tried to approach it was to tell the administrators they had the authority to run their own departments. I told them that none of my staff was going to tell them what to do. I had my own staff of planners and fiscal personnel, but I told the heads of each of the different transportation modes that my staff wasn't "operational" and that I didn't want them to think that they were. My staff could pass on to them things I had agreed could be done, but I didn't want *them* telling a Joe Stanton or a Dave Fisher what to do.

One thing we did, for example, was to reexamine the whole highway program. The old State Roads Commission had its own bonding authority, the maximum level for which was set in state law. When Tawes was governor, he wanted to increase that bonding authority from $300 million to $360 million. To round up the votes he needed to get that change through the legislature, a lot of highway projects were promised. I often kidded my old colleagues in the legislature that everybody in the Senate got a highway project but me.

One of the first things we did in the new department was to go through all of the projects that had been approved over the years. We found that the $60 million in new road projects was actually going to cost the state more than $400 million and that the total projects on the books would have cost well over $1 billion. Even if the state had the money to do it, it would have taken twenty years or more to complete the projects. It was really unrealistic. Some of the roads on the list had been promised so long ago that they had been forgotten. We had quite a job whittling the list of projects down to something that was more realistic.

This turned out to be the beginning of the development of the state's first comprehensive transportation plan, one that included not only highways, but also mass transit. The privately owned Baltimore Transit Company was in bad shape and there were efforts to have the state take it over. Before the department was started, the legislature set up a steering committee to look at the Baltimore City transit company's problems and, with the creation of the new department, the state took over the bus company. When this sort of thing happened in other states, an independent transit authority was usually created. But in Maryland, the state

1. On Labor Day 1938, FDR campaigned in Denton for Davy Lewis, but incumbent Millard Tydings won anyway. *Courtesy of the* Baltimore Sun.

2. President Roosevelt, waving his hat from the car on the left, turns the corner in front of the Brick Hotel in Denton. I used to sit on chairs on the hotel's porch and talk to Denton old-timers. The hotel has since been demolished and replaced with a bank. *Courtesy of the* Baltimore Sun.

3. Bill Greenly and I were friends when we were kids and have been friends all our lives. *Courtesy of Governor Hughes's personal collection.*

4. I worked with Slim Baynard (left) and Woody Lord at Nuttles's sawmill and cannery. *Courtesy of Governor Hughes's personal collection.*

5. My brother and I both played on the 1941 Caroline County High School soccer team. (Left to right, back row) Jonathan "Buddy" Hughes, Wesley Thawley, Sam Young, Tommy Baker, Alfred "Boobie" Smith, Paul Wright, John Andrews and me; (front row) Frank Zeigler, Mac Lord, Charles "Froggy" Irwin and Leslie Lutz. *Courtesy of Governor Hughes's personal collection.*

6. The Denton Town Team circa 1942. (Front, left to right) Me, Dick Snead, Nick Pender, William "Cy" Cole; (second row) Earl Hignutt, Joe Scurto, Wesley Thawley, Charles Shaube (who was killed in WWII), Doug Bennington (third row) Charles "Doc" Baker, John Andrew, John Cahall (manager), Robert Hooper Thawley, Albert Biess, Paul Wright. *Courtesy of Governor Hughes's personal collection.*

7. I was never a great trumpet player, but I enjoyed playing it all through my life. This was when I was governor. *Courtesy of Maryland State Archives.*

8. In my U.S. Navy pre-flight school uniform. *Courtesy of Governor Hughes's personal collection.*

9. Pitching for the University of Maryland baseball team in 1947–48. *Courtesy of Governor Hughes's personal collection.*

10. Pat and I married in Delaware in 1951. (Left to right) Dorsey Donoho (Pat's father), Blanche Donoho (Pat's mother), Bill Adkins, Jonathan L. Hughes (my father), Jonathan L. Hughes Jr. (my brother), Helen Roe Hughes (my mother), Bill Greenly, maid-of-honor Ann Burton, Pat, Cynthia Sheaffer, me, Michael Omstead, Joan McGeogh, Edwin Miller, Marjorie Mullikin, Paul Mohr, Emma Morel, Michael Sedmak and Elaine Marks. Other than family members, the rest were bridesmaids or ushers. *Courtesy of Governor Hughes's personal collection.*

11. I will always be grateful to Tom Everngam for offering me my first chance to go into a law practice. *Courtesy of Sally Croll.*

12. In the late 1950s, we attended several Halloween costume parties hosted by my friend L. Tayloe Lewis on the second floor of his Chrysler dealership in Denton. One year, I dressed as a French fisherman...

13. ...and Pat as a French "Lady of the Night." *Courtesy of Governor Hughes's personal collection.*

14. Jack Logan became my friend and political mentor. We spent many hours together talking politics. *Courtesy of the* Baltimore Sun.

15. Building Chesapeake Community College was one of the best things to happen on the Middle Shore. Here I am at the groundbreaking with (left to right) Comptroller Louis L. Goldstein, state Senator Robert Dean and George Silver, the school's first president. *Courtesy of Chesapeake Community College.*

16. Senator Fred Malkus became one of the longest serving elected officials in Maryland history. He and I clashed over civil rights and many other issues. *Courtesy of the* Baltimore Sun.

17. Governors had traditionally played a major role in picking the Senate leadership, but in 1962 we picked our own leaders without intervention of Governor Tawes (right). With me are Senator Winnie Wheatley, the majority floor leader, and my close friend, Bill James, the Senate president. *Courtesy of Maryland State Archives.*

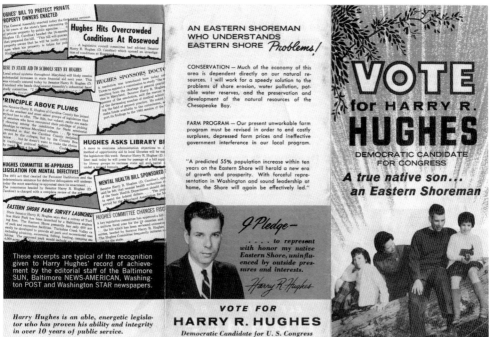

18. First District Congressman Rogers C.B. Morton was originally from Kentucky, so when I ran against him in 1966, I did my best to highlight my Eastern Shore roots. *Courtesy of Maryland State Archives.*

19. Paul Cooper was one of the most resourceful men I ever met. *Courtesy of the* Baltimore Sun.

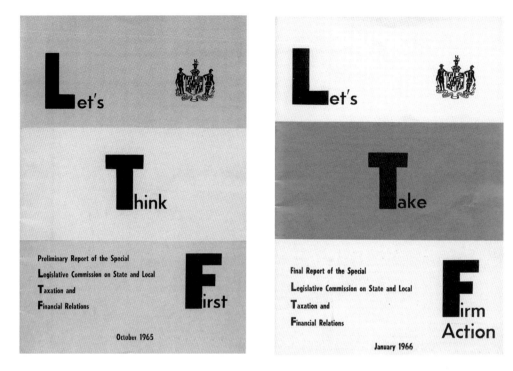

20. With these two little pamphlets, we set the stage for the most comprehensive tax overhaul in Maryland history: the Cooper-Hughes-Agnew program. *Courtesy of Governor Hughes's personal collection.*

21. Spiro T. Agnew was an enigma. At first he seemed moderate, then he changed and became a staunch conservative. He is pictured with his wife, Judy. *Courtesy of Maryland State Archives.*

22. An unidentified representative of the Ralph M. Parsons Company meets with Airport Administrator Bob Aaronson, me and contractor Victor Frenkil, whose later attempt to tamper with a Baltimore subway contract led to my resignation as secretary of Transportation. *Courtesy of the* Baltimore Sun.

23. Governor Marvin Mandel and Comptroller Louis Goldstein join me at the ribbon-cutting ceremony for the opening of the parallel Bay Bridge. *Courtesy of the* Baltimore Sun.

24. Political neophyte Joe Coale ran my '78 campaign on a shoestring budget. *Courtesy of Joseph M. Coale III.*

25. During our 1978 primary election campaign, Pat pitched in by working the phones and keeping contact with our "Zip Code" captains around the state. It was Pat's plan to organize our network of supporters by Zip Code districts. *Courtesy of the Baltimore Sun.*

26. After my primary upset victory in '78, *Sun* cartoonist Mike Lane had fun with state Senator Harry McGuirk's earlier dismissal of my candidacy as a "Lost Ball in High Grass." *Courtesy of Joseph M. Coale III.*

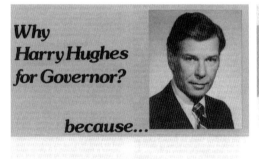

Why Harry Hughes for Governor?

because...

"A vote for the right man is never wrong!"

A Case for Hughes
The Evening Sun, Baltimore, Monday, August 21, 1978

Harry Hughes should be your next Governor because:

- He won't give in to the political bosses campaign for politics as usual.
- He can't be bought (but the people who buy politicians are all trying to beat him).
- He won't make promises he can't keep.
- He is a man of proven integrity and proven experience.

Harry Hughes will be your next Governor if:

- You vote for him on September 12.
- You get your friends and neighbors to vote for Harry Hughes for Governor.

Vote Democratic Primary September 12th

Elect

Harry Hughes / **Sam Bogley**
Governor — Lt. Governor

Hughes for Governor Committee
Lord Baltimore Hotel
Baltimore, Maryland 21201
(301) 837-7444

Hughes/Bogley Prince Georges
and Montgomery County Headquarters
Brady Building - Bowie, Md. 20715
(301) 262-3556

By Authority of Hughes for Governor Committee, L.F. Rodowsky, Treasurer

27. After we won the *Sun's* endorsement, we used it in our campaign brochures. I always liked the phrase, "A Vote for the Right Man is Never Wrong!" *Courtesy of Maryland State Archives.*

THE SUN

K 4   BALTIMORE, SUNDAY, AUGUST 20, 1978

WILLIAM F. SCHMICK, JR., President and Chief Executive Officer, The A.S. Abell Company
DONALD H. PATTERSON, Publisher • PAUL A. BANKER, Managing Editor • J.R.L. STERNE, Editorial Page Editor

Hughes for the Democrats

The 1978 gubernatorial elections offer Marylanders a needed opportunity to break cleanly with the politics of the past. For too long this state has been plagued by a system that has fostered corruption, petty and monstrous. It is a system that has ended in the criminal conviction of Maryland's last two elected governors. It is a system oiled by private profits gleaned from the manipulation of political power. It is a system that has demeaned this state in the eyes of the nation, and it must be broken.

All four Democratic candidates portray themselves as men unsullied by the system. But only one —Harry R. Hughes—seems to have the experience and capacity both to overcome the system and to govern. Although his campaign to date has lagged behind his major competitors, many citizens regard him as the best in the field—if only he could win. The Sun considers him the best of the Democratic candidates. To help him win, this newspaper offers its early and enthusiastic endorsement.

About Blair Lee

Acting Governor Lee came to office under trying circumstances that offered him an extraordinary opportunity. He had acquired a reputation for being well-versed in government, particularly in fiscal and education matters. After long working in the shadow of a governor dragged down by corruption, he now had a chance to show his gubernatorial mettle and to establish independence from the old system. He did not live up to his promise, as witness his appointments of Mandel cronies and his ties with the various political organizations.

Despite nice flashes of candor and a refreshing disdain for the pomp of office, Mr. Lee's incumbency has been flawed by an excess of flexibility. He comes through as a Governor lacking in steadfastness and purpose. Too often he has staked out positions on important issues only to reverse himself in the face of the prevailing political winds. The prison issue and state pension reform were clear—and appalling—examples. So, too, was his ill-fated property tax relief proposal, which would have had a serious adverse impact on the counties and a devastating impact on Baltimore.

That tax relief proposal offered a glimpse at another troubling side of Blair Lee, his apparent inability to understand fully the plight of Baltimore. Although his record in the last General Assembly on state aid to the city was generally satisfactory to the Schaefer administration, his often-disparaging attitude toward the city raises questions about the kind of commitment to the city's welfare he will have if elected. Mr. Lee's decision to form an all-suburban-Washington ticket heightens our unease.

About Walter S. Orlinsky

Of Mr. Lee's three opponents, Walter S. Orlinsky has demonstrated as a state delegate and City Council president for seven years that he is articulate and imaginative. He has spent months traveling the state trying to learn Maryland's problems. Some of his campaign position papers have been impressive.

But Mr. Orlinsky is without executive experience. At City Hall he has done things which, though he no doubt wants to help Baltimore, have not been in the city's best interests. His long, bitter feud with Mayor Schaefer raises questions about how well he as governor could work with the Mayor. Mr. Orlinsky, we believe, is not temperamentally suited to be governor.

About Theodore G. Venetoulis

Theodore G. Venetoulis, a city native, understands Baltimore and indeed has tried in a limited way to foster a more sympathetic attitude toward the city in Baltimore county. As county executive, his greatest achievement was his defeat in the 1974 primary of a corrupt machine and his conduct of a scandal-free administration. Yet Mr. Venetoulis fumbled about for a year after taking office and then, more interested in politicking than governing, became bored. Now, he is hurrying on to other things.

Though Mr. Venetoulis has made contributions to Baltimore county, he also is leaving much uncompleted work for his successor. His government experience is limited to these 3½ years. And, he has

shown more than once during the campaign an inadequate grasp of some issues and, on others, a willingness to act contrary to the public interest.

Mr. Venetoulis portrays himself as a pure-as-the-driven-snow alternative to traditional politics. Yet he is one of the best practitioners of the old politics, even if he goes about his work with an emphasis on reform and volunteerism that gives his candidacy its special flavor and appeal.

About Harry R. Hughes

The fourth Democratic candidate, Harry R. Hughes, offers Marylanders a rare combination: integrity, experience, compassion. He is eminently qualified to be Governor. Over 16 years in the General Assembly, he became its leading expert on fiscal matters. He was the chief legislative architect of the state's graduated tax system, Maryland's last major tax reform. He was heavily involved in the state's efforts to devise an adequate and equitable system for providing financial aid to Maryland schools. Tax reform and school aid are two issues confronting the next Governor. We believe Mr. Hughes is better qualified than his opponents to develop sound solutions to those problems.

After leaving the legislature, Mr. Hughes spent six years as the state's first secretary of transportation. He took disparate agencies jealous of the autonomy they were losing and welded them into a department devoted to producing a balanced transportation system. He worked diligently to achieve that balance, watching out for the port, the city subway, for Western Maryland roads and Eastern Shore railroads. He had to do that in the face of a fiscal crisis that hit his department three years after its creation. Soaring construction costs and oil prices combined with a recession to undercut the department's revenues. Mr. Hughes made the best of a bad situation while relentlessly pressing the Governor and General Assembly for a solution.

Harry Hughes has made integrity and political independence a major issue. His detractors accuse him of hypocrisy, of having remained long in the Mandel administration only to abandon a sinking governor. Yet Mr. Hughes is the only candidate who quit his job over a matter of principle. He resisted the wheeling and dealing of a contractor desperately trying to get in on a major contract. When he got no support from the State House, Mr. Hughes resigned. Though Mr. Lee eventually accepted the Hughes recommendation, he initially was more critical of the resignation than of the contractor and the politicians whose machinations prompted it.

Born and raised on the Eastern Shore, Harry Hughes is now a Baltimorean. He long has recognized the port's interests. Even as a legislator from Caroline county, he showed understanding of the city's peculiar problems by supporting state aid to the city and acknowledging society's obligations to the disadvantaged and deprived. He was one of only two Eastern Shore senators to vote for the state's public accommodations law.

Harry Hughes is a reserved man of intelligence, background-in-depth, sound judgment, and steadiness of purpose. His election would bring Maryland an excellent governor and bring new faces to Annapolis. The Sun urges his nomination.

28. We needed a miracle to win that 1978 gubernatorial primary. It appeared with this editorial in the *Baltimore Sun* on Sunday morning, August 20, 1978. *Courtesy of the* Baltimore Sun.

29. Victory in the 1978 Democratic Primary was really a great moment. *Courtesy of the Baltimore Sun.*

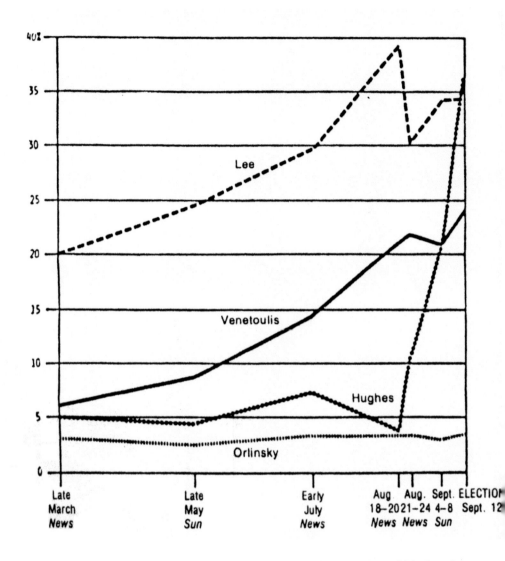

40%

35

30
Lee

25

20

15
Venetoulis

10

5
Hughes
Orlinsky
0

| Late March News | Late May Sun | Early July News | Aug 18–20 News | Aug. 21–24 News | Sept. 4–8 Sun | ELECTION Sept. 12 |

30. There may not be another political graphic like this in America. The 1980 chart by consultant Sidney Hollander, of Hollander, Cohen and Associates, Inc., showed how I went from nowhere to victory in the span of about three weeks. Thousands of undecided voters decided at the last moment that they wouldn't be wasting their votes if they voted for me. *Courtesy of Maryland State Archives.*

shouldered the responsibility. I don't think there is another state in the country that owns and operates a metropolitan bus company.

To his credit, Governor Mandel gave me a free hand to pick my staff. I brought in James J. O'Donnell to be my deputy. Jim was a good man who had headed the Department of Public Improvements, an agency that oversaw the state's capital construction program and was a predecessor to the Department of General Services.

The Motor Vehicle Administration (MVA) is always a lightning rod agency because it has more direct dealings with the public than any other agency by far. For that job, I picked Ejner J. Johnson. Johnny Johnson, as he was known to everyone, was a good, hard-working administrator. He originally came to Annapolis as a reporter for the *Baltimore News-American*, then served on Governor Tawes's staff and had been assistant to Motor Vehicle Commissioner John R. Jewell. While Johnny was at MVA, we set up a lot of regional offices around the state, which proved to be very helpful. Prior to that, most of the work done in those regional offices had been done by mail. When I became governor, Johnny became my chief of staff, a trusted adviser and one of my closest friends.

Walter Addison headed the Transit Administration. He was very efficient, but he didn't hesitate to make his opinion known. Joe Stanton was the same way. I wanted them all to feel that way.

My staff at MDOT was top-notch. In addition to Canning, who dealt with the press, Verna Harrison handled the department's dealings with the General Assembly for four years; Gerry Glick dealt with the multitude of financial issues that arose from management of the newly consolidated Transportation Trust Fund; Clyde E. Pyers was my able director of Systems Planning and Development, looking at the state's overall transportation network; and Irv Feinstein was in charge of all the new department's many administrative tasks. Irv was so good you had to be careful what you said in front of him because if you casually mentioned you might want something done, he would go out and do it before you had a chance to reconsider. We all got along really well, enjoyed each other's company, respected each other's abilities and actually had a lot of fun together at work.

The other important person on my staff was not a veteran transportation expert, but rather a young man fresh out of college. Joe Dore had been a student at the University of Maryland when I first hired him as an assistant while I was still in the Senate. I invited him to come with me to Transportation and he became my personal aide, a trusted and all-purpose "go-for." Whenever I needed something done, I could trust Joe to carry my instructions to the right people. Over the years, we became very close. Joe Dore worked with me the six years I served as secretary and then stayed on to work for my successor, although he said he wasn't very happy after the change. Shortly before I was elected governor, Joe was tragically killed in a traffic accident on his way home to Columbia. I always regretted that he never got to see me win that next election and work with me back in Annapolis.

The Transportation Trust Fund

The new department had its own bonding authority, but we couldn't issue bonds until my staff and I could get the new consolidated Transportation Trust Fund up and running. This was a monster fund, with all of the state's gas taxes, titling fees, bus fares and other transportation-related revenues going into it. To this day, the decision to pool transportation revenues in one large, multi-purpose fund has provided Maryland with unprecedented flexibility for financing new transportation projects.

When we were finally ready to solicit bids for our first bond issuance, we requested proposals to provide us with financial advice both on the issuance of the bonds and on how to manage the new Transportation Trust Fund. I had a team review the proposals and it recommended we accept a joint proposal from Baker Watts (now Ferris Baker Watts) and the Wertheim Company of New York. The review team was impressed by the amount of time the Baker Watts's proposal devoted to management of the Trust Fund.

This decision, however, rankled executives at Maryland's premier investment house, Alex. Brown & Sons, who thought they should have received the work. I met with the top people from Alex. Brown, who said they had always done the bond work for the State Roads Commission, which prior to consolidation had also overseen the bonds for the state's toll facilities. They were really upset and said the Baker Watts decision would cause a "ripple in the Street." When they said, "the Street," I didn't know what they were talking about. I told them we had made the choice based on what we thought was in the best interests of the department, particularly regarding management of this new Trust Fund. I pointed out that the Alex. Brown proposal hardly addressed that issue.

The top people at Alex. Brown, Barton Harvey and others, refused to accept my decision. They said in a somewhat threatening tone, "We'll have to go see somebody about this," and when I said, "Who?" they said, "We'll have to go see the governor or the treasurer about this."

At the time, Mandel was the governor and John Luetkemeyer was the state treasurer. I said, "Well, go ahead, but we've done what we think is right and we're going to stick with it." We went ahead and awarded the contract to Baker Watts and nobody changed a thing. The Alex. Brown people were really upset with me, but maybe they learned a lesson. It was the first time Baker Watts had been able to get any state business.

Friendship Airport

Our first aviation administrator was David Snyder. When I took over the department, the Aviation Administration had not been very active. That, however was about to change. The state was about to take over Friendship Airport.

Twenty-four years earlier, in May 1947, the city of Baltimore had borrowed $12 million to buy about 3,300 acres in Anne Arundel County to build an airport to serve the city and the surrounding metropolitan area. On June 24, 1950, with President Harry Truman presiding, air service was initiated at the new International Airport.

By the late 1960s, however, it became increasingly obvious that Baltimore—facing financial troubles of its own—could not keep up with the maintenance and expansion needs of a major airport. As population in the Baltimore-Washington corridor rapidly expanded and the importance of the airport to the region's economic vitality became more obvious, pressure grew for a state takeover.

In June 1967, Robert H. Levi, the chairman of the Greater Baltimore Committee, an activist business organization, sent a thick report to Governor Agnew and Baltimore Mayor Theodore McKeldin recommending a state takeover, suggesting that Friendship could become "an area airport for the Baltimore/Washington complex just as Newark is to the Newark/New York complex." In December 1967, while I was still in the Senate, I was appointed to serve on a Special State Committee on Friendship Airport, which was to determine the best possible means of transferring the airport to state ownership.[49]

We wasted little time moving forward with the state takeover of Friendship. During the 1968 session, we passed legislation[50] in which the General Assembly formally recognized the importance of the airport to the state, discussed plans for expanding and developing it and created a Maryland Airport Authority to acquire Friendship from Baltimore. It was clear to legislators that the state could provide better highway and transit connections and coordinate the airport's activities with smaller satellite airports elsewhere in the state. Statistics showed that about 80 percent of the passengers who used Friendship were from around Maryland and only about 20 percent from the city.

In 1968, the city authorized the sale of the airport to the state for $22 million. Almost immediately, opponents sought court injunctions to stop the transfer, saying, among other arguments, that the city did not have the authority to sell it.

The Maryland Court of Appeals invalidated the transfer, saying the state had improperly established a debt without a revenue source to pay for it. The city and the state then agreed to lease the airport for forty years to an independent airport authority, but that effort was short-lived when it became clear that the authority was unable to convince airlines using the airport to help finance some $20 million in needed improvements.

Based on a subsequent study that indicated the city had invested about $29.6 million in the airport, Governor Mandel and Mayor William Donald Schaefer cut a new deal in 1972 to sell the airport to the state for $36 million.[51] Legislation

49. Other members of the Special Committee on Friendship Airport included: Senators William S. James and George R. Hughes; Delegates Marvin Mandel, J. Glenn Beall Jr., and William M. Houck; and gubernatorial appointees Charles B. Allen, James P. Slicher and Vladimir Wahbe.
50. Senate Bill 185, 1968 session of the Maryland General Assembly.
51. Gilbert A. Leuthwaite and G. Jefferson Price III, "City, State Set Price on Airport: $36 Million," *Baltimore Sun*, March 30, 1972.

authorizing the sale was cosponsored by Senator Jervis Finney, a Republican from Baltimore County, and Victor Crawford, a Democrat from Montgomery. By then, I was the transportation secretary and our plan was to use the $1.4 million a year generated by the airport to pay off bonds to cover the sales price. The sale finally was ratified in July 1972.

Once my staff at the new Transportation Department began to look closely at airport operations, however, we realized we needed to practically rebuild the terminal. It was totally inadequate and badly maintained. The city just couldn't afford to do anything. We also needed to improve baggage-handling facilities, parking and approach roads and broaden the airport runway aprons.

We sold bonds to cover the cost of the improvements and decided to fast track the work. That means you don't wait until you get everything designed and engineered, but rather you design the changes just ahead of construction. To do it that way, you have to know what you're doing, so we knew we had to get a construction management firm. The state had never done that before. So we put out a proposal and subsequently hired the Ralph M. Parsons Company, which had done work for the Honolulu airport and others.

Once again, however, I encountered Victor Frenkil. His firm, Baltimore Contractors, had joined in the Parsons's contract. I called in the man who headed the job for Ralph M. Parsons and said, "I want you to know something. You didn't get this job because you got Baltimore Contractors involved. You got it despite Baltimore Contractors, and we're holding you, Ralph M. Parsons, responsible, solely, for this job."

In the end, they did a good job and the fast tracking worked. It was touch and go at times, but it worked. We decided not only to build a new airfreight terminal, but that we should plan for the expansion of the airfreight terminal. We put in the plumbing, piping, sewage lines and everything that would be needed when time came to expand it, which was later done.

We also anticipated that the airport would one day be connected with rail transit, which has happened, but not the way we planned. When we were renovating the terminal, we installed a big tube for transit right under airport terminal. It was a pretty good idea, but it has never been used. Instead, the airport has been linked with an above-ground light rail line. I assume that tube is still there, although I don't know what condition it might be in. If it is still there, it is probably just a big metal tunnel that would need to be finished.

The man who oversaw all this work was Robert J. Aaronson, who I hired on the recommendation of Lowell Bridwell and later promoted to become the aviation administrator under the consolidated Transportation Department. Bob had broad transportation experience and did a good job on that project. He went on to become responsible for management and development of six major airports in the U.S., including the three operated by the Port Authority of New York and New Jersey.

The change that was most visible to the public was the renovation and expansion of the original passenger terminal. The only problem I can recall that didn't turn out too well was the floor. We picked an octagonal-shaped tile for the floor and the tiles kept popping up. Eventually, the flooring had to be replaced.

The unexpected problem we had with the newly named Baltimore-Washington International Airport[52] was competition from a new federally financed international airport in Northern Virginia. Promoted by the Eisenhower Administration and named after Ike's Secretary of State John Foster Dulles, the new airport was built on ten thousand acres, some twenty-six miles from Washington. It took flights and passengers away from Friendship from the day it opened in 1962. I always thought federal support for Dulles represented a breach of faith because everyone knew the city of Baltimore had taken the initiative with Friendship (later, BWI) and that it was to be the international terminal for the Baltimore-Washington region. But the way growth in the region has spread, I suspect we probably need all three airports: Dulles, National (now named after President Ronald Reagan) and BWI (which now is named after Thurgood Marshall).

The Parallel Span

When I took over as secretary, the pilings for the new parallel span of the Chesapeake Bay Bridge had already been built and we assumed responsibility of completing the construction, which had begun in May 1969. Traffic headed to and from the Eastern Shore had really begun to pick up. By 1960, only eight years after the original span opened, the only way to handle weekend rush hour traffic was to limit the bridge to one-way traffic.[53] We were scrambling to get the new span done as soon as possible. But to do that meant we would have to start pouring concrete in cold weather.

Contractors hired to do the work came to the department with an aggregate they said would help firm up the concrete quickly in cold weather. The J.E. Greiner Co., which engineered and designed the bridge and was one of Maryland's largest engineering firms, tested it, as did the State Highway Administration lab. Then they put it on my table and said, "We can't tell you for sure, but we think it will work," leaving the decision to me. I told them to "go ahead" and it worked. In fact, it held up longer than the other, heavier concrete.

One big problem surfaced. When the underwater test borings for the new parallel span were taken, a decision was made not to take as many borings as were taken for the original span. When they were preparing to put a big bridge pier down, for example, they might have done two or three borings instead of the four or five that might have been taken had there not already been another bridge built close to the same alignment. Because they did that, they never realized how sharply the bottom fell off at one of the four huge anchor piers that supported the suspension span.

---

52. The airport was renamed on September 30, 1973.
53. Douglas Watson, "New Bridge Span Opens Over Bay," *Washington Post*, June 29, 1973.

What that meant, of course, was that we had to put down a much deeper pier than originally expected. That would mean a lot more concrete, a lot more time and, of course, a lot more cost. The bottom of those piers is a big area to fill with concrete. I don't know if it is true, but somebody once told me that each of those piers is as big as Baltimore's Belvedere Hotel.

The obvious question arose: who was responsible for the overrun? Was it the state? Or was it Greiner? It was for exactly this kind of question that I decided the department had to hire an outside counsel to give us advice.

I contacted an engineering consulting firm in New York and they recommended that the department hire its own independent counsel because the job of dealing with contractual claims for cost overruns had become such a highly specialized field of law. I was told that in New York the attorney general's office had lost every case it represented on these kinds of matters because they just didn't have the expertise. As a result, we retained a law firm in Washington that had this expertise and later hired one of the firm's attorneys, Marty Ellis, to work for the department full-time. We had all kinds of overrun claims coming in. I remember Marty had a small office and the paperwork was so high you could hardly move around.

In the end, the independent experts came to the conclusion that it was a fair engineering judgment to do what the bridge designer had done: to cut back on the number of test borings. The extra borings that could have been made never would have cost the state as much as the eventual overruns, but it was determined that the decision to reduce the number of borings was what a prudent man would do.

By the time the second parallel span opened on June 28, 1973, the cost was approximately $120 million, about three times what the original span cost to build, but it could have been a lot more. Governor Mandel came to the ribbon cutting, as did the widow of former Governor William Preston Lane Jr., after whom the parallel bridges were named. The ceremony opened with a parade of antique cars traveling east on the new three-lane, 3.9-mile-long westbound span. The $1 toll remained in effect.

A couple years later, Mike Canning came to me with the idea of holding a Chesapeake Bay Bridge walk. Mike had been at a meeting in the Midwest with his public relations counterparts from other state transportation agencies and got the idea from an annual walk across the five-mile-long bridge up in Mackinac, Michigan, which had been going on since about 1958. Mike, Don Riley, a former State Highway administrator whom I had appointed to head the Toll Facilities Administration, and other staff discussed it at great length because we were concerned about what might happen—everything from crowd management, to how many might show up or whether there was any risk walkers might suddenly take a leap over the side. At one point, someone on the staff suggested we would have to get the written permission of all the bridge's bondholders before we could suspend the collection of tolls for a day. Someone else said we might have to require everyone who walked on the bridge to sign a release form to keep the state from being sued. These were obviously impossible tasks that, in the end, we decided were unnecessary.

Finally, in 1975, we decided to go ahead and do it. We lined up Mass Transit Administration buses to carry walkers to the starting point on the Eastern Shore side of the bridge. Since then, the Bay Bridge walk has become an extremely popular annual event, attracting thousands of participants. There has never been a major problem that I know of. The funny thing is I've never done the walk myself.[54]

The World Trade Center

For years before the new Maryland Department of Transportation (MDOT) was created, the state Port Authority began pushing for construction of a World Trade Center along Baltimore's waterfront. The project was authorized in a Port Authority law that predated formation of MDOT. But port officials could never get the project past the state's Board of Public Works.

Bill James, the Senate president, had been very much in favor of it, as was "Young Tommy," the name everyone used to refer to Baltimore Mayor Thomas L.J. D'Alesandro III. I remember one of the meetings I had with Tommy and he said, "We've really got to have that World Trade Center. I've moved it up and down the waterfront depending on who I've talked to. If I'm talking with General Electric, I say, 'Yes, it's going to be right by you.' Talk to someone else and say, 'It's going to be right by you.'" When I became secretary, we decided we would really push to get the project approved.

By then, Senator James had become the new state treasurer and William Donald Schaefer had become the new mayor of Baltimore. The first thing I had to do was to get Schaefer to agree to get the city to give a little bit on the taxes. We finally worked it all out and went before the Board of Public Works. This time, however, the opposition came from Comptroller Louis L. Goldstein. He kept saying to me: "Well, you're going to put this out on public bid, aren't you? You're not going to have one of those secret deals." He said that two or three times before I finally said, "Comptroller, I've told you three times that we're going to have it on public bid. It is a construction contract and you know as well as I that it has to be on public bid and that is what it will be." I was really angry. Then Louie jumped on Mayor Schaefer, asking if "We're going to build that thing down there in the city where we have all those rats running around?" Schaefer started turning purple and getting angry and Louie realized he had gone too far. "Alright, Mr. Mayor," he said, "don't get too excited." Then, strangely, Goldstein said to Schaefer, "What you need is a nice little woman, a nice little woman. There's a nice little woman up there in Garrett County who'll take care of you. That's what you need, a nice little woman."

What had apparently upset Goldstein was a contract negotiated years earlier by the Port Authority to have Baltimore developer Bernard Manekin's firm manage

---

54. The first governor to do it was Parris N. Glendening in May 1997.

the new building. That's what Goldstein was complaining about when he referred to "secret deals." To get the project approved, I met Manekin at BWI Airport just before he took a plane to Israel to visit his son, who lived there. I said, "Bernie, we can't get this thing built. Goldstein won't give up as long as this contract is out there." Bernie agreed to give it up, even though he didn't have to legally. That was what got the project approved. In the years after that, Manekin and I became very good friends.

Once we had approval, there was concern that private contractors might find the job of building the foundation in the water too risky. So the Department of Transportation built the foundation at a cost of about $3 million and then put the tower portion of the project out for bid. The winning bid was around $23 million—lower than any of us thought it would be.

Highways to Rail

In support of the state's new comprehensive transportation plan, my staff and I began visiting every jurisdiction each year to discuss transportation needs with local officials. This practice of holding what became known as the annual "pothole hearings" was well received and is still a regular function of the department to this day. This comprehensive approach to statewide transportation planning represented a big change from the old system in which funds for transportation projects were often handed out as pork barrel rewards for certain elected officials or jurisdictions.

The real action—and the big money—in those days was at the federal level. The interstate highway system had been authorized under President Eisenhower in the 1950s, but actual construction stretched out through the 1960s and 1970s and beyond. In 1963, Baltimore and Wilmington, Delaware, were connected by I-95. South of Baltimore, I-95 was supposed to go all the way into downtown Washington, but because Washington officials couldn't agree on an alignment, the road terminated at the Capital Beltway, another interstate highway that opened in 1963. In 1970, I-70 opened between Frederick and Hancock and other projects were underway.

One project we spent a lot of time on was Interstate 68, the highway that went from Hancock west through the mountains of Allegany and Garrett Counties to Maryland's western border with West Virginia. The road had been proposed for a long time. Everybody out there said it was desperately needed to help boost the faltering western Maryland economy. So we really went to work on it. We hired Lowell Bridwell's consulting firm to study all kinds of alternative alignments.

No matter which alternative we picked, one obstacle stood in the way: the road had to go over or through Sideling Hill, a mountain ridge that runs all the way from the banks of the Potomac River north into Pennsylvania. There is no natural gap in it. The big question was whether to tunnel through it or excavate a large gap through which the road could pass. We knew that if we had to dig a gap in the ridge, it would have to be deep so the grade of the highway on either side would not be too steep for large trucks.

We finally decided to do the cut because a tunnel would have been more expensive, more subject to sabotage and would have bigger maintenance problems. We realized we were probably going to get environmentalists coming out of the woodwork in opposition, but for some reason that never happened. It really surprised me.

As anyone who has driven through the Sideling Hill gap knows, it is a huge, V-shaped cut. The unexpected benefit from this project is that the cut has become such a popular site for geological study that the state has established a Visitors Center there.

That western Maryland highway was really an engineering feat. I am not sure whether it has meant that much to the economy of western Maryland to let big trucks pass through more quickly. But I suppose it opened up access to the Deep Creek Lake area probably more so than it otherwise would have been.

Although we worked on this project while I was secretary of Transportation, it wasn't completed until I was governor. On the day it was opened to traffic, I flew up there by helicopter and was met by William K. Hellmann, who was then my secretary of Transportation. Bill told me there were some people demonstrating in the back because their businesses had been cut off by the new road and they were losing a lot of clientele. It was windy and cold and they had a few placards, but Bill said, "We've talked to them, but there's nothing we can do for them, and they've been pretty quiet."

During the ceremony, everybody got up and said a little something. I was sitting next to Bill when Louis Goldstein got up and said, "You people standing back there with the placards: we're going to take care of you. We're going to fix your problem. I've already talked to the secretary of Transportation. We'll take care of that for you."

Hellmann looked at me and said, "That sonuvabitch!" That was pure Goldstein, always putting you on the spot. He was promising something that not only he couldn't do, but did it in a way that made him come across as the big guy while putting somebody else in a box. He did that time and time again. I'll never forget that one.

The Baltimore Subway and Resignation

WHILE ENORMOUS AMOUNTS OF MONEY were being poured into interstate highway construction in Maryland and throughout the United States, the federal government also was beginning to finance major transit systems and transit studies around the country, paying 80 percent of the cost. Relying primarily on this major infusion of federal funds, the new Washington subway system began running its first trains in 1976.

There was also a big push for transit in the Baltimore area and we began studying a six-legged subway system. Around that time, however, cities all over the country — Buffalo, Denver and elsewhere—began to plan rapid rail systems that would cost billions and billions of dollars. The projected cost to the federal government got so large so quickly that the feds suddenly had second thoughts. They began to demand that transit plans in one city compete for funds with plans from other cities and they required studies to look at all different modes of transit—light rail, heavy rail, buses and preferred highway lanes—to come up with the most cost-efficient transportation system. That really slowed things down.

An Era of Scandal

Another, more insidious problem had also cropped up in Maryland that influenced our actions at the Department of Transportation: allegations of kickbacks to public officials in exchange for government contracts. The initial focus, though, was not at the state level, but rather at the county level.

It began in August 1972, when U.S. Attorney for Maryland George Beall, the younger brother of Maryland's then newest U.S. Senator, Republican J. Glenn Beall Jr., launched an investigation into allegations of kickbacks from highway contractors in Baltimore County. His target was Agnew's successor as county executive, Democrat Dale Anderson. Beall began by issuing dozens of subpoenas to construction companies, but when that turned up nothing he turned his attention— and a new wave of subpoenas—to architectural and engineering firms. In those days, Baltimore County could award contracts to architectural and engineering firms without going through a formal competitive bidding process.

As I look back on it now, it seems like there was just one scandal after another in Maryland in those years. In 1968, an Eastern Shore congressman named Thomas F. Johnson was convicted for his involvement in a 1960s Maryland savings and loan scandal—a scandal that also brought down powerful Maryland House Speaker A. Gordon Boone. Just three years later, Johnson's successor one time removed, Congressman William O. Mills, committed suicide after he was unable to explain an unreported $25,000 in cash he received from President Nixon's campaign organization. In 1972, even my friend Danny Brewster pled *nolo contendere* (no contest) to accepting an illegal gratuity while serving as a U.S. senator.

Of course, President Nixon was mired in a major scandal of his own: Watergate. Nixon and Agnew had been reelected by a landslide in November 1972, but Nixon became cornered by Watergate allegations of dirty tricks and a massive cover-up. It would lead to his resignation in August 1974.

By the summer of 1973, a special federal grand jury impaneled by Beall the previous December indicted Anderson on forty-three counts of bribery, extortion, conspiracy and tax evasion. Beall accused the county executive and his aides of receiving kickbacks from architectural and engineering companies in exchange for contracts to do business with Baltimore County. Later that same year, Joseph W. Alton Jr., the county executive of Anne Arundel County, acknowledged that he, too, was under investigation in the expanding kickback investigation.

By August 1973, Vice President Agnew, who had developed a national reputation as a man of honesty and integrity and had become the spokesman for the so-called "Silent Majority" of Americans, was notified he, too, was under federal investigation. On October 10, 1973, the former Maryland governor resigned as vice-president under an agreement with the Department of Justice. He pleaded *nolo contendere* to a single charge: that he had cheated the government of $13,551 on his federal income tax payment for 1967. The judge declared that the plea was "the full equivalent of a plea of guilty."

To me, this was a stunning revelation. I never suspected Agnew was accepting bribes and was really surprised. Once he resigned as governor, I never saw him again and never knew about any of this until after he became vice-president. I don't think anybody I knew had any idea Agnew was doing anything illegal.

According to a subsequent book about the investigation and resignation of the vice-president,[55] Agnew had been receiving cash payments since 1962, the year he became Baltimore County executive, through his years as governor and even when he was serving as the nation's vice-president. The scheme began when architectural and engineering firms that received Baltimore County contracts were asked in exchange to kick back 5 percent of their fees to Agnew.

55. Richard M. Cohen and Jules Witcover, *A Heartbeat Away: The Investigation & Resignation of Vice President Spiro T. Agnew* (New York: The Viking Press, 1974).

The scandals embarrassed me and many other honest public servants who felt tarred by the same brush.[56] I was determined that this stain of corruption would not touch the Department of Transportation while I was secretary.

By 1974, the Maryland General Assembly finally responded, enacting legislation[57] to clamp down on government procurement of professional engineering services. Staff from my department was very much involved in drafting the new laws designed to tighten and protect the procurement process. The legislation established two new professional services evaluation boards. It also stipulated that all contracts valued at $25,000 or more must be evaluated on both price and technical merit and that neither can be the sole criterion. The purpose was to try to take politics out of the awarding of contracts.

Meanwhile, I took action on my own within the department. As a result of the scandals that started with Dale Anderson, my staff and I decided to put several engineering consulting firms on a "black list" of firms that the state would not do business with until all of the legal allegations were cleared up. After we did that I remember receiving a telephone call from Joseph H.H. Kaplan, then a Baltimore attorney, complaining that we had put the firm of one of his clients, Matz, Childs and Associates, Inc., on the black list.

I said, "I'm sorry, Joe, but that's the way it is going to be." He said, "Well, you can't do that," and I replied, "I'm doing it, Joe. They've had it pretty good for a long time. Now they're just going to have to put up with this until this is all cleared up." Kaplan told me that eventually I would find that Matz, Childs "is the clean one" of all of the firms then under investigation. "Maybe that is so," I said, "but until that is determined, they stay on the list." Ultimately, of course, it was shown that Lester Matz, a close friend of Ted Agnew's, delivered kickbacks to Agnew at every stage of his political career.[58]

Throughout this period, I worked very closely with George Beall, the federal prosecutor. I wouldn't make a move or make a statement without clearing it with George. We were moving very cautiously.

Our department turned over tons of paper related to state contracts—so much that Beall's staff had to take the files away in a pickup truck. They were looking for some sort of *quid pro quo*, but they never really found anything. (The bribes Agnew was accused of accepting as governor in exchange for contracts from the old State Roads Commission predated formation of the Department of Transportation).

56. At a Cabinet meeting in the Reception Room of the State House shortly after I became governor, Attorney General Sachs nodded toward Agnew's official portrait on the wall and quietly said to me, "Don't you get tired of looking at that?" I said, "Yeah, I do," and he said, "Then why don't you have it removed?" I did. Mandel's official portrait was not even completed until after I had left office and was not hung in the State House until his friend, Governor Schaefer, had it added to the group of portraits of recent governors that traditionally hangs in the ceremonial second-floor Reception Room. As I think back on my decision to remove Agnew's portrait, I am not sure it was the right thing to do because, regardless of what he did, he had been Maryland's governor.
57. House Bill 640, 1974 session of the Maryland General Assembly.
58. Cohen Witcover, *Heartbeat Away*.

I later learned why the prosecutors probably didn't find anything in all those records. If you were a contractor and you were going to bid on a state highway contract in Maryland, it was in your interest to get your performance bond from the Tidewater Insurance, Inc., which was Harry Rodgers's insurance company. The reason was obvious: Rodgers was a close friend of Mandel's and had entree to the governor. That meant that if a contractor ever had a problem with cost overruns or claims, he was confident he had entree to the governor through Rodgers. That sort of thing doesn't show up anywhere in the records. All that shows up is that the contractor got a performance bond from Tidewater.

Getting the Subway Back on Track

Even with all of this going on, my department was still trying to move forward with the Baltimore subway project. With the feds cutting back on funding, we had to scale back our Baltimore transit plans. As a result, a lot of planning went into deciding which of the six lines we should build first.

We studied a north-central alignment through Baltimore up to Timonium and south into Anne Arundel County, but found it was not economically feasible to build a light rail line there. We spent half a million dollars studying that because the feds required us to do so, but what we found was that the rail line virtually paralleled the best highway into the city, the Jones Falls Expressway, so it was redundant. The study indicated that it wasn't going to get very high ridership and the feds recommended we consider express bus service instead.[59]

Years later, when Schaefer succeeded me as governor, it seemed ironic that one of the first things he did was say the state was going to build that light rail line for $290 million. I remember the figure because I can remember saying at the time, "There is no way they are going to build that for $290 million." Within two years of Schaefer's original proposal, the cost was revised upwards by 69 percent, to $489 million.[60] The last figure I heard was that the real cost turned out to be well over $600 million, and that was before the state paid the additional funds to double-track the entire route. Fares cover only about a third of the system's operating costs and taxpayers pick up the rest.[61]

Why the legislature stood still for that, I'll never know. But you know Schaefer—he likes to build things. Education programs or things like that, he could care less. But building things is easy, particularly if someone names them after you. It is amazing they didn't call that the "Schaefer Light Rail!" I'm sure that thing is losing

59. Kenneth T. Barents, "Transit Advice Sought," *Baltimore Evening Sun*, June 4, 1979.
60. Doug Birch, "Light Rail's Price Rises $43 million; Md. Officials Lobby for Gas Tax Increase," *Baltimore Sun*, November 28, 1990.
61. Peter Jensen, "Light Rail Shows Rise in Ridership," *Baltimore Sun*, December 22, 1993.

money like mad. It has always amazed me that nobody has really done a good, objective study since then to see what we got for our money.

Governor Mandel, like Schaefer, was also from the city and really wanted the subway to be built. He made me the point person for the project. I met with every legislative delegation to explain what we were doing and why we were doing it, but it was really a struggle.

We finally decided to start with the route from downtown northwest toward Owings Mills. We eventually saved a lot of money on that alignment by running the tracks down the highway median of the Northwest Expressway. For transit projects, the state only received 80 percent federal money, but on a highway project the split was 90/10. By using the highway right-of-way, the feds covered a much higher share of our right-of-way acquisition costs.

When the subway legislation reached the House floor, John Hanson Briscoe from St. Mary's County was the Ways and Means chairman and floor leader for the bill. I was up in the second-floor gallery on a telephone to him on the floor, advising him as the debate went on. The measure passed, but the margin was slim.

The vote was very close in the Senate as well where opponents filibustered it for eight days and rural senators like Fred Malkus did everything they could to kill it. The filibuster was only broken after Mandel signed an executive order that threatened to extend the legislative session another thirty days.[62] I always thought it was amusing that Mandel convinced a senator from northern Anne Arundel County to switch his vote, which was the final vote we needed to get the subway project approved. I remember the senator telling me with a straight face how his sudden change of heart was the result of learning more information about the subway project. Shortly afterwards, Mandel named the senator to be a deputy secretary in the Department of Licensing and Regulation. Just a coincidence, I guess.

On Mandel's Cabinet

The best way to describe my relationship to Governor Mandel is that he was hands-off. I think it surprises a lot of people when I tell them that. Mandel and I had served on a lot of committees together and we got along fine, but I wasn't one of his close associates like I was with Bill James or others. But Mandel never bothered me. There were a couple occasions when a member of the governor's staff might call to ask me to do something, but if I had any doubts I would ask them to have the governor call me personally, but he never did. In six years, this probably only happened a couple of times.

The person in the State House with whom I dealt with the most was Blair Lee, because he handled the budget for Mandel. When I went up to the governor's office to talk about my budget, it was usually with Blair, not with Marvin.

---

62. Richard Ben Cramer and Barry Rascovar, "City Likely to Get its Heavy-Rail Line," *Baltimore Sun*, April 7, 1976.

The governor left us alone, so a lot of what we did originated in the department. With big transportation projects, for example, contractors are required to put up a performance bond to assure that they do what they are being paid to do. At that time, there was work going on building a portion of the Capital Beltway and the contractor was really not doing his job. So, I said, "Let's go after the performance bond." This was a new thing for the state. I was told the old State Roads Commission had never before gone against a contractor's performance bond. But we did it and Marvin never said a word.

When I was secretary, it was our department that started the process of annually appropriating funds for the new Washington Metro system. We also started a rural bus system. What got me interested in that was actually my mother's situation in Denton. At the time, most of the medical facilities that served the area were she lived in Caroline County were over in Easton in neighboring Talbot County. An elderly person like my mother could only get to Easton by having someone drive her or by taking a taxi. The state was providing transit services in the Baltimore and Washington regions, but there also was a lack of public transportation in rural areas, particularly for the elderly and the ill. So we started a rural bus service and Mandel never interfered.

The only time Governor Mandel ever called me in about anything had to do with a complaint from Harry Rodgers, who said the State Highway Administration was taking too long to settle claims by contractors, many of whom I am sure had performance bonds from Rodgers's insurance agency. We looked into the allegation and concluded it was a legitimate complaint. In some cases, it was taking the State Highway Administration a year or two before they took action on a claim. Rodgers said the contractors just want to know—give them a yes or a no, but don't hang them out there for a year or two. We thought he was right and changed our whole system for handling claims as a result.

What happens a lot of the time is that contractors try to make their money on cost overruns. They lowball their bid going in and figure they'll make it up on the overruns. If they have an entree through the powers that be, then that just makes them more confident that their scheme will work. We put precautions in place to try to keep that sort of thing from happening and to this day I am proud to say that with all of the scandals in those years, none of it involved our department.

Unexpected Trouble

It wasn't long after we received legislative approval to build the eight-mile, $721 million first leg of the Baltimore subway that it became apparent we needed a construction management firm to oversee the construction. Little did I know the trouble that idea would cause.

The Department of Transportation had used a construction management firm when we redid the airport and felt we needed one to oversee the building of the subway because it was such a complicated, specialized and massive undertaking. Under the new procurement law enacted in 1974, we first had to ask the new Transportation Professional Services Selection Board to allow us to hire a construction management firm. Approval was granted in June 1975.

Because the federal government was picking up 80 percent of the subway costs, we next had to get federal approval of the firm we wanted to hire.

We started by setting up a team to conduct the selection process. The team invited firms to submit written proposals and make oral presentations and then had them respond to questions. We were trying to gauge the level of each firm's expertise: what kind of personnel they were going to assign to the job, which principals would be involved in the job and so on. To some extent, we were making a subjective decision. We were also asking the firms to provide us with unit prices: how much an hour will we be charged for each principal? How much an hour for an electrician, or whatever? What was each firm's estimate of the number of hours it is going to take to do the whole job?

After we went through all of that, we ranked the eighteen applicants and, in early November 1976, selected the Ralph M. Parsons Co. of California, as first among the top five firms. We submitted the results of this process to the federal Urban Mass Transit Administration and asked for its approval.

On November 18, 1976, UMTA Regional Director Franz K. Gimmler approved the procurement process that resulted in the selection of Parsons. The five-year, $24 million contract was referred to the state Board of Public Works for what I thought would be almost a *pro forma* approval. Boy was I wrong. That is where the trouble started.

During the bidding process, Baltimore Contractors, the politically connected Baltimore firm run by Victor Frenkil, had become part of a team that submitted a proposal, but that proposal wasn't included in our review team's list of the top five. After those five firms were picked, one of the teams asked if they could substitute Frenkil's firm for one of the partners in their original proposal. I said no. "You can't change the rules in the middle of the game. Your team was picked because of who your team is, and it is in the top five."

Despite my decision, Frenkil's firm was brought in to do 30 percent of the work, not as a principal or partner but as a subcontractor to Singstad, Keyhart, November & Hurka, the team that was ranked fifth. At least on paper, Baltimore Contractors was to assume most of the responsibility for work that was to have been performed by Tisch, a well-qualified New York firm with expertise in tunneling. We thought this was wrong. We told them that one of the reasons we picked their team to be among the top five was the New York firm's expertise and suddenly that firm had been cut back to a very minor role to make room for Baltimore Contractors. The team was still ranked fifth, but now Baltimore Contractors was part of the mix and so was Frenkil, whom the *Washington Post* would later describe as "an immensely audacious and pugnacious man."[63]

63. Editorial, *Washington Post*, May 30, 1977.

In the fall, we presented our proposed contract with Parsons to the Board of Public Works, which was then made up of Mandel, state Comptroller Louis Goldstein and state Treasurer Bill James. Under Urban Mass Transit Administration rules and state law, the state—in this case, the Board of Public Works—could reject the firm that we had selected, but if it did so the Department of Transportation then had to negotiate a contract with the firm ranked second on the list, and so on.

It was a fairly complicated presentation to the Board, but not as complicated as Louie made it out to be. When Louie opened the questioning it was clear he was trying to treat the contract as if it was a straight bid contract, like a construction contract that went to the lowest bidder. It wasn't, it was a contract based on unit costs, but that is what Louie kept saying meeting after meeting. The first time I realized there was going to be any problem with that contract was when I got before the Board that day.

It didn't take me long to figure out what was going on. Louie didn't want Parsons to get the contract because, I am sure, he wanted it to go to the firm to which Victor Frenkil had become a subcontractor. Louie was doing most of the talking, not Marvin and not Bill James. But it became obvious to me as the months dragged by that Marvin was just as opposed to this contract for Parsons as Louie was.

Louie had a history with Frenkil. At one time, he and Frenkil together owned Barren Island, off Dorchester County. They were more than just acquaintances. But you could also tell something was going on because of the way he was acting, not paying any attention to the facts or established procedures.

We were answering every question. At one point, we explained to the Board that part of the proposal from a construction management firm is an anticipated construction timetable. In such a timetable, there are going to be peaks when the level of work will be most intense. The top four firms in our ranking all estimated that the heaviest work would peak at about the same time. Singstad, the firm Frenkil was associated with, estimated that the peaking would occur at an entirely different time than the other four, which indicated to us that they really didn't know what they were doing. In addition, it had grossly underestimated the amount of man-hours required for the project.

We kept telling Goldstein and the other members of the Board that there was no way to know what the total final price of this work would be because all a construction management firm could do at this stage was make estimates, but that they would be on the job until it was done. I said each of the firms had bid on unit prices, so we had that information, and emphasized that the federal government had approved the plan.

I consistently said to the Board, "You have the right to approve or reject, but you do not have the right to select the contractor. If you reject, that is your decision. Then we will go back and negotiate with the second firm on the list." Louie raised objections to that because he knew we would never get to number five with that process. I said the Urban Mass Transit Administration says if the first bidder is rejected, you go to the number two firm and negotiate a fair and reasonable price with them. Finally, we got a legal opinion from the attorney general saying just what we had been saying: the Board had the right to accept or reject, but it did not have the right to select a specific firm.

The Board kept postponing a decision and the fight dragged on for months. I began to get worried that construction was going to be delayed as a result. To keep from wasting time, we got the State Highway Administration inspectors who normally inspect highway projects to start doing inspections on the rapid rail construction.

The Singstad/Frenkil consortium then launched a new line of attack, letting the Board know that it could do the job for $5 million less than Parsons.

By February 1977, I was beginning to get fed up. I went to Bill James, who was a good friend, and I said, "Bill, this isn't getting anywhere and I can't put up with this any longer. I'm really thinking about resigning and maybe it'll bring this thing to a head some way." But he said, "No, no! Don't do that, don't do that! We can work out something."

On March 2, the contract was again on the Board of Public Works's agenda. Parsons had been the unanimous selection of the Mass Transit Administration team; the selection had been approved by the Transportation Professional Services Selection Board; approval was strongly recommended by me, the secretary of Transportation; and UMTA's regional office had approved the procurement process that resulted in the selection of Parsons, noting that Parsons's estimated contract was comparable to other major transit construction projects around the country.

I told the Board that the integrity of the consultant selection process, as prescribed by law, was at stake, as was the state's credibility with the private engineering sector. I said the state's long-term relationship with UMTA, which was critical to the future of the Baltimore project, was also being jeopardized, as was the public's perception of the state's commitment to professionalism, integrity and good judgment. I told the Board,

> In my almost six years as Maryland's Transportation secretary, this is the first time I have ever seen many of the activities that have transpired in the last six months. This process has degenerated into a price bidding contest—an auction—after the books were closed. It has been totally inconsistent with accepted practices in the selection of professional services as well as that prescribed by law and UMTA.

I warned that if a construction management firm was not approved by July that I was going to halt work on the project.

The Board still refused to budge, the contract remained unapproved and Mandel further undercut my authority by saying the subway project would not be stopped.

By then, even Parsons had had enough. Two days after the Board meeting, Joseph Volpe Jr., a Parsons's vice-president, wrote UMTA seeking their intervention.[64] On

---

64. Joseph Volpe Jr. (vice-president, Ralph M. Parsons Co.) to General Counsel, U.S. General Accounting Office, March 21, 1977.

April 21, Charles F. Bingham, the acting administrator at UMTA, replied in a letter to Walter Addison, the state's Mass Transit administrator, saying, "While UMTA does not recommend selection of any specific firm, we do not understand why Parsons was not approved by the Board of Public Works."[65]

Finally, on May 25, with Mandel out with an illness, there was a meeting in Blair Lee's State House office to try to resolve this. It was Blair, Louie, Bill James, Walter Addison and me. The meeting started with a discussion of how we could resolve this impasse. Louie said, "Well, we ought to go to Washington and talk to the people over there in the Urban Mass Transit Administration. We ought to go there and tell them there has been a defect in the selection process and we want to start all over again."

I said, "I'm not going to do that. There hasn't been any defect in the process and I'm not going to do that. They have already approved our process and everything about it." I kept repeating, "If you want to reject it, that's up to you. I'll go back and negotiate with number two." The meeting went until about six o'clock but, in the end, it amounted to nothing.

Resignation

That evening, Pat and I were to have dinner with our close friends Bill and Anne Boucher at the University Club on Charles Street in Baltimore. They were already there when I arrived late. I sat down and said, "This isn't working out. I'm going to resign." I don't even remember if we discussed it. I had made up my mind and I went in the next morning and wrote out a four-page resignation letter and had it delivered to Mandel. But Mandel was surely distracted by his own problems: he and five codefendants were scheduled to go on trial in federal court the following week on unrelated political corruption charges.

There had been a previously scheduled meeting in my office with all of the modal administrators that morning so I told them of my decision. They were upset. Addison approached me afterwards in the hall and said, "Please don't do this. You can work better from within." I said, "Walter, I've been working from within for months and months and it is not working and I'm not getting anywhere. They're playing games with me and I've had enough." I remember that Joe Dore, my longtime personal aide, cried. I felt frustrated because I had some really good people working for me there and I felt bad about leaving them.

After word of my resignation spread, I agreed to hold a press conference to explain my decision and refused to mince words. Frenkil, I said, had tampered with the selection process and tainted its integrity. I noted that Frenkil had telephoned members of the selection committee and also officials at Parsons.

65. Charles F. Bingham (acting administrator, U.S. Urban Mass Transportation Administration) to Walter J. Addison (administrator, Maryland Mass Transit Administration), April 21, 1977.

"He suggested he could pave the way for them if they took him on their team," I said. "It seems obvious that Mr. Frenkil has been tampering with the system to try to get part of this work. It was obvious many months ago."[66] Parsons had already requested the U.S. General Accounting Office to investigate the situation and I pledged to assist anyway I could.

Reaction

Reaction was predictably mixed. Senator Edward J. Mason, a Republican from western Maryland and then the Senate's minority leader, called me "the best man in the Cabinet" and said, "It's unbelievable; you've got the governor waiting to go on trial and the Board of Public Works is still playing the same old games."[67]

Blair Lee, however, said I had "overreacted," saying the selection procedure "was just no good." "It was comparing apples, oranges, raspberries, watermelons and bananas," he said. As for Frenkil, Blair said, "It's a cutthroat business, it's a cutthroat competition. Victor is a hard-nosed businessman. I have no basis for knowing, one way or another, what old Victor was up to."[68]

Mandel simply released a written statement saying he had accepted my resignation "with regret and appreciation for [my] many years of outstanding service to the state of Maryland."

Goldstein seemed happy to see me go. "There's no indispensable individual in this state," he said. "I feel the state of Maryland will go on, the Department of Transportation will go on."[69]

"This is typical of Mr. Hughes," Goldstein said. "He goes and calls a press conference before he lets anybody know what he's doing. I had no idea Mr. Hughes was contemplating resigning." Later that night, Louie went on television to say I had an allegiance to the Ralph M. Parsons Company and was actively pushing the firm! Of course, that was ridiculous. The process selected Parsons, not I.

In many ways, I think the press fell down on its job on this story. They let Goldstein get away with murder. It was obvious what he was doing: he was trying to get this contract down to the fifth-ranked firm. The press knew about Frenkil, but they didn't make anything of it. We did that contract absolutely right—absolutely right! And we stuck by our guns.

In the end, of course, we were vindicated when the Mandel administration eventually brought back the Parsons's contract and approved it. Alan Wilner, Mandel's chief legal counsel, wrote a memo saying the contract had been renegotiated and the price reduced, but that was just a face-saving technique. The

66. Robert A. Erlandson, "Hughes Quits, Charges Frenkil 'Tampering,'" *Baltimore Sun*, May 27, 1977.
67. Ibid.
68. Ibid.
69. Ibid.

reason they could reduce the price was that a lot of the work had already been done by the state highway inspectors that we put on the job months earlier. Some years later, after I became governor, Parsons came back before the Board of Public Works with a change order for a cost overrun. We approved it, but I did so with a smile because the change order brought the price almost up to the penny of what we had submitted in the first instance to the Board of Public Works. Goldstein never said a word.

My deputy, James J. O'Donnell, was appointed as interim secretary. I had no idea what I would do next. I was fifty years old and had been in public life for the past twenty-three years.

Not long afterwards, Clarence Miles, who was a partner at the Baltimore law firm of Miles and Stockbridge and had himself been a candidate for governor in 1966, asked me to be a partner in the firm. I remember him saying, "If you want to run for governor, go ahead and take all the time that you want."

I thought that was a pretty good offer. So I took him up on it. I've always felt sorry that Clarence didn't live long enough to see me elected governor.

11
"Lost Ball in High Grass"

I DID NOT RESIGN AS SECRETARY of transportation as part of any premeditated plan to run for governor, but there is no doubt my resignation is what launched me into the 1978 gubernatorial race.

It took the press no time to connect the dots, linking my resignation and my sudden statewide name recognition with the approaching election. In newspaper stories the day after I resigned, reporters immediately speculated as to whether my resignation would be a "springboard" for a campaign for governor.

"I've been too busy with this [subway contract dispute] to think about other things," I said at the time, but conceded that I planned to consider the idea of running for governor a little harder in the near future.[70]

And why wouldn't I? The newspaper editorials written about my resignation were far more glowing than anything I had ever before experienced or expected. The *Baltimore Sun*, then the most influential newspaper in the state, for example, catapulted me into the race, saying, "Harry R. Hughes has injected himself into the 1978 gubernatorial campaign by abruptly resigning as Maryland secretary of transportation. He didn't declare his candidacy, but he is considering it...His timing hits the Mandel administration squarely in its political solar plexis."[71]

The editorial went on to observe, "Mr. Hughes is not ready to say how far he is willing to go politically in the name of integrity. While his defiance of the administration conveniently positions him for a white-hat run for governor, a campaign constructed against 'the same old crowd' is likely to open deep Democratic wounds and aid the Republican nominee."

Several days later, the *Washington Post* weighed in with its own editorial: "Backstairs maneuvering over state contracts is, sadly, nothing new in Maryland. What is unusual though is for a top state official to resign in protest, as Transportation Secretary Harry R. Hughes has just done...[By resigning,] Mr. Hughes is laying on the line his considerable reputation for integrity and managerial competence... With the state's top elected officials up to their elbows in the mess, it's little wonder that Mr. Hughes, who seems to take the new rules seriously, got fed up and got out. Perhaps the next election will bring changes."[72]

Three weeks after my resignation, when it was announced I was to become a partner at Miles and Stockbridge, I publicly acknowledged my interest in becoming governor.

70. Ibid.
71. Editorial, *Baltimore Sun*, May 27, 1977.
72. Editorial, *Washington Post*, May 30, 1977.

"I have not abandoned a career in public life and will spend considerable time assessing the feasibility of running in the Democratic gubernatorial primary in September 1978," I said. To make clear I was not angling to be tagged for lieutenant governor on someone else's list, I added, "The governorship is the only office I would seek."[73]

A week later, I was dragged back into the still smoldering dispute over the subway contract when Acting Governor Blair Lee told the *Baltimore Sun* that the effort to select a construction manager for the subway operation had been "flawed from the start," creating a situation where "everyone was playing games." Lee, of course, was the frontrunner for the Democratic nomination for governor and the candidate I would have to beat if I was to win the party nomination. I might have been out of office, but I wasn't going to stay out of sight. At the beginning of a formal four-page statement, I said:

> Since my resignation four weeks ago, I have kept relatively quiet regarding the controversy over the construction management contract for the Baltimore subway…However, some recent public statements by certain members of the Board of Public Works compel me to break that silence. These kinds of statements are simply more of the same old story which eventually caused me to resign and now cause me to respond in order to put the record straight.

I again went through the step-by-step process the Department of Transportation had followed, noting yet again that it was carried out "in strict compliance with Maryland law, regulations of the Professional Services Selection Board and federal rules and regulations."

"No one has disputed this fact," I said.

After relating once again the actions my department had taken in bringing the Parsons's contract before the Board, I noted that, "The distortion continues. Mr. Lee says the selection effort was 'flawed from the start.' Why didn't he say so long ago if he really believed that? Maybe because the documented facts do not support such a statement and now the overriding issue is to 'save face.'"

I concluded that Lee was searching for a scapegoat because

> the record will not justify what has happened. A perfect spot for a scapegoat and the best scapegoat in this instance is to say the process was "flawed." It blames no one specifically, only by implication, is plausible in what appears to be a complicated matter, although it really is not, and tends to substantiate the confusion deliberately created over the last several months.

---

73. David F. Woods, "Hughes Considers Run," *Baltimore Sun*, June 15, 1977.

And, more importantly, it diverts everyone from the real reasons which brought about this sorry mess—the reasons which caused me to resign as secretary of transportation in protest over "tampering" with the integrity of the consultant selection process. The perfect "face saver," the perfect "sweeper under the rug"—a scapegoat named "flaw."

By summer's end, I had decided privately that I was going to enter the race for governor. I felt like I had some momentum, a long career in the legislature of which I was proud, some newfound statewide name recognition and, frankly, nothing to lose by trying. I hadn't practiced law for seven years and just felt this was an opportunity that may never come my way again. I made up my mind, and Pat was supportive of this, that I had to do it. And I felt that if I didn't do it, I may regret it for the rest of my life. If I ran and lost, okay; at least I would have gotten it out of my system.

The Hiring of Joe Coale

Late that summer, I asked Mike McWilliams, with whom I had become friends during our years together at the Department of Transportation, to contact an aide to Mayor Schaefer named Joseph M. Coale III to see if he might be interested in helping out with our campaign. Mike knew Joe, who had been working for about two years as a general trouble-shooter for Schaefer, although I did not. Mike called Joe at City Hall and suggested the three of us meet over lunch at the Merchants' Club, but Joe was worried about being spotted with a potential candidate for governor at a time when Mayor Schaefer had not decided whether he was going to enter the race himself. Coale later recalled feeling sympathetic toward me because I had been forced to resign as secretary of transportation.

"His reputation was that of a competent, honest administrator, which represented a valuable and rare resource in state government," Coale was to write in his own personal account of the 1978 election.[74] Instead of the Merchants' Club, Joe and I had a "secret" rendezvous at McWilliams's home and several other subsequent meetings at my house in Cross Keys. By summer's end, I asked Coale to be my campaign manager, knowing full well he had never done such a job in his life. Joe was a stockbroker by trade and had only worked in the mayor's office for a couple years. Outside of being president of his class for three years at Washington College, he was essentially a political neophyte.

The problem was that I didn't know anybody who had the kind of campaign experience I needed. Well, that's not quite true. I knew some, but the ones I knew I wouldn't want. I had always run my Senate campaigns myself. The bigger problem was that I didn't have any money. That was the big sticking point. Joe was assured

---

74. Joseph M. Coale III, "A Maryland Political Revolution: The Election of 1978," draft, 1.

that the Hughes for Governor Committee would raise enough money by the end of summer to pay him. Naïvely, we both believed that. Joe went off for an end-of-summer vacation with plans to return and open our campaign headquarters in September.

The core group backing my campaign was as lacking in political skills as Coale—maybe more so. It included Edgar Boyd, a stockbroker at Baker Watts; Harry Wells, who had been with the old Maryland Port Authority; Francis D. Murnaghan Jr., a partner with the Baltimore law firm of Venable Baetjer and Howard[75]; Bill Guy, who was involved in real estate; Bob Koch, formerly with the Arundel Corporation; Lucian Brush, a professor at the Johns Hopkins University; Harry Ratrie, a Baltimore County contractor; Chic Allen, who was connected with Greiner Engineering and served as the informal chairman of our committee; and Larry Rodowsky, a lawyer with the Baltimore firm of Frank Bernstein.

I got Rodowsky to be my campaign treasurer and he was really a stickler for details. He made copies of everything: every check, every receipt, everything. He wanted everything to be right, so I was always comfortable with that.

In the late spring of 1978, I also brought in Mike Canning, who had handled public relations for me at MDOT. The campaign needed someone with Mike's talents to deal with the press.

This core group stayed with me throughout that campaign—supporting me even in the darkest, most depressing days when our chances of winning seemed nonexistent. To this day, I feel nothing but gratitude to each of them. The group was a mixture of Democrats and Republicans. For several of them, I have no idea what their party affiliation was. None were politicians—none of them! Most, I suspect, had never been involved in a political campaign before. It was really a neophyte group.

The first order of business for this group, of course, was to fan out and raise money for the campaign. We were all excited to get the campaign going, but as it turned out, we were naïvely optimistic as well. This group would have more than a little trouble raising the money we needed.

We opened our campaign headquarters in the Lord Baltimore Hotel in downtown Baltimore. The morning we went there for the first time, Mike, Joe and I had breakfast in the hotel's coffee shop and Mike charged the meal ($7.85) to the campaign. Joe worried whether we had enough money to cover it.

The headquarters was in a fifth-floor hotel room initially equipped with a bed, nightstand, house phone and barely enough room for the three of us to stand. One reason we went there was that it was cheap. The hotel also had a ballroom that we thought would be available for events, but as it turned out we never used it except for our opening announcement and again on election night.

At the time, our campaign treasury contained one $1,000 check from Murnahan and a promise from Bernie Manekin to pick up the tab for the Lord Baltimore, if

---

75. Murnaghan, a Phi Beta Kappa graduate of the Johns Hopkins University and a cum laude graduate of Harvard University Law School and editor of the *Harvard Law Review*, was appointed in 1979 to the U.S. Fourth Circuit Court of Appeals in Richmond, Virginia.

our campaign went broke. Even the two desks that were later sent up to our hotel headquarters were donated by Mike Asner, who had been Joe Coale's wife's boss and who provided the furniture because he thought I'd make a good governor.

Almost immediately after establishing the headquarters, Joe met with a graphic designer named John Rouse, who came up with ideas for brochures and bumper stickers. Unfortunately, we had no money to pay him so Joe had to put the plan to purchase campaign materials on hold until the money started rolling in.

Honesty and Integrity

Our other immediate need was to develop a campaign theme. Someone at Johns Hopkins had done a study that pointed out that Maryland was losing manufacturing jobs and that economic development was becoming a problem in the state. Joe and the others in our campaign group thought this would be our winning issue.

In retrospect, it is hard to understand why all of us failed to see the real issue of the campaign from the start: it was integrity in government. More precisely, it was the need to restore integrity to government and who better to do that than a former Cabinet secretary who resigned rather than give in to shady dealings involving a high stakes subway contract?

By then, of course, Mandel had added his name to the long and growing list of Maryland politicians who had been tainted by scandal, indicted by grand juries, convicted by courts and—in some cases—sentenced to prison.[76]

It is hard to overstate how badly these scandals tarnished Maryland's reputation. A former governor who had become vice-president of the United States, an incumbent governor, a U.S. senator, at least two congressmen, various state legislators, county executives and other public officials were all implicated in various acts of wrongdoing. By the mid- to late 1970s, Maryland was regularly mentioned in the same breath as states like New Jersey or Rhode Island that had earned their own unsavory reputation for political corruption.

I think the public was really unhappy about what was going on. There was a lot of talk about it. You heard people say that when they went to another state they were embarrassed to say they were from Maryland.

To some extent, Blair Lee became tainted by his association with Mandel, even though the two men could not have been more different. Blair and I were good friends, but we never discussed this issue. Some people said he should have gotten rid of Mandel's staff when he took over, but he wasn't governor—he was only the acting governor.

76. Mandel and five other codefendants, W. Dale Hess, Harry W. Rodgers III, William A. Rodgers, Irvin Kovens and Ernest N. Cory, would later be indicted and convicted of mail fraud and racketeering. On June 4, 1977, Lieutenant Governor Blair Lee III began serving as acting governor following Mandel's conviction. Mandel served nineteen months in federal prison before being pardoned by President Ronald Reagan. In 1989, the U.S. Supreme Court upheld a 1987 lower court decision overturning his conviction on a technicality.

I really didn't have any professional political strategists. That might have been good for me in the long run. If I had had a political strategist, it might have worked out differently. They might have said the same thing about me that they ended up saying about Kathleen Kennedy Townsend, whose 2002 campaign for governor failed partly because of the bad advice she received from her campaign aides and political handlers. If I had had professional campaign strategists, I might have lost, too.

In his personal campaign memoir, Coale recalled that none of us sensed at first that "honesty and integrity in government" was the real underlying issue of the campaign. "It was good that our energies were not spent pursuing or trying to capitalize on it because these efforts would have seemed self-serving," he wrote. "It had a life all its own and didn't need television promotion, slick brochures, a lot of money or talk show hosts to promote it."[77]

It was a good thing, because we had virtually no money, no television spots and, at least at first, not even any brochures. I really didn't have much of a political base. My legislative political base was in the thinly populated counties in the center of the Eastern Shore, and I hadn't represented those areas for nearly eight years. I didn't even live in Caroline County anymore; Pat and I moved to Cross Keys in Baltimore not long after I became transportation secretary. Moreover, by resigning I no longer had a political office to use as a platform from which to wage my campaign.

By contrast, my Democratic opponents were all current office holders: Blair Lee III, the acting Governor of Maryland; Theodore G. Venetoulis, the Baltimore County Executive; Francis "Bill" Burch, the state Attorney General; Senate President Steny Hoyer of Prince George's County; and Baltimore City Council President Walter S. Orlinsky.

Brochures and Television

In October, Coale paid a visit to a Baltimore advertising executive named Harold C. Donofrio, who began developing ideas for a brochure and bumper stickers. Working with a Republican political consultant named Bobby Goodman, Hal Donofrio developed a $620,775 media budget for the campaign. I did not know Goodman—Donofrio knew him. And we got to Hal Donofrio only because Joe's wife, Kim, had done interior decorating for his office.

As if to jump-start our media effort, Donofrio contributed a $1,000 check of his own to the campaign. Combined with other expected expenses, the overall campaign budget approached $1 million. Joe showed it to our core campaign committee and, after that, attendance at meetings seemed to drop by half.

Hal's campaign brochure was top notch. It contained pictures of me from my days at the Department of Transportation, as a University of Maryland baseball player, in

77. Coale, "Maryland Political Revolution," 3–4.

uniform in the navy and a picture of Pat and me together. Our color scheme was a yellow background and bold black letters: Maryland colors. When they first showed them to me, somebody had made up a mock bumper sticker that proclaimed, "Harry Whose?"

Hal never provided me with much political advice, but Bobby did. I met with Bobby and I guess he just took a liking to me. I don't know any other reason he would support me. He had always worked with Republican candidates—people like Pete Wilson of California or Alan Simpson of Wyoming. I think he did this work for me sort of *sub rosa*. He surely wasn't in it for the money, because we didn't have any. I had long talks with Bobby. To him, it was all about television. He was concerned about issues, but more importantly, how to portray me on television.

Several people suggested I get some tutoring on how to improve my appearance and delivery on TV—to "delegalize" my presentations and make them more exciting. For a while, I met regularly with a woman in Baltimore named Ginny Corino. She was the wife of the director of one of the local television stations and she tried to train me for my TV appearance—how to sit, how to hold my hands, what to do with my arms and legs, all of that. I thought she was very good.

A friend of ours at Maryland Public Television suggested I consult a media specialist in New York named Roger Ailes. But when Joe contacted his office, he discovered that a twelve-hour session would cost us $4,000, at a time when we had less than $300 in the campaign treasury. Still, we decided an introductory conversation would be worth our time so Joe and I went to New York. Before going up there, Joe had me tape a short speech and sent the tape up to Ailes to review before we got there.

I remember that meeting clearly: after talking with me, Ailes said he didn't think I had the fire in the belly that was needed to run for governor. When he said that, I thought he was probably right. Yet, I don't know what he was expecting. He kept saying, if you're going to do this, you really have to go after it, and I thought, "God, I thought I was going after it, and with no resources." I think he was talking about more visible energy.

When I returned, I wrote a "memo for record" on November 15, 1977, about the meeting.

> People must say they like that guy. Goal is to reach an emotional level. If you can't do that, forget it. Concentrate on the heart issues, not the head issues. You have a restrained energy level. Government and politics are two different things. You must make the audience comfortable, then you will be comfortable. The candidate is the message. He must be a performer in emphasizing what is already there in his personality, but not an actor. At the moment of entrance to a meeting, the candidate controls the atmosphere. He must immediately take the initiative with the crowd. If not, he loses control within 10 seconds and can never effectively regain it. People want to like the candidate and they will like him if they see he cares about people and can show a concern for them.

In my memo, I noted Ailes's reaction to the tape of my speech. "HRH appeared reluctant, reticent, low energy, internal conflict, as if to say, 'Why is he doing this?'"

"The real trick," Ailes advised me, "is getting to the point where you can say that you enjoy campaigning and you're having fun doing it. When this happens you can do practically anything and still have the crowd love you."

With the cynical approach to governance that political consultants often take, Ailes said, "It is critical that HRH be interesting. It is not necessarily what you say in regard to the issues, but what you say that makes people respond and feel good about you. HRH must get in touch with his real emotions and emphasize them in campaigning. We all have these emotions but some keep them under control more than others. It is a matter of 'coming out of the closet,' so to speak."

After receiving advice like that, Joe and I shared a mighty quiet train ride back to Baltimore.

"Political Corruption is the Issue in 1978"

We decided I would make the formal announcement of my candidacy in the week between Christmas and New Year's, an attempt to take advantage of an always-slow news time for reporters. We scheduled the event as a lunchtime buffet in the ballroom of the Lord Baltimore Hotel. We had a table of sandwiches to one side and three bars in the back of the room opposite the platform and podium. We also hired a three-piece band. We were worried the crowd would be small and the TV coverage minimal, but, fortunately, we were wrong on both counts.

Jack Logan, Wayne Cawley and other old friends from the Shore brought several busloads of supporters over from Caroline County. A large contingent from the Department of Transportation also showed up. TV crews from all three Baltimore stations and two from Washington covered the event.

About the only glitch involved our only two hundred campaign buttons, which for some reason lacked the legally required "by authority of" line. I remember watching the ever meticulous Larry Rodowsky frantically stuffing his coat pockets with the buttons before anyone could pick them up. Given the sad state of our campaign treasury, Joe worried that we had wasted twenty-three cents apiece on the unusable buttons.

In my announcement speech, I hit hard on the issues of integrity and honesty in government, pointing to my own resignation and the continuation of "business as usual" in Annapolis.

"Incredibly, just three weeks ago, Marvin Mandel stated that corruption should not be an issue in this campaign," I said. "In effect, Marylanders have been asked to put their blinders on again…to pretend that nothing has really happened…to help sweep the past under the political rug. That we would be asked to do this is both appalling to me and insulting to the electorate."

Then I turned my attention to Blair Lee, criticizing him for referring to "those who tamper with the system" (that is, to Victor Frenkil) "[as] just 'good old' overzealous businessmen."

> Political corruption in Maryland is the issue in the 1978 gubernatorial campaign! And nothing Mr. Mandel says—or anyone else says—can alter that fact.[78] We've had enough for those who have betrayed the public trust. We've had enough of "business as usual." Maryland is desperately in need of a new direction. You can feel it. I can feel it. This can be a turning point—an opportunity for a clean sweep—a chance to restore public faith.
>
> [The Democratic Party needs] a clean, untainted candidate who can win the general election for those good and honest and decent Marylanders—and they are legion—who care about their party and who care about their state. So today, I ask you to join me in a crusade—a crusade to redeem our state from the morass of corruption into which it has sunk. This can be a turning point—I know that we can restore integrity to the leadership of Maryland. I know that we can clear the atmosphere of the past and bring a new perspective to the issues that face us.
>
> I don't have all the answers and I'm not going to make promises I can't keep. But I do pledge to you that my actions will always be guided (as they have been in the past) by the belief that the public trust is the highest honor to which a citizen can respond. This can be a turning point.
>
> And so, I say to you here today—and to Marylanders everywhere—to all who understand what old-fashioned morality really means—I want to be your next governor.

A *Washington Post* reporter asked me if I didn't think I owed Mandel a favor for appointing me secretary of transportation.

"No, I don't believe so," I replied. "I believe Mr. Mandel owes me a favor for the job that I did for him as secretary."[79]

The campaign got a boost out of the announcement. We had a get-together the night of the announcement at Mike McWilliams's house to watch the TV coverage and were certain the money and support would start rolling in.

To keep up momentum, we immediately scheduled our first big fundraiser. Sponsored largely by a group of Baltimore lawyers who supported my candidacy, we called the February 28 event the "Bar Review." We really had some significant names involved in this effort. It was headed by Eli Frank, a lawyer with Frank Bernstein, and Vernon Eney, whom I thought was probably the best lawyer in the state of Maryland. Our honorary chairman was Clark Clifford, the former secretary of Defense and distinguished adviser to several presidents.

78. "Harry Hughes for Governor" campaign, press announcement, December 28, 1977.
79. Robert Bomboy, "Hughes Joins Governor's Race," *Baltimore News-American*, December 29, 1977.

Eney was a wonderful man. He was a top lawyer with Venerable Baetjer and Howard, one of Baltimore's premier law firms, and had been chairman of the state's Constitutional Convention in 1967 and '68. Vernon spent two or three years working on changes in the state constitution, only to have them rejected by voters. It was a tremendous disappointment to him. When Vernon would talk to you or present something to you, it was as if he was talking in outline form. Everything was right where it should be, and everything followed what it was supposed to follow and it was just beautiful to hear. I was never quite sure why Vernon supported me, but I was proud to have his help.

Around the same time, Bobby Goodman volunteered to write three thirty-second television spots for the campaign, Hal Donofrio produced them and we premiered them at a pair of fundraisers hosted by Chic Allen at the Greenspring Inn and the Maryland Club. Again, we hoped the ads would spark donations so we could afford to put them on TV.

At the Maryland Club event, we showed the television spot, I said a few words and then we asked for donations to pay to put the ad on the air. There was a fellow in the audience, a squat Irishman, who had apparently been at the Maryland Club since lunchtime and had had more than a few drinks. He struggled to stand and, his speech slurring a bit, announced, "I pledge $500." He was the first one to pledge. The next day, he called Mike McWilliams and asked, "Did I pledge anything at that event yesterday for Harry Hughes?" Mike said, "Yes, $500." And he paid it. But I later jokingly said to Mike, "You should have said $1,000!"

The money, however, did not pour in. Despite a good turnout at the "Bar Review" event, most of my supporters saw me as a dark horse candidate running fourth in a five-way field. They donated once because they liked me or knew me or as a friendly gesture, but for most of them once was enough.

Without the funds to do TV, Joe and I took to the road. We went to Democratic clubs, bull roasts and crab feasts, women's clubs, church fairs and American Legion halls. As winter turned into spring, I campaigned in Dundalk, and at the Inner Harbor and just about anywhere anyone would have me. When someone at one of these events commented about having seen me on television, it just made me more frustrated that we couldn't seem to raise the money to do TV ads.

"Lost Ball in High Grass"

I didn't get much press coverage, but from time to time reporters came to interview me and I did my best to explain why I was running for governor and my positions on the issues of the day. For the most part, this worked out well, until one night in May when a *Sun* reporter named Matt Seiden and I drove out to an event in Carroll County.

We thought that having Matt tag along was a real break because we hoped his story would give the campaign the attention it deserved. It was the first time a reporter had followed me for the day.

That night, we drove out to Carroll County to attend a "political forum" at an Eldersburg elementary school. It was not a fundraiser or an event for me, but rather one in a series of events they were doing to promote voter registration. They had asked public officials and candidates to stop by to engender enthusiasm so people would register to vote. But when we got out there, there was nobody there and a sign on the door that said, "Forum cancelled due to lack of interest." But that was not the way Seiden reported it.

In a story a couple days later, Seiden used the cancellation sign as a metaphor for my entire campaign.

"The words read like the handwriting on the wall for the former state secretary of transportation, who has been waging an uphill campaign for governor since his resignation from the Mandel administration a year ago this month," Seiden wrote.[80]

Then Seiden dropped the hammer, quoting a veteran Baltimore wheeler and dealer, state Senator Harry J. McGuirk, about my chances. "Harry Hughes," said McGuirk in words that would resonate in different ways for the rest of my political career, "is a lost ball in high grass." Seiden went on to say that McGuirk's political predictions "are rarely wrong."

When I read the paper that day that was a pretty low point. There were a lot of low points during that campaign, but that was one of the lowest.

We had another major fundraiser scheduled just two weeks later, but after that news story hit the bottom just fell out of everything. By summer about all I could do was campaign along the Inner Harbor, with Joe on a bullhorn exhorting passersby to "Step up and meet Harry Hughes, Democratic candidate for governor." My daughter Beth would march back and forth wearing a sandwich board and hand out campaign brochures. We were campaigning like that one afternoon when Beth, then twenty-two, walked up to a man and said, "I'd appreciate your support," or something like that, and the man took the brochure, looked at it and replied, "Oh, he's a loser." Beth, who has always been quite a competitor, fired back, "So are you in your white socks!"

In retrospect, the "lost ball" story probably helped in some way—it gave our campaign some notoriety and got my name in the paper. But I sure didn't think that at the time.

Throughout the campaign, the newspapers were regularly polling voters and publishing stories about the results. From our perspective, those results were never good. We just hovered at 5 to 7 percent, usually mired in fourth place and showing no movement whatsoever. When I think back on it, I wonder, "Why in the hell did I stay in that race?"

The only numbers in the poll that gave us any semblance of hope were the high percentages of voters who consistently polled as "undecided" or "uncommitted."

---

80. Matthew J. Seiden, "Hughes's Bid for Governor 'A Lost Ball in High Grass,'" *Baltimore Sun*, May 14, 1978.

Lieutenant Governor

As summer approached, we faced two serious problems. The first was that Maryland law requires candidates for governor to run on the same ticket with another candidate for lieutenant governor. With a July filing deadline fast approaching, I either had to give up my dream of becoming governor and try to hook on as a lieutenant governor on someone else's ticket, something I had said publicly I was not interested in doing, or find someone to run for lieutenant governor on my ticket.

The second problem was our chronic lack of money. That forced me to consider getting out of the race entirely. McWilliams had arranged a $30,000 loan to cover some of our campaign debts. Five members of our committee, McWilliams, Al Decker,[81] Chic Allen, Donofrio, Coale and I had cosigned a note in which each of us guaranteed $5,000 toward repayment. Things weren't looking good, so we met with the group and I said, "I'd better withdraw." But they said, "No, you stay in. If you want to stay in, you stay in and don't worry about that $30,000 note." I was gratified when they all agreed I should continue the race despite my low standing in the polls.

As the deadline drew closer, I decided I had to speak with Lee and Burch about possibly joining their tickets and arranged private meetings with both. I also spoke with my friend Steny Hoyer about the possibility of him joining my ticket, but he declined.

In early June, I went to Government House in Annapolis and spent over an hour in the mansion's first floor den discussing the election with Lee. It was just the two of us. We had known each other for years, had worked together on many issues and, despite our current competition, were genuinely fond of each other. But it became clear to me during that meeting that Blair and his people had already made up their minds to pick Hoyer as Blair's running mate. When the state's political pundits learned that Hoyer, the Senate president, was going to join the ticket with the lieutenant governor, most of them concluded the race for governor in 1978 was all but over. But it wasn't.

Burch, first elected in 1966, was completing his third term as attorney general. He was smart. He had attended Loyola College in Baltimore on a scholarship and finished first in his class. He went on to Yale Law School, where he finished fourth in his class. He had been the state insurance commissioner, city solicitor in Baltimore, president of the National Association of Attorneys General and, in 1975, had received an award as the Outstanding Attorney General in the United States.

I met with Burch on June 13, but went into the meeting worried about some of the people who might be supporting his candidacy. I told Burch that if I were to join his ticket, his campaign would have to assume my campaign's $60,000 in outstanding debts. I also said I wanted authority to review his list of campaign

81. Of the family that founded the Black & Decker hand tool-manufacturing company.

contributors and to direct that contributions from individuals whose support I could not accept—people such as Victor Frenkil—could be returned. Nine days later, Burch rejected these conditions and instead picked Joseph G. Anastasi, who was Mandel's secretary of economic and community development, to be his running mate. We later discovered that Burch's campaign was also in debt and in no position to accept my conditions.

Venetoulis, meanwhile, picked Anne Stockett, an Anne Arundel County councilwoman, as his running mate, and Orlinsky picked Ron Young, the mayor of Frederick. Everyone had someone on their dance card but me and I had less than two weeks to find a partner or my campaign was over. This was another low point in the campaign: we had very little money, no movement in the polls and now no running mate.

I do not know how many different people I asked to be my lieutenant governor, but there were a lot. I had already asked Steny and Anastasi, but both hooked on with other candidates. I put out feelers to Fred Wineland and Ann Hull, both of whom were legislators from Prince George's County, and to James Clark Jr., a farmer and state senator from Howard County. I always joked later that there were ten people who could have been lieutenant governor, but that's probably a little bit of an exaggeration.

We were desperate. Canning brought up the name of a Prince George's County councilman named Samuel Bogley III. I didn't know Sam at all, but Mike had known him through his involvement in Prince George's County politics. I had known Sam's father years before when he was on the old State Roads Commission and thought he was a good guy. Canning knew Sam's family and served as the go-between. Over the long Fourth of July weekend, just before the filing deadline, Sam agreed to join the ticket, but only after he and Canning had several long telephone conversations.

The thing I remember hearing about Sam was that he was really an independent voice, which to me was rather appealing. I did not know at that time about the extreme views on abortion that he and his wife, Rita, shared, but they would surface soon enough. I knew none of that at the time. We were frantically searching for a running mate and, at the last moment, Sam Bogley became our guy.

Coale liked to say we were running "a campaign of firsts: first to announce; first on TV; first to have a fundraiser." But in picking a lieutenant governor, we were dead last.

The *Sun* Editorial

Not long after the filing deadline, Burch surprised us all by dropping out of the race. That made it a four-way race, with Lee the clear leader, followed by Venetoulis. Orlinsky and I brought up the rear. Other than receiving a lonely endorsement from the Southern Howard County Democratic Club, my campaign just seemed stuck.

But Venetoulis wasn't doing that much better; he was only a few percentage points ahead of me in the polls. Coale used to call the energetic young Baltimore County executive "kissy-face" because he would come into an event and kiss all the women whether they wanted him to or not. But he was smart, stylish and articulate and, at first, I thought he would have a chance to catch Lee. As the summer wore on, though, his campaign appeared to be as stuck as mine. Lee's numbers weren't changing either and there was always a big bloc of voters who said they were still undecided.

By then, of course, I had realized that my running mate and I had opposing views on the issue of abortion and that once this problem became public, we were going to be in trouble. In mid-July, Joe Coale and I met with Bogley at the family business in Prince George's County to discuss the issue. Our goal was to contain it, at least until the September 12 primary was over.

Polls showed I had around 7 or 8 percent of the vote. I had been campaigning for almost a year and our numbers just hadn't moved. I was really frustrated. In August, I participated in four televised gubernatorial debates, which provided me with television airtime I otherwise could not afford. Lee and Venetoulis spent much of those debates bickering with each other, and I think I benefited from that. I tried to put the best face possible on our situation. I wrote supporters on August 15, saying, "Each week I am encouraged by positive signs that our efforts are paying off. There are now just four weeks left before the primary and we are in good position to make a run at the nomination." But I knew better. Pat was trying to organize "Zip Code Captains" around the state to generate volunteer support, but it was clear that what I needed the most was a miracle.

The miracle arrived on Sunday morning, August 20, 1978. On the front page of the Sunday *Baltimore Sun*, in a small box jammed between stories about Congress and NATO and positioned just below the word "The" in the masthead title, The *Sun*, it said: "Sun Endorsements for Governor."

> The editorial page offers its endorsements today in the gubernatorial primaries. In the Democratic primary, the paper endorses Harry R. Hughes in the belief that he is the one candidate with both the experience to govern Maryland and the capacity to rid state government of a political system that in the last decade has helped give it a reputation for corruption.

Inside the paper, the editorial itself, entitled "Hughes for the Democrats," was beyond my wildest expectations. It opened by noting,

> The 1978 gubernatorial elections offer Marylanders a needed opportunity to break cleanly with the politics of the past. For too long this state has been plagued by a system that has fostered corruption, petty and monstrous. It is a system that has ended in the criminal conviction of Maryland's last two elected governors. It is a system oiled by private profits gleaned from the manipulation of political power. It is a system that has demeaned this state in the eyes of the nation, and it must be broken.

One-by-one, the editorial then sized up Blair Lee, Wally Orlinsky, Ted Venetoulis and, finally, me.

> The fourth candidate, Harry R. Hughes, offers Marylanders a rare combination: integrity, experience, compassion. Over 16 years in the General Assembly, he became its leading expert on fiscal matters. He was the chief legislative architect of the state's graduated tax system, Maryland's last major tax reform. He was heavily involved in the state's efforts to devise an adequate and equitable system for providing financial aid to Maryland schools.

At the Department of Transportation, the editorial went on to say,

> He took disparate agencies jealous of the autonomy they were losing and welded them into a department devoted to producing a balanced transportation system. He worked diligently to achieve that balance, watching out for the port, the city subway, for Western Maryland roads and Eastern Shore railroads.
>
> Harry Hughes has made integrity and political independence a major issue. His detractors accuse him of hypocrisy of having remained long in the Mandel administration only to abandon a sinking governor. Yet Mr. Hughes is the only candidate who quit his job over a matter of principle. He resisted the wheeling and dealing of a contractor desperately trying to get in on a major contract. When he got no support from the State House, Mr. Hughes resigned.

It went on to praise me for "acknowledging society's obligations to the disadvantaged and deprived" and noting I was one of only two Eastern Shore senators to vote for the state's public accommodations law.

> Harry Hughes is a reserved man of intelligence, background-in-depth, sound judgment, and steadiness of purpose. His election would bring Maryland an excellent governor and bring new faces to Annapolis. The Sun urges his nomination.

Even today, it is hard for me to find the words to describe my personal feelings about that endorsement, not to mention what it meant to my campaign. Here was the most influential newspaper in the state swinging its power through an unprecedented front-page endorsement to a candidate who had never risen higher than about 8 percent in any of the pre-primary polls. It was a stunning rejection of Lee, the front-runner, and even of Venetoulis, who to many, seemed the only alternative to Lee with a chance to be elected.

I had been campaigning on the Eastern Shore that Saturday before the announcement appeared, and ended the day at a union hall in Dundalk. Coale, knowing the endorsements were likely to appear in Sunday's papers, stopped by a drug store in Loch Raven to pick up the early edition of the Sunday *Sun*, which came out late Saturday afternoon. And there it was! Coale later told me he got into his car and speeded to meet me in Dundalk, screaming at the top of his lungs the entire way. He actually beat me there and his voice was shot by the time I arrived. "Harry, look at this? Isn't this wonderful?" he croaked. I was talking to someone else at the moment and said to Joe, "Oh, that's great," but I didn't show the excitement I think Joe expected.

The next morning, however, as I was standing outside a Jewish grocery on Reisterstown Road handing out literature, the importance of the endorsement began to sink in and I was elated. And surprised. I had a pretty good rapport with some of the *Sun*'s editorial writers, like Brad Jacobs and Jerry Kelly, but none of them had said a word to me in advance. It wasn't until after Brad died that I learned that he had been instrumental in having the *Sunpapers* endorse me.

The next day, the *Baltimore Evening Sun*—the afternoon sister paper of the *Sun*—followed with its own editorial that said, "The candidate armed with the sturdiest promise for running Maryland's government honestly and well, Harry Hughes, apparently is being overlooked by party voters." It later described me as "no whirlwind campaigner, no backroom money-raiser, no spinner of utopian dreams [but rather] a proven leader on both the two broad avenues a governor must travel, legislative and executive."

The editorial ended by noting that some pundits had suggested that a vote for anyone other than Lee or Venetoulis would be wasted, but concluded with a sentence I will never forget: "A vote for the right man is never wrong."[82]

For me, the impact was obvious, if not immediate. Suddenly, I was seen as a viable candidate. We reprinted two hundred thousand copies of the editorial and had volunteers distribute them statewide. The endorsement was a way of telling voters that they would not be wasting their votes by voting for me. It also served as a warning to big campaign donors not to put all their eggs in Blair Lee's basket.

Throughout my campaign, I had to combat the belief that I just couldn't win. People would say, "I'd like to vote for you, but I don't want to throw away my vote." The editorial got people to thinking for the first time that, "Maybe he can win."[83]

---

82. Editorial, "A Case for Hughes," *Baltimore Evening Sun*, August 21, 1978.

83. On August 25, 1978, I wrote a short thank you letter to William F. Schmick Jr., the president and chief executive officer of the A.S. Abell Company, publishers of the *Sunpapers*: "Dear Mr. Schmick: I wish to express my sincere thanks for your splendid endorsement of my candidacy for the Democratic nomination for Governor. There are many rewards of public office and political life, but I have had none that excels receiving this endorsement, regardless of the outcome of the September primary. It was beautifully written, beautifully reasoned and has given my campaign a beautiful boost. Sincerely, Harry R. Hughes"

Down in Crisfield; Up on Primary Night

But things didn't start to turn around right away. We expected a big and immediate spike in our polling numbers—an expectation that set us up for what was probably the lowest moment of the entire campaign.

On the Saturday of Labor Day weekend just after the editorial came out, we made a campaign swing down to Crisfield and Ocean City. The big newspapers like the *Sun* and the *Baltimore News-American* always put out an early edition of their Sunday papers on Saturday afternoon. That Saturday, the *News-American* was to publish its latest gubernatorial primary poll and we had made arrangements to give a call to their political reporter, David Ahearn, who would tell us the results over the phone.

We were down at the Crab Derby in Crisfield. A friend of mine had a boat there, so Pat stayed on the boat while Joe and I went to a pay phone to call Ahearn to find out how well we were doing. What Ahearn told us, however, left us stunned: our numbers not only had not gone up, they had actually dropped, from 8 percent to 7. By the time we returned to the boat, we had the longest looks on our faces you can imagine.

We were supposed to go on to Salisbury to open a headquarters and from there go to the boardwalk in Ocean City to meet some volunteers, several of whom had worked for me at MDOT. The news about this latest poll made me almost sick to my stomach and I said, "Let's can the whole thing." But we couldn't. We drove over to Salisbury to open the headquarters, but there was hardly anyone there. Again, I tried to end the campaign swing, saying, "Let's not go on to Ocean City," but Joe and the others insisted, saying the volunteers were expecting us.

I relented and we drove to Ocean City. When we got to the boardwalk, Joe pulled out a bullhorn to alert the beach crowd that I was there. Within minutes, however, the Ocean City cops pulled Joe aside and threatened to arrest him because he was using a bullhorn on the boardwalk, which apparently was illegal. I was doing my best to shake hands with as many people as I could when I suddenly realized most of the people I was meeting were from Virginia or West Virginia or Pennsylvania. There were hardly any Marylanders there. It was a miserable end to a miserable day.

We rode back to Baltimore that night and all I could think was, "This is it. It's over."

Just one week later, however, the tide finally turned. It is hard to say whether it was the *Sun*'s editorial finally sinking in or the fact that undecided voters were being pushed by the calendar to decide, but suddenly the lift we had been seeking for more than a year finally came. On Saturday, September 9, we picked up early editions of the *Sun* that carried the paper's latest poll and a huge headline that said: "Hughes Surges—Neck and Neck with Venetoulis." Lee still had a 3-percentage point lead, but we had all of the momentum.

That night, Joe called a meeting in Donofrio's office to raise all the money we could to go on TV in the final days. Donofrio even committed to cover the cost of TV time through Monday with his own funds.[84] We were also aided by Lee himself,

84. Coale, "Maryland Political Revolution," 27.

who stumbled at a news conference the previous Friday when he refused to identify the source of a mysterious $25,000 donation to his campaign. Lee's campaign had already gained notoriety as the first in state history to exceed $1 million in contributions, but when he would only say that an unidentified "rich uncle" had given him the $25,000, it raised anew all of the swirling questions about integrity and honesty in government.

I released a statement to the *Sunpapers* that day promising that, if elected, I would manage the state government on "three important bases: integrity, independence and issues—the same bases that have marked my 22 years of public service and my campaign."

"I want to be your governor because I want to lead Maryland in a new and different direction—a direction that will make you proud, once again, to be a Marylander," I said.[85]

The day before the primary, the *Sun* weighed in one last time in an editorial entitled, "Chance for a Change." The editorial writers again suggested that a vote for me would not be wasted. "Harry Hughes can win," it said flatly, adding, "He will win if the tens of thousands of Marylanders who normally stay home from the polls come out tomorrow and vote."[86]

On primary election day, we were publicly predicting a major upset in the making, but privately were in a state of high nervous anxiety. At headquarters around midday, McWilliams fielded a telephone call from a volunteer in Dundalk who reported that exit polls were showing voters backing me by an 8-to-1 margin. Reports from elsewhere in the state fed our growing optimism.

In early afternoon, Baltimore station WJZ-TV sent reporter Frank Luber to our headquarters to set up to cover what we hoped would be our victory party. But Luber confided to Coale that in fifteen years with the station, he had never covered a winning candidate on election night. Coale told him his luck was about to change.

About 7:20 p.m., the results started to come in. The first came from a city precinct on Belair Road: Hughes 195; Lee 61; Venetoulis 38; and Orlinsky 12. Even state Senator Harry McGuirk's home precinct went for me by a two-to-one margin. I was emerging from the "high grass." By 8:30 p.m., other news reporters began to arrive at our headquarters as they became aware that I was likely to be at the center of one of the biggest and most unexpected political upsets in Maryland history.

Pat and I had been watching the returns on TV in a room upstairs in the Lord Baltimore. I hadn't prepared a victory speech or a concession speech. Around 9:30 p.m., I took the elevator downstairs to the ballroom and when the doors opened the swelling crowd was just ecstatic and a band struck up the song, "I'm Just Wild About Harry."

I guess a lot of people really don't make up their minds until right up to the time of voting, and I think that is what happened to me. There had been a large bloc of voters,

85. "Harry Hughes for Governor" campaign, *Sunpapers*, September 10, 1978.
86. Editorial, "Chance for a Change," *Baltimore Sun*, September 11, 1978.

maybe as much as 40 percent at one point, that described themselves as "undecided." I think it was the combination of the editorials, the debates and the feelings about scandal in state government in Maryland that turned the election my way. All of that welled up until, in the last few days, people just decided to vote for me.

I had a young fellow named Paul Farley who was my driver on Election Day. We traveled all around the region and the reaction was so obvious at all the polls—it was just so obvious.

About 6:00 p.m., we were on our way back to Baltimore from Columbia and I said, "Paul, what do you think?" He said, "I think you're going to win. From what I've seen today, I think you're going to win."

I felt good. I felt really good.

A Mandate for Change

I BEAT ACTING GOVERNOR BLAIR LEE III by more than 20,000 votes—210,623 to 190,303. In the four-way race, I won a little more than 37 percent of the vote—a far cry from the 7 to 8 percent levels I had endured during almost the entire campaign. Lee finished with just under 34 percent, Venetoulis with about 24 percent and Orlinsky with a little more than 4 percent. I won Baltimore City and twelve of the twenty-three counties.

As well-wishers jammed into the Lord Baltimore Hotel ballroom that night, I described my victory as a repudiation of the corruption scandals that had plagued Maryland for so long.

"What you have said is you want something different," I said. "The people of Maryland can win an election. You can beat the machine."[87]

Blair Lee, gracious in defeat, hurried to my victory party to pledge his support in the general election, in which I would face former U.S. Senator J. Glenn Beall Jr., easy winner in the four-way Republican primary.[88] "Harry is a fine man and I really do hope that all of you will join hands in supporting him in November," Blair said that night.[89]

In May 1980, Sidney Hollander Jr. of Hollander, Cohen Associates, Inc., a marketing and opinion research firm in Baltimore, analyzed the effect of the *Sunpapers*'s endorsement of my candidacy in an article for *Public Opinion Quarterly*. The endorsement fell in the midst of polling by the *Sunpapers*'s competitor, the *Baltimore News-American*, which showed that I had 4 percent of the vote on the Friday and Saturday before the endorsement and 11 percent on the Monday to Thursday afterward. "This was readily interpreted as the size of the electorate who would follow the *Sun*'s idealistic or sentimental move in support of the candidate who at that point represented more of a protest than a challenge," Hollander wrote. Lee showed a corresponding drop from 38 to 30 percent. As Election Day neared, however, the surge in my candidacy continued, which Hollander attributed to a change of heart by "the large number who hesitated to vote their convictions because they were afraid of 'throwing away' their votes. The newspaper endorsement made Hughes a plausible candidate and the voters did the rest."

87. Robert Timberg, "Hughes Topples Lee, Will Face Glenn Beall in November," *Baltimore Evening Sun*, September 13, 1978.
88. Beall received 73,765 votes, or 57 percent of the total, against opponents Carlton G. Beall (no relation), 29,439; Louise Gore, 21,155; and Dr. Ross Z. Pierpont, 4,835. Political observers speculated that Carlton Beall, a one-time Prince George's County sheriff, received an unexpectedly high number of votes because of the name confusion with J. Glenn Beall.
89. G. Jefferson Price III, "Lee Concedes After Midnight; Sachs Wins Attorney General Race," *Baltimore Sun*, September 13, 1978.

The reality in heavily Democratic Maryland in 1978 was that the winner of the Democratic primary for governor was almost certain to be elected governor in November. Glenn Beall was a fine man. In a state in which voters were evenly divided between the two major political parties, he might have been a formidable opponent. But that was not Maryland in 1978. By winning the primary, I could finally allow myself to believe with some certainty that I was about to become governor of Maryland.

Ironically, the biggest problem I encountered in that general election campaign came not from Beall, but from my own running mate for lieutenant governor, Sam Bogley. The real problem was Sam's wife, Rita, and her extremist views on abortion. I had learned of Sam's views on abortion after he joined my ticket and we had discussed it during the primary campaign, but we were so far back in the pack that no one ever asked or cared whether my running mate and I had differing views on this politically sensitive issue. The day after we won the primary, however, Rita made sure the press knew.

We were at our old headquarters in the Lord Baltimore and I heard a commotion out in the hallway. When I went out to investigate, there was Rita talking with the press about abortion and handing out photographs of fetuses. We had just won the nomination and she was obviously intent on using that as a platform for her views.

I called Sam into the office and said, "We've got to do something about this and we're not leaving here until we get this issue resolved." Women's rights organizations were very upset about this. They weren't concerned about me. They knew I favored a woman's right to choose. They were concerned about what would happen if something happened to me and Sam had to take over as governor. So I got Sam to agree that if anything ever happened to me, my policies would be carried out through the rest of that term. Two weeks after the primary, Sam issued a statement that we had agreed upon.

"I have said in the past and repeat, as lieutenant governor, I will support all the policies and programs of Harry Hughes as elected governor of Maryland," he said. "If for some reason I have to assume the office of governor during our four-year elected term, I will continue those policies and programs, unless they are changed by action of the General Assembly or by the vote of the people."

There also had been speculation that because of this disagreement, I was about to dump Sam from our ticket or that Sam was going to resign. He addressed this issue by saying, "In no way have I ever considered resigning from the Hughes-Bogley ticket over any disagreement regarding the state's funding of abortion or any other issue. And in no way has Harry Hughes ever considered the possibility of me leaving the ticket...I am not resigning, nor will I resign, and it is my intention and purpose to support totally the candidacy of Harry Hughes for governor of Maryland."[90]

90. "Harry Hughes for Governor" campaign, Bogley statement, September 29, 1978.

That put the problem to rest for a while, although it cropped up again the night of the general election when Rita, then a thirty-five-year-old mother of six, was asked if her anti-abortion campaign was now over. "It's not, believe me," she told the *Baltimore News-American*. "I wasn't elected. My husband was. But I am a wife. As a wife, I cannot see myself not having some input into what my husband says and does."

I was beginning to think I had made a mistake in choosing Sam. Long before my first term was over, I realized he and I would have to part ways. Yet, under the circumstances at the time I filed for governor, I really had no choice. I had to have a running mate and candidates were not exactly flocking to join my desperate campaign.

Sam turned out to be a pretty good campaigner. He raised some money, although not a lot. We campaigned both separately and together and I grew to like him. I continue to like him, although sometimes I think he would have been better suited as a priest or a minister than as a politician.

After I became governor, our relationship was distant, even though his office was just across the State House hall from mine. I tried to use him as a liaison with local governments. I thought he could be of help there because he knew and understood the workings of county councils. But he started doing little things I didn't like, things that were disloyal in a way.

For example, during each General Assembly session, I usually hosted a series of dinners at Government House for members of the legislature. One year, one of those dinners conflicted with the annual Agriculture Dinner, a big affair hosted by the Maryland Farm Bureau at a banquet hall near Baltimore. I couldn't go to the Ag Dinner, so Sam went in my place, but when asked to speak he made some nasty remarks about me not being there. My friend Jack Logan happened to be in the audience and called Sam aside and really chewed him out.[91]

General Election Sweep

The problem with Sam and Rita during the general election campaign, however, blew over pretty quickly and the momentum was all ours. In contrast to the problems of our primary campaign, people actually started donating money to our general election campaign! I was no longer "Harry Whose?"

On November 7, 1978, five months after I had nearly dropped out of the race for lack of money and support, I was elected by a landslide to become Maryland's fifty-seventh governor. I beat Beall by a margin of 416,526 votes—701,046 to 284,520—and swept Baltimore City and twenty-one of the state's twenty-three counties. The only counties I lost were the two rural and predominantly Republican

91. By January 1980, a year after we had taken office, Sam was quoted as saying: "My political instincts tell me I will not be on the Hughes's ticket for lieutenant governor next time. I know they don't consider me gubernatorial timber. This doesn't bother me so much. Maybe I'm not." He added that he did not believe the job he was doing was worth the money the state was paying him.

counties in the mountains of far western Maryland, Allegany and Garrett. That night, I received a congratulatory telephone call from President Jimmy Carter.

Blair Lee marveled at the strength of my position, saying I would come into office with "a tidal wave of popular support accompanied by almost zero advance promises and commitments of any sort." That was undoubtedly true—I was beholden to no one because, at least until the end, no one had asked for anything because no one supported my candidacy. I remember going to several events—a wine and cheese party in Baltimore, an outdoor dedication ceremony in Calvert County—where I showed up, but no voters did. Joe Coale used to say that we made more U-turns in the state of Maryland than anybody in history. Joe would drive, or Paul Farley would drive, or sometimes I'd drive myself to an event, but I can tell you, there were a lot of lonely rides.

Transition

The first thing I had to do, of course, was assemble a government. Based on the government reorganization recommended by the Curlett Commission, Mandel had set up a Cabinet system of government. After I was elected, I kept waiting for the Cabinet members to submit their resignations so I could choose which ones I wanted to keep, but none of them did. When there is a change of administration at the federal level in Washington that is what Cabinet secretaries do. But none of Mandel's secretaries tendered their resignations except for Thomas W. Schmidt, the budget secretary. I was so miffed that I decided to let the whole bunch of them go, although I later reconsidered and kept James B. Coulter at natural resources, J. Max Millstone at general services and Schmidt at the state budget office. My friend Paul Cooper had come out of retirement to help with the transition and was very impressed by Schmidt.

I later found out that Henry Bosz, Mandel's secretary of personnel, had been advising Cabinet secretaries not to submit letters of resignation because it would adversely affect their pensions. The only ones I spoke with were Schmidt, Coulter and Neil Solomon, the physician who had been Mandel's health secretary. Solomon, who had a syndicated newspaper column and a national reputation, asked to see me and pleaded to keep his job, but I wasn't interested in having him stay. As for the rest of them, I felt if I wasn't going to keep them on there was no point in talking to them. If they didn't have the courtesy or the professionalism to submit a resignation, I figured I didn't have the responsibility to call them in.

Mike Canning and Joe Coale naturally formed the core of my new State House staff and Mike McWilliams remained a close adviser, but from the outside. Through McWilliams, I hired attorney Judson Garrett to head my legislative office and Louise Keelty as my appointments secretary. Louise had started off life as a nun and Jud had started off in a seminary. I brought in a lawyer with the Baltimore firm of Frank, Bernstein, Conaway & Goldman named George W. Liebmann to prepare briefing books on issues and later to be my energy adviser and liaison with the Cabinet. His reports were thick and detailed. Some six years later, one of Liebmann's memos to me would play a bigger, more problematic role in my administration.

To run my press office, I hired Gene Oishi, a Japanese-American who had distinguished himself as a national political correspondent for the *Baltimore Sun*. I brought in Ann Hull, a very smart former legislator from Prince George's County, as my staff person for welfare, health and social services issues. I kept Sheila Tolliver, who had worked under Mandel, as my liaison on higher education issues. And I brought over several people from my years at MDOT: Wayne McDaniel would be my liaison on transportation issues; Verna Harrison would join my legislative office; Sylvia Ramsey would become an executive assistant with the principal responsibility as liaison with the horse racing industry; Irv Feinstein would handle administrative issues related to our State House quarters; Canning would serve as staff director; and Annette Silverman would become my primary secretary and gate-keeper. There is no one more important to an executive than a very competent and loyal secretary and I could not have asked for a better one than Annette. Almost all of these MDOT veterans had been volunteers in my campaign.

Throughout November and December, I sifted through recommendations for my Cabinet. I appointed my old deputy, Jim O'Donnell, to be secretary of Transportation and Ejner J. Johnson to be secretary of Licensing and Regulation.

I hired Kalman "Buzzy" Hettleman, who had worked for Schaefer in the city, to head the Department of Human Resources. Buzzy was great. He had once been a top aide to former Baltimore Mayor Thomas L.J. D'Alesandro III, served on the city school board and then headed the Legal Aid Bureau in Baltimore, which provided legal assistance to the poor. Buzzy really cared about poor people and turned out to be a very good secretary.

I also picked another city official to run the state prison system. Baltimore City Jail Warden Gordon C. Kamka had been highly recommended to me by the state's newly elected attorney general, Stephen H. Sachs. Gordon thought there should be more emphasis placed on rehabilitating prisoners so they could return to productive life once they were released and that seemed like the right approach to me.

For the Department of Agriculture, I tapped Wayne Cawley, an old friend of mine from Denton. Wayne had been three years ahead of me in school and we were lifelong friends. "I've known Harry since we were old enough to talk," Wayne told reporters.[92] I don't think Wayne had ever thought of becoming secretary of Agriculture, but he did a fine job. He brought an interesting combination of experiences to the task: he had been a farmer all his life, but he also had worked for the Denton National Bank advising farmers on the equipment they should buy without putting themselves in financial jeopardy. Wayne brought a business sense to the job as well as a deep understanding of farming and agricultural issues.

---

92. Donald P. Baker and Michael Weisskopf, "Hughes Appoints Two, Retains One for Cabinet," *Washington Post*, January 12, 1979.

Max Millstone had only been general services secretary for about a year before I was elected. He did a good job, but Max was a worrier and always seemed to be wiping the sweat off his brow. We used to kid him by asking him whether he was having a three-handkerchief or four-handkerchief day. Years later, I appointed Max to the Workman's Compensation Commission and he was so relieved to have a politically and financially secure job that he was forever grateful. Other members of my initial Cabinet included Constance Leider to head the Department of Planning, Martin M. Puncke to head the State Lottery Agency and Charles R. Buck Jr. as secretary of Health and Mental Hygiene.

The one Cabinet position I had trouble filling was secretary of economic development. That briefly proved embarrassing because I had made such an issue during my campaign of the need to boost economic development in the state. After a couple of false starts with other candidates, I finally hired James O. Roberson to fill the post, but not until June 1979, five months after taking office. Roberson was vice-president of the Howard Research and Development Corp., a subsidiary of the Rouse Company, the developer of Columbia, Maryland.

This was an important post for me to fill with the right person. A report issued toward the end of the Mandel administration indicated that Maryland had lost an estimated forty-one thousand manufacturing jobs between 1972 and 1977.

The Return of Marvin Mandel

Piece by piece, I began to pull together a staff and Cabinet and prepare for my January 17, 1979, inauguration. But three days before I was to be sworn in, Marvin Mandel's conviction on political corruption charges was overturned by a two-to-one vote of a federal appellate court.[93] The next day, unembarrassed by his years of legal trouble and insensitive to the fact that Lee was in the final days of his own long political career, Mandel revoked Lee's designation as acting governor and triumphantly returned to the State House to reclaim his throne. For two days, we had a governor, a former acting governor and a governor-elect roaming the State House halls. Blair complained that he no longer had a desk at which to sit.

The day prior to my inauguration, Goldstein was sworn in for a new term as state comptroller before a joint session of the General Assembly meeting in the House

93. Bradford Jacobs, *Thimbleriggers: The Law v. Governor Marvin Mandel*, (Baltimore, MD: The Johns Hopkins University Press, 1984). Mandel's legal problems followed a tortuous course. His first trial in U.S. District Court ended in a mistrial because of attempts at jury tampering. After he and his five codefendants were later convicted, a three-judge panel of the U.S. Fourth Circuit Court of Appeals vacated the conviction on a 2–1 vote. Federal prosecutors appealed and a six-judge panel of the court reinstated Mandel's conviction in summer 1979 on a 3–3 tie vote. Pressed for a more definitive ruling, an eight-judge panel affirmed the conviction again in November 1979, this time on a 4–4 tie vote. In 1980, the former governor and House Speaker began serving a nineteen-month sentence in a federal prison in Florida. Years afterward, the conviction would be overturned on a technicality.

chamber. Immediately after that, Mandel was officially reinstated as governor and the entire Assembly serenaded him with the state song, "Maryland, My Maryland."

One result of this unexpected game of gubernatorial musical chairs is that I ended up with two commissions as governor for the same term: one signed by Lee before he knew Mandel was going to take over, the other signed by Mandel. When a rabbi at my inauguration "blessed the governor," Blair later said he thought the rabbi was going to add, "Whoever he may be."

Regardless of his new legal status, I did not want Mandel at my inauguration and did not invite him. Nor did I invite Agnew. After resigning in protest over tampering with a state contract, after the state had endured years of embarrassing political corruption and after I had campaigned so hard on a theme of restoring integrity to government, I just felt it would have been hypocritical to invite Mandel or Agnew to my inauguration.[94] But I did invite J. Millard Tawes, the only living ex-governor of Maryland who had not been convicted of a federal crime.

Inauguration

Inauguration day was damp and bitterly cold, with a mix of sleet and freezing rain. We had set up the stage on the opposite side of the State House from Government House, near the statue of Supreme Court Justice Roger Taney. In that location, the stage sat high on the hill and the thousand or so well-wishers who braved the awful weather were forced to stand or sit in a semi-circle far below the stage looking up. That was the last time an inauguration was held on that side of the State House. From the stage, you could see the Circle Theater (now an office building) immediately across the street, where the marquee read, "Goodbye Marvin, Hello Harry."

My goal was to bring some dignity back to the office of governor and so I tried to dress appropriately. I wore a formal morning coat, a silk ascot and striped trousers. Former U.S. Secretary of Defense Clark Clifford, a true statesman who had become a steady supporter of mine, introduced me. In electing me, he said, the people of Maryland made it clear, "We not only want a new deal, we want a new deck."

---

94. Jacobs, *Thimbleriggers*. Toward the end of my first year in office, Attorney General Sachs—acting with my blessing—brought a lawsuit against Mandel that alleged that when the former governor left office he had stolen $23,800 in furniture, liquor and other goods, including toothpaste, dog food, a five-piece bedroom set, Waterford crystal, redwood patio furniture and two historic wooden sculptures that were chopped from a pair of carved doors that once graced the front of the mansion. The sculptures were later found hanging in the Mandel home. Mandel claimed there was simply a mix-up; that he had taken some items by mistake and left some of his own belongings at the mansion. We identified some items that were probably his, put them in a truck and tried to return them, but he wouldn't accept them—probably because that would have required him to admit that what we were saying was true. The dispute lasted five years, bracketing the period Mandel served in federal prison at Eglin Air Force Base in Florida. He ultimately settled the case by keeping some of the furniture, returning some, and reimbursing the state for $9,250.

In my remarks, I said my inauguration was more than tradition and more than transition, but rather "a celebration of real change."

> *In all humility and with all gratitude, I come before you as the governor with the greatest mandate in Maryland's history to effect change. This mandate will be fulfilled. This obligation will be met. I will live up to the electorate's expectations.*
>
> *The people of Maryland have had enough political manipulation; enough unfulfilled promises; enough scandal, shock and shame…Integrity and independence will be the hallmark of this administration.*

I said my style ("the Hughes style") would be to act, not react. "I will propose comprehensive solutions. I will not govern by crisis. To a certain extent, this means Maryland may have a very quiet administration, but I think I can speak for every citizen when I say we've had enough media events; we need meaningful events."

I spoke of what I saw as a "corrosion of public confidence in representative government…a rising provincialism; the fragmentation of special interests; the self-defeating politics of selfishness." To that, I suggested, "Acting with integrity is the first step to restoring public confidence," and promised to set "an example of moral conduct which is beyond reproach."

I did not have to mention Mandel or Agnew by name when I said, "The highest standard of ethical conduct will begin with the governor and permeate throughout the state service."

I concluded by thanking those who had voted for me, saying, "I am grateful for your trust and will never betray it…Today, we begin the noble, exciting mission to resurrect the image of Maryland's government as the most respected, most efficient, most progressive in the nation." My last words were from Abraham Lincoln: "I like to see a man proud of the place in which he lives. I like to see a man live in it so that his place is proud of him."

13

The "Hughes Style"

N EITHER THE LEGISLATURE NOR THE press was accustomed to the new style I brought to the governor's office. My style was steady and deliberate. The tone of my administration would be one of honesty and integrity. Legislators accustomed to being strong-armed by Mandel and his aides would find in me a governor respectful of the separation of powers and the rightful role of the General Assembly. My appointments would be based on merit, professionalism and results, not on politics, connections and paybacks, and would emphasize the inclusion of women, blacks and other minorities.

For reporters who had become addicted to the rat-a-tat flurry of political scandal emanating from the State House's second floor, my administration would seem tame, uninteresting and, yes, probably boring. I was interested in good governance; they were more interested in stories about Agnew accepting cash bribes in unmarked envelopes, or the salacious intrigue of the married Mandel carrying on a secret tryst with a southern Maryland divorcee, or the disheartening tale of a state legislator arrested on narcotics charges on the State House grounds and later being gunned down in a Baltimore parking garage.

I remember one headline in a Baltimore newspaper shortly after my election that predicted, "4 Competent, Colorless Years Seen Ahead,"[95] and thought to myself that that was probably just what Maryland's citizens needed.

It posed an interesting problem for me. On the one hand, the press, the legislature and even the public seemed disgusted by the heavy-handedness and scandalous conduct of my predecessors, yet somehow felt short-changed with the quiet, low-key approach I brought to government. It left me open to criticism that I was a weak leader, being led around by the suddenly more powerful General Assembly.

I heard all that "do nothing" stuff. That is a favorite phrase of the press. If the session goes smoothly and there is nothing sensational or big, then the press writes it is a "do nothing legislature" or a "do nothing governor." I've seen that for years. It is part of the game. Reporters want certain things. They want sensationalism or flamboyance, and that's fine, but I'm not that and I'm not going to worry about it.

The night my first legislative session as governor ended, I went to a *sine die* party, where a *Washington Post* reporter found me standing alone sipping a drink. He seemed to expect the governor of Maryland to be in the middle of a noisy crowd.

"I don't see any reason why they should treat me any different now than they did before

95. Kenneth T. Berents, "4 Competent, Colorless Years Seen Ahead," *Baltimore Evening Sun*, November 8, 1978.

I was governor," I said. "I've sensed a warm feeling, but you know I don't believe in the crown system. You know there are no constitutional requirements for being governor except being a certain age. It doesn't make me any different from anyone else."[96]

In a *Baltimore Sun* editorial appraising my first six months in office, even my supporters at the newspaper criticized my first legislative session as "lackluster," but they said that was okay as long as my administration did more in 1980. "He prefers to avoid confrontation and seek consensus," the editorial said, an assessment I took as a compliment.[97] The truth was, I wasn't satisfied with the way the second floor was operating.

I decided to make some adjustments to my staff, which was frankly pretty light on State House experience. That fall, I brought in Johnny Johnson to be my personal liaison with the legislature, but within three months I made him my new chief of staff. To do that, I had to shift Mike Canning to more of a supervisory role with the Cabinet and with the staff that served as my liaison to the various secretaries. Johnny had been my Motor Vehicle administrator when I was transportation secretary and when I became governor I initially appointed him as secretary of the Department of Licensing and Regulation. I had confidence in his organizational abilities and felt he would help us develop strategy and deal with the legislature.

The son of a Brooklyn cop, Johnny had what one reporter described as "Swedish good looks and Scotch-Irish charm and humor."[98] His mother was from an old Worcester County family and he had spent many of his summers in Snow Hill. He graduated from the University of Maryland and settled in Severna Park. He came to Annapolis initially as a newspaper reporter and later worked in the Tawes's administration and at MVA under Mandel. At MVA, where about two-thirds of the workforce were women, Johnny was credited with moving more women into top management positions. In less than a year at Licensing and Regulation, he also showed he was not afraid to get rid of employees who had been hired in the past because of their political connections, and he immediately set about the task of professionalizing the nearly forty boards and commissions under his control.

When Johnny moved into the State House, he signaled his arrival—and his newfound power—by first moving into the office that had been occupied by Irv Feinstein, sending Irv into cramped new quarters in the State House basement. He then ejected Deputy Press Secretary Ginny Friedlander from her office to make room for his own secretary, Carol Salmon. Next, he set his sights on the office then occupied by Secretary of State Fred Wineland. A few days later, Wineland found himself in the unfortunate position of denying to a reporter the rumor that the secretary of state's offices were being moved to another building across the street just as workmen came by carrying his desk out the door.[99]

96. David A. Maraniss and Michael Weisskopf, "Hughes Gets His Way Watching from the Wings," *Washington Post*, April 11, 1979.
97. Editorial, "Six Months with Mr. Hughes," *Baltimore Sun*, July 23, 1979.
98. Timothy M. Phelps, "Johnson Unabashedly Asserts His Primacy in the Laid-Back Hughes' Administration," *Baltimore Sun*, March 2, 1980.
99. Ibid.

I felt this change was necessary, but wanted to do it in a way that did not embarrass Canning or hurt his feelings. We had been through too much together. At a September 28, 1979, press conference, the day these changes were announced, I explained that Mike would continue to answer directly to me, but felt he had been spread too thin. "He agrees and, as a matter of fact, this is mostly his recommendation," I said of the staff changes. I also explained that I needed "to free my time more because of the many details that I take care of in that office. I am in there a long time every day and mostly on weekends and I need to have more time to get out and to think and to look at the big picture. I think my whole staff has recognized this." To replace Johnson at Licensing and Regulation, I appointed John J. Corbley, who had helped set up the Maryland Automobile Insurance Fund, the state-run insurer of last resort for motorists.

In retrospect, I feel bad about the way Mike was treated during this time. I think everyone would have been better off if I had made Mike my press secretary, which is what he had been when we were together at MDOT. I have often regretted not doing that.

Around the same time, I also brought in John F.X. O'Brien to improve my relationship with the legislature. O'Brien, who had first been elected to the House of Delegates from Baltimore in 1966, was a close friend of many of the senators and delegates who now were deciding the fate of my programs. Some of them were complaining, both privately and in the press, that they weren't getting the personal attention from the governor's office they felt they deserved, so O'Brien's initial task was to try to calm them down and elicit their support.

One of the first things O'Brien did was convince me to initiate a series of breakfasts at Government House for legislative leaders. More frequently, we had morning meetings with legislative leaders in the Reception Room outside my office. These get-togethers allowed me to exchange ideas on issues with legislators and let them know I was fully aware of the problems they were confronting.

These staff changes, as important as they ultimately were to me, however, did nothing in the short run to deter writers from routinely describing the administration as "boring." I took note of this in my second state of state address in 1980. After listing our first session accomplishments in tax relief, pension reform and the imposition of new ethical standards for state government employees, I told lawmakers: "To some extent, this shared mission has been accompanied by the criticism that we are not flamboyant. This seems a small trade-off, which I gladly accept, for delivering the services and for the efficient, business-like and especially for the honest management of government that our constituents want."[100]

---

100. Governor Harry Hughes, state of the state message (House-Senate Joint Session, January 16, 1980).

First Priority

My first priority as governor was to restore a sense of integrity in government. In my initial state of the state address, I discussed the condition of the state's budget and explained the various programs I would be proposing and why I thought they were necessary. I spoke with a level of programmatic and budgetary detail that modern governors have since abandoned in favor of more general philosophical or even blatantly political rhetoric. It may have been dry stuff, but I felt it was the substance of governance. As chief executive, I felt it was my responsibility to report to the legislature the factual "state of the state" and outline the changes I believed state government should make. This is the approach I took in all eight of my state of the state addresses.

In that first speech, for example, I spoke about the increase in state spending I was proposing in both percentage terms and in real dollars. I explained how I could have used accounting tricks to make the overall increase seem smaller than it really was and thus deflect criticism, but said, "That would have been accounting gamesmanship and this administration is not going to play games."

"The electorate has spoken for honesty and they shall receive it, in accounting as well as administration. We may not look as good, but what the public will see is clean, clear facts and figures. So long as I am governor, Maryland's citizens will be told the fiscal not the figurative truth," I said.[101]

I was fortunate to be elected in a year in which the members of my own political party retained their overwhelming dominance in the General Assembly. Democrats controlled 40 of 47 seats in the Senate and 125 of 141 in the House of Delegates, but many of them were new, as were the presiding officers in both houses. I knew and liked Jim Clark, the new Senate president, but did not know as well young Benjamin L. Cardin of Baltimore, the new House speaker. But I knew Ben was smart and believed I could work with them both.

"State of the State Has Never Been Better"

During my first two years in office, Maryland enjoyed budget surpluses that were so large that legislative leaders and I made a determined effort to give much of it back in tax relief. That first year, we enacted the largest tax reduction the state had ever seen. We tripled the standard deduction on the income tax from $500 to $1,500, eliminated the 2 percent sales tax on manufacturing equipment and farm machinery and eliminated entirely the sales tax on fuel oil and utilities for residential properties.

Because some of this tax relief would siphon funds away from local governments, I also proposed an increase in state aid to local subdivisions. "This assures that the

---

101. Governor Harry Hughes, state of the state message (House-Senate Joint Session, January 19, 1979).

state taxpayers' relief will not be eroded by increased local taxation," I explained. "This guarantees that tax relief…will be real rather than a case of the state giveth and the subdivision taketh away."[102]

The following year, revenues continued to pour in. In 1980, I was able to propose a budget that would increase overall state spending by 6.7 percent and still rank as the smallest increase in state spending in seventeen years. At the time, the national inflation rate was 13 percent.

I began my second year in office by confidently telling the General Assembly that "the state of the State has never been better."[103] My budget called for additional tax relief, but also for a 7 percent salary increase for all state employees, increases in state aid for public schools and community colleges and an 11 percent increase in welfare grants, the largest single grant increase in the state's history (which came just a year after we had given welfare recipients a 10 percent increase).

The back-to-back increases in the Aid to Families with Dependent Children program represented "an unprecedented state effort to confront the long-standing gap between welfare grant levels and the need of low-income families for minimal, decent subsistence," I said.[104] I had been interested in social issues since I was in the legislature. Suddenly, I had people on my staff or in the Cabinet, such as Buzzy Hettleman at Human Resources and H. Louis Stettler III in my budget office, who also were interested in those issues. We were in good fiscal shape at the time, we had an opportunity to do it and so we did it.

I have always felt we never got much credit for the tax relief we put in place. It is funny: people just don't seem to remember tax reductions. You can stop ten people on the street and ask them what kind of reduction they got on their Maryland income tax in the last few years and they don't know. They don't even know if they had a tax reduction. Eliminating the sales tax on utility bills was a big deal—and it would be a much bigger deal today because utility bills are so much higher. But that is all soon forgotten. Once it doesn't appear on the bill, it is out of sight, out of mind. That's the way with most tax relief, I think, but not so with tax increases.

Spending Limits

Despite these tax reduction efforts, legislative conservatives—and political opportunists—still complained about the overall growth in the state budget. They characterized the size of the state workforce as bloated and proclaimed the need to impose caps on spending, perhaps embedded in the state Constitution. Proposition 13, which capped property taxes in California, had just been enacted and tax cap

102. Ibid.
103. Governor Harry Hughes, state of the state message (House-Senate Joint Session, January 16, 1980).
104 Ibid.

fever had spread to the East Coast. I warned the legislature that Maryland could face similar demands for statutory or even constitutional limits if we failed to enact significant tax relief.

During my second legislative session, two Baltimore County conservatives, Republican Delegate Ellen R. Sauerbrey and Democratic Senator Francis X. Kelly, pushed hard for passage of a package of Proposition 13-style caps on state spending. I opposed rigid spending limits. Whatever limit was set would be arbitrary, I thought. To tie our hands that way should not be necessary, as long as we did our jobs properly. More importantly, I could see that spending limits could cause problems in future years as we tried to provide the services government needs to render.

My staff and I were fairly confident this sort of restraint on spending would not fare well in the relatively progressive General Assembly and, consequently, we simply ignored it. That almost proved to be a serious mistake. The package of spending limits bills unexpectedly emerged from the Senate Budget and Taxation Committee and was sent to the Senate floor where passage suddenly seemed likely. Some of the bills in the six-bill package had more cosponsors (twenty-eight) than the twenty-four votes needed for passage.

We hastily called a staff meeting to figure out what to do and O'Brien recommended that we start our defense by talking to the nineteen senators who were not listed as cosponsors. By the next morning, I had eighteen of the nineteen in my office. I told them that supporting these bills was a threat to the oath of office they had taken and that they would be relinquishing their authority to some automatic, robotic clause in the Constitution. By the time the meeting was over, fourteen of the eighteen were on our side. I needed ten more to assure a majority against the bill.

The next day, I summoned another dozen legislators to my second floor office and, one by one, we tried to persuade them. That evening, a little before midnight, the spending limits bill came up for preliminary approval on the Senate floor, normally handled by voice vote. But, working through Senate Majority Leader Rosalie Abrams of Baltimore, we called for a roll call vote and defeated the spending limit bills that night. It was important to kill those bills because of the constraint they would have placed on state government, but it was perhaps just as important for me to show the General Assembly that the administration was not going to roll over. It was this fight that I believe began to change my image.

Ultimately, we fended off the effort to impose inflexible spending limits by agreeing to keep future spending within a less formal, non-statutory "spending affordability limit" roughly tied to the annual increase in personal income. House Speaker Ben Cardin was a big help in working out this compromise. Succeeding governors and legislatures have, for the most part, abided by this voluntary check on spending ever since and I believe this record of budgetary self-control shows that it was unnecessary to put rigid spending limits in state law or the Constitution. Such an arbitrary limit would have undoubtedly limited the state's ability to respond to crises, changing times and the inevitable fluctuations of the state and national economy.

Downturn

You might say my first term as governor went from riches to rags, although the rapid deterioration of the state's financial fortunes was not of my doing. The brewing national recession finally hit Maryland with a vengeance in late 1980 and 1981. After two years of big surpluses, we suddenly faced a deficit.

To adjust to the downturn, I ordered my agencies to take steps to contain costs and scale back plans for new spending. The budget I unveiled in 1981 contained no pay raise for state employees, no increase in welfare benefits and no new state aid for education. The overall increase in the general fund portion of the budget was only one-half of 1 percent, the lowest growth rate in two decades. "In two short years, we have gone through a period of apparent plenty and arrived at one of scarcity," I told the General Assembly.[105]

Faced with this sudden dearth of money, we turned our attention to changes that were important, but were not costly. For example, we pushed a package of legislation to raise the penalties and lower the threshold for convicting drunken drivers; set up a state corporation to promote energy conservation and the development of alternative sources of energy; pushed a surprisingly controversial measure to require motorcycle riders to wear protective helmets; and an ill-fated effort to remove state circuit court judges from the partisan election process. I felt strongly about separating the circuit judges from the electoral process, but was never able to convince the legislature to approve it.

Another project I initiated in 1980 was an agreement with Governor John Dalton of Virginia to have our two states jointly establish a regional veterinary school. At the time, Maryland did not have a vet school and we were sending our young students to colleges in New York or Alabama or elsewhere at considerable cost to the state. The federal government at that time was offering money for states that worked together to create a regional veterinary school, so Dalton and I agreed to develop one between the University of Maryland and Virginia Tech, two land-grant universities. The main part of the vet school is located at Virginia Tech in Blacksburg, Virginia, but a smaller, affiliated center is in College Park and an equine center is located in Leesburg, Virginia. This vet school has been quite a success for students from both states and I think of it as a real accomplishment.

By focusing on proposals that could be enacted without imposing a big new cost to the state, I told legislators, "Together, we are establishing a management record of self-discipline of which we can be proud. We are proving through action, not just words, that in Maryland we do not need arbitrary spending restrictions on the decision-making powers of the executive or the legislature."[106]

105. Governor Harry Hughes, state of the state message (House-Senate Joint Session, January 21, 1981).
106. Ibid.

"It's Cold Out There, Mr. President!"

Our new president wasn't helping. Ronald Reagan, a conservative who kept the decent Jimmy Carter from winning a second term, pushed a brand of "federalism" intended to shift more power from the federal government to the states. He shifted the programs, but did not shift the federal money with it. We lost millions of dollars when he did away with the federal revenue sharing program. At a time of recession and falling tax revenues, these cutbacks just exacerbated the problems faced by Maryland and other states. To me, the Reagan administration approach was heartless and uncaring.

Already battered by inflation, high interest rates, high unemployment and a bust in the housing and automotive industries, states were now reeling from federal cuts. Hundreds of state jobs had been either fully or partially funded by the federal government, so when the feds cut back, there suddenly was no money to pay these men or women. As a result, the Senate's Budget and Taxation Committee voted to eliminate many of these federally supported jobs. I thought that was wrong. These were good, hard-working people doing good work for the state and just to eliminate their jobs—and their livelihood—without exploring other options made no sense.

I called in officials from the health department, transportation, human resources and other departments to identify which of these jobs were most critical to keep and we began to compile a list. I then dispatched O'Brien to talk with Senator John A. Cade to see if he would try to get these positions restored in the budget, but paid for with state dollars. Cade, a Republican from Anne Arundel County, was an interesting character. Big as a bull and sometimes mean as a snake, he also was one of the smartest men in the General Assembly. He was conservative on fiscal matters, but had a tender heart and more of a social conscience than many of the Democrats in the legislature. And, although he was a member of the minority party, he wielded more clout in the Senate's Budget and Taxation Committee than anyone other than the chairman. Even though his position was contrary to that taken by his own committee, Cade led the fight on the floor to restore the jobs as we had requested and he succeeded.

This and other problems caused by the federal cutbacks, however, began to anger me. Just before I was to deliver my fourth state of the state address in January 1982, I decided that rather than give my standard, detailed, programmatic summary of the health of the state (which I submitted separately in writing), I would instead address my remarks more broadly to "the people of Maryland and to the president of the United States as well."

"It's cold out there, Mr. President, but we intend to warm things up," I said in a short substitute speech that was such a departure from my normal speaking style that reporters were left scrambling to find out who had drafted it and why.[107] "To me, and to my colleagues in forty-nine other states, you have said in effect: do more

107. The substitute speech was largely inspired by my old campaign adviser, Bobby Goodman.

with less. Do better with what you have. The White House has its hands full. It's up to the states. Sink or swim. It's cold out there, Mr. President, but this is one state that is ready to handle the weather."[108]

I wanted to demonstrate the determination of the state of Maryland to persevere through the problems brought on by the national recession and federal indifference. There was mixed reaction to the speech, which I expected. Some thought it was too theatrical and said it didn't sound like me. But I had fun doing it.

"What kind of state are we?" I asked rhetorically, and then answered my own question: "We [are a state that] finds ways to make ends meet without hurting people."

Staff Adjustments

As I moved into my third year in office, I made several important staff changes that helped set the course not only for the remainder of my first term, but for most of my second term as well. Louise Keelty, my appointments secretary, left in September 1980. I had hired Louise to help me bring more women and minorities into government and to take politics out of the appointments process. She was good at the former and, frankly, almost too good at the latter. Legislators complained that she wouldn't return their phone calls, did not consult them on appointments and when they did get through to her, they were often put off by her sharp tongue. In December 1980, I brought in Constance R. Beims, who then headed the state's Commission for Women, to replace Louise. Although I didn't know her well, Connie had been an early supporter of mine, chairing my Harford County campaign in 1978, and had been recommended for the job by Harford County Senator Arthur Helton.

At the end of my third legislative session, Gene Oishi left to begin work on a book. I replaced him as press secretary with another veteran newspaperman, Lou Panos, a longtime Annapolis reporter who had become deputy editor of the editorial page and a political columnist for the *Baltimore Evening Sun*.

For most of the rest of my years as governor, Johnson, O'Brien, Beims and Panos became my sounding board. Usually joining the group was my legal council, first Jud Garrett and in later years Carl Eastwick and Ben Bialek. In one grouping or another, we would meet almost daily to discuss personnel, legislative issues, strategy and politics. Connie Beims, who was ably assisted by Frances R. Smith, became much more than just my patronage chief; she became a critically important adviser. Whatever successes I achieved as governor would not have been possible without the faithful hard work of these aides and many others.

---

108. Governor Harry R. Hughes, state of the state address (Maryland General Assembly, January 20, 1982.)

A New Approach to Prisons

I never dealt much with prison issues when I was a legislator, so consequently I knew little about the state prison system when I became governor. I quickly learned, however, that Maryland's prisons were woefully outdated, dangerously overcrowded and poorly staffed. The oldest portions of the maximum security Maryland Penitentiary in Baltimore had been built in 1811. The House of Correction in Jessup had opened in 1874. One reason prison systems are allowed to deteriorate is that there is little political capital to be gained by politicians who work to improve the conditions for staff or inmates. As long as inmates are locked up and the citizenry feels safe, no one gives the prisons or the prisoners a second thought unless there is a riot, a murder or some other crisis.

Gordon C. Kamka, the young man I tapped to be my secretary of Public Safety and Correctional Services, felt it was time for the state to take a new, more modern, more constructive approach to the thousands of men and women who were incarcerated for various crimes. He envisioned a system that relied more on parole and less on incarceration.[109] As a candidate for governor in 1978, I had opposed plans then pending in the legislature to build a major new prison on what was known as the "Continental Can" site in Baltimore, saying I opposed "warehousing" criminals.

But in the early 1980s, long before we could even think about rehabilitation programs, it was all we could do just to keep up with the surge of inmates pouring into the prison system. Crime and violence, mostly drug-related, was on the rise. Moreover, a federal court had ordered the state to halt the practice of placing two inmates in cells built to accommodate only one. That meant we needed to build several expensive new prisons. The high cost of this prison construction program would be one issue, but a much bigger political problem would be location: where in the state could we build new prisons? Who wanted a big new prison next door?

In my second legislative session, I tried to confront the growing prison crisis head on. I proposed building a new 500-bed maximum/medium security prison in Jessup and a 250-bed minimum security pre-release center in Baltimore. I budgeted funds to create nearly 700 new positions within the Division of Corrections, including 147 new correctional officers to staff two new prison facilities that were already under construction and expected to open in the coming year and that would house some 900 inmates.

I also tried to set in motion a proposal initiated some years earlier by the General Assembly to establish community adult rehabilitation centers (CARCs) throughout the state and proposed that the state cover 100 percent (rather than 75 percent) of the cost of constructing these facilities. There would be about twenty of these live-in, work-out CARCs. "We know that warehousing people doesn't work," Kamka said at the time. "We've got 200 years of consistent history to show that."[110] The theory behind CARCs was that it would be better for everyone if offenders were incarcerated

109. Alan Doelp, "Kamka's Views on New Prison Unrealistic, Judge Murphy Says," *Baltimore Evening Sun*, January 25, 1979. This idea was immediately attacked as "unrealistic" by, among others, Robert C. Murphy, the chief judge of the Maryland Court of Appeals.
110. Doug Struck, "Kamka's Program Gets Another Hard Look," *Baltimore Sun*, February 15, 1981.

closer to their homes. That would provide them with support from friends and family and social pressure to mend their ways; local officials could develop programs that would benefit both the offender and the community; and the state would save money it otherwise would have to spend on costly prison cells.

When Kamka tried to sell these ideas to the legislature, however, he was blasted. I thought Gordon was good. But this was an era in which legislators, probably reflecting the views of their constituents, wanted to "lock 'em up and throw away the key." Legislators felt Gordon was disdainful of the General Assembly's oversight role. From day one, he had a very poor relationship with the legislature. Every time he testified they would go after him.

Kamka's—and my—experiment with rehabilitation came to a screeching halt in March 1981. The last straw was the mass arrest of twenty-seven inmates from the Brock Bridge Correction Center who were on work- or college-release programs, but were charged with crimes ranging from escape to rape, robbery, drug offenses and even murder—crimes allegedly committed while these inmates were supposed to be attending classes or at their jobs. Kamka and his Commissioner of Corrections, Edwin R. Goodlander, submitted their resignations on March 30.

"Mr. Kamka as an individual has become the focal point for anyone who was critical of anything, whether he was to blame or not," I said as I accepted their resignations. "That position is probably the most difficult in state government. It requires the utmost support, not only from the governor's office, but from the legislature and from within the department. Without that, the secretary of corrections doesn't stay around very long."[111]

When Kamka finally left, I moved Tom Schmidt over from the budget office to take over at Corrections and Public Safety.[112] Tom was what the legislature was looking for: a hard-nosed, no-nonsense "lock 'em up" kind of guy. His tenure represented a sharp shift in my approach to prison policy and may, in some respects, have been a mistake, but it had the short-term effect of quieting down a lot of the yelling from the legislature.

The most serious problem I had with the legislature was over selecting a site to build a major new state prison. The arguments dragged on for months until I finally picked a site on the Lower Eastern Shore in Somerset County. I kept reminding people that the Somerset County commissioners had said they wanted the prison as a way of easing the county's chronic unemployment,[113] but locals were happier to blame me and did what they could to embarrass or humiliate me. When I attended the annual J. Millard

111. Michael Shultz, "Hughes OKs the Shakeup of Prison Aides," *Baltimore Evening Sun*, March 31, 1981.
112. H. Louis Stettler III, Schmidt's deputy, took over as budget secretary.
113. "Somerset Alters Stand on Prison," *Associated Press*, January 29, 1983. The Somerset County commissioners met with my staff and expressed interest in the new prison being built in any of six proposed locations in the county, but when news of their comments became public they quickly voted, 3–2, against a prison in Somerset. We, nevertheless, moved ahead with the project. "Local and political reaction must be taken into consideration, but if local and political reaction dictated [sites], there would be no prisons in this state," Mike Canning on my staff explained.

Tawes crabfest in Crisfield that summer, a small plane flew over pulling a banner that read, "Harry Hughes Memorial Prison." That prison, however, has turned out to be the biggest economic asset in one of the poorest counties in the state. The average wage at the prison is way above the average wage elsewhere in the county and it employs a lot of people down there. Some four hundred county residents were initially employed by the prison, helping to drop the unemployment rate in Somerset from 17 percent to about 12 percent.[114] Most people down there now think the prison was a wonderful thing.

By the time I finally left office in January 1987, we had opened prisons with a design capacity of 1,882 beds and had authorized construction of other facilities that would add another 1,632 beds. That represented more prison capacity than had been built in the first eighty years of the century. In addition, we hired 1,300 additional correctional officers, an 88 percent increase. We performed extensive reconstruction of the Penitentiary and the House of Correction and revamped programs at both institutions, including expansion of drug and alcohol abuse programs. Despite legislative resistance to rehabilitation efforts, inmate education and work programs were expanded and diversified.[115]

I caught a lot of flak for our handling of the prison system, but am proud that we not only expanded the system to meet current needs, but improved the overall condition and performance of the prison system. You don't win votes with that kind of work, but it was the humane thing to do and a necessary function of government that demanded our attention and resources.

Violence and Extremism

Toward the end of the 1981 legislative session, I hosted a meeting in my office with leaders from a group called the Coalition Opposed to Violence and Extremism. These men and women were concerned about the noticeable increase in acts of violence and intimidation motivated by racial, ethnic or religious prejudice both in Maryland and elsewhere around the country. Convinced that the state could and should do something about this abhorrent practice of religious and racial bigotry, I appointed Connie Beims to chair a special Task Force on Violence and Extremism, which I believe was the first of its kind in the nation.

In a 1982 speech to the legislature, I said,

> Intimidations, desecrations, cross burnings, [and] distribution of hate literature are all part of a sickness that would mock the principles upon which our government was founded.[116] I want you to know that, as a

114. Doug Struck and Mary Corddry, "Maryland Estimates Impact of Prison on Somerset," *Baltimore Sun,* January 28, 1983.
115. Governor Harry R. Hughes, "The Record and the Legacy: A Report to the People of Maryland," *Baltimore Sun,* January 1987.
116. Ibid.

governor, and as a human being, I am affronted by the re-emergence of this violence and extremism and have taken action through a special task force and through other means to make those acts, in fact, intolerable within our borders. We will not be intimidated!

The Maryland Task Force discovered that little existed at the national level to help states address these problems. As a result, we conducted a feasibility study and I established the National Institute Against Prejudice and Violence, promised three years of state funding and named former U.S. Senator Birch Bayh of Indiana as chairman of its board of directors. The Institute conducted research, provided assistance and advice to victims, provided technical assistance to communities that were targets of hate crimes and became a clearinghouse for information on the issue. Establishment of this Institute was one of my proudest achievements, but I am sorry to say that in a few years it was allowed to go out of existence.

14

An American Governor in China

IN THE FALL OF MY first year as governor, a small delegation from the southeastern Chinese province of Anhui visited Maryland. This sort of international exchange may seem commonplace today, but in 1979 it was almost unheard of.

Earlier that year—some seven years after Richard Nixon's historic visit to China—Vice Premier Deng Xiaoping visited Washington and the United States finally established full diplomatic relations with the communist superpower. Long closed to the West, China was taking its first tentative steps to open itself to new ideas.

The September visit by the Anhui delegation was led by Wan Li, the provincial governor, whose own political fortunes in China had risen, fallen and risen again. The visit was arranged by Dr. John S. Toll, then president of the University of Maryland; Nobel laureate physicist Chen Ning Yang, who had been recruited to the Stony Brook campus of the State University of New York when Toll was president there; and a Chinese-born physicist at the University of Maryland named Dr. Chuan Sheng Liu.[117]

Wan Li and his entourage spent about two weeks in Maryland and we took them all over the state, to manufacturing plants, farms and on boat trips on the Chesapeake Bay. The Chinese delegation was housed in the historic Paca House in Annapolis and a Chinese cook brought in to prepare some of their meals. In my welcoming remarks at a ceremony on the State House lawn, I said Americans had long admired and respected the people of China for their proud traditions of three thousand years, their self-discipline and resourcefulness and their contributions to mankind in the fields of science, philosophy, medicine and literature. To emphasize the mutual interest of our two countries on economic globalization, I relied on a ship's manifest dug out of the Maryland Archives that showed the first cargo ship importing goods from China to the newly formed United States had arrived in Baltimore on August 12, 1785. I quoted the *Maryland Journal* newspaper's report on the ship's arrival: "It is a pleasing sight to see the crew of this ship, Chinese, Malays, Japanese, Moors and a few Europeans employed together as brethren; it is thus commerce that binds and united all the nations of the globe."

We hosted two state dinners, entertained the entourage with a performance by the Baltimore Symphony at St. John's College and took them to a banquet hosted

---

117. Chuan Sheng Liu, "The Tale of Two States: Anhui and Maryland," draft (commemorating the twentieth anniversary of the signing of the sister state agreement), September 7, 2000.

by Dr. Toll at the University of Maryland. Since the Chinese were new to America, Joe Coale came up with the idea of buying them all cowboy hats. I still have a ten-gallon Stetson at home left over from that visit. At a parting press conference, Wan Li said the thing that impressed him most during his visit was "the spontaneous friendship he encountered everywhere."[118]

This visit was a big deal. It was the first state-to-state exchange since the normalization of relations with China and it was supported at the highest levels of the Chinese and American governments. Vice President Walter Mondale hosted a large party for the Chinese at his home in Washington, with a large tent on the lawn and an invitation list that featured a "Who's Who" from Washington power circles. Mondale even wrote a poem for Wan Li for the occasion. We received briefings by State Department officials in this country and the Chinese ambassador referred to me as one of the "founding fathers of our new relationship." I think both countries were interested in demonstrating that the thawing relationship had already begun to trickle down to lower levels of government as well as to businesses and universities. Secretary of State Cyrus Vance later sent me a letter on October 12, 1979, personally thanking me for "giving the Chinese visitors a varied and stimulating series of impressions of Maryland and of the United States."

Wan Li and I immediately hit it off. He was an absolutely delightful person. He also was a close friend of Deng Xiaoping. They had fought together in the Communist revolution, then became enemies of the state during China's Cultural Revolution, only to return to prominence once the Cultural Revolution was over. Wan Li told me that during the Cultural Revolution he was confined for a number of years and his wife was made to work in a factory ten hours a day. Later, however, as the party leader in Anhui, Wan Li became one of China's earliest reformers.

Anhui is an inland province south of Beijing located on the lower reaches of the Yangtze River and has always been one of China's poorest provinces. It may be best known to some Americans as the setting for Pearl Buck's 1931 Pulitzer Prize–winning bestseller, *The Good Earth*, about a rural family in famine. It was a later famine in 1960, one that resulted from Mao Zedong's disastrous adventure in creating "people's communes," which led to the deaths of millions of Chinese. This was part of Mao's "Great Leap Forward" program in 1958. Twenty years later, when Wan Li became the governor of Anhui, the province suffered from a terrible drought. To avoid further famine, Wan Li quietly permitted the breakup of communes, allowing individual peasants to be responsible for production on their own small plots of land: a program called the "Household Responsibility System." This breakup of the communes, initiated by the peasants, was a courageous act by Wan Li.

"Knowing this could be considered anti-revolutionary and they could all be put in prison for it, farmers wrote a contract that they were in this together and if misfortune should befall on any one, the rest would take care of his family. Then they signed in blood," Chuan Sheng Liu later recorded in a history of the time.[119]

118. Ibid.
119. Liu, "The Tale of Two States."

This land use reform was credited with staving off further famine by sharply boosting food production. In the first year, the yield from the farms doubled. The reform later spread to other parts of China and began a transformation from a controlled economy to a market economy that is still evolving today.

Wan Li's trip to Maryland was such a success that he invited me to visit him in China the following year. So in the summer of 1980, I became the first American governor to make an official visit to China after the establishment of diplomatic relations. I took with me a delegation mostly consisting of businessmen: Charlie Cole of First National Bank, Gene Allen from Black & Decker, George Bunting from Noxell, Henry Rosenberg of Crown Central Petroleum, Dr. Richard S. Ross, dean of the Johns Hopkins University School of Medicine, John Deely of Fairchild Industries, and Wayne Cawley, my friend and Agriculture secretary. Dr. Toll, Chuan Sheng Liu, my wife, Pat, and my daughter, Beth, were also part of the delegation, as was Joe Coale, who really did most of the organizing for the trip. While we were there, we established a sister-state relationship between the state of Maryland and Anhui Province.

By the time of my visit to China, Wan Li had risen to become the national vice-premier in charge of Chinese agriculture and rural reform, which is why we met him in Beijing (which was formerly called Peking) rather than in Anhui. Years earlier, before he became governor of Anhui, Wan Li had been vice-mayor of the capital city and in 1959 was responsible for construction of the Great Hall of People.[120] He held a banquet in our honor there and showed us around the place. I soon discovered that in Chinese cities, the vice-mayor was the man of importance. The mayor is usually more of a ceremonial position, but the vice-mayor really runs the place.

In Wan Li's new position of national authority, he rubbed shoulders with diplomats from other nations and from time to time played tennis with America's envoy to China, George H.W. Bush. Wan Li also loved to play bridge.

He arranged for me to meet Deng Xiaoping, which was very interesting. Deng was barely five-feet tall, more than a foot shorter than me, and he smoked like a fiend. I remember Deng asking, "Do editorial writers bother you?" I replied, "Yeah, they do sometimes. They sometimes don't have their facts right or I don't agree with their opinion. Yeah, they bother me sometimes." And he said, "They don't bother me!"

Deng was particularly impressed by the youthfulness of our delegation, particularly Joe Coale, my young assistant, who was thirty-six at the time. Most of the Chinese leaders were war veterans in their sixties. Suddenly, they were face to face with a group of young, well-educated Americans, a cultural difference they hadn't anticipated. Deng remarked that they needed more young leaders in China and as a result of this experience later established criteria designed to attract more young people into the Chinese leadership.

120. Ibid. The Great Hall has a capacity for ten thousand people. Employing three shifts of workers a day, Wan Li saw that it was completed in just six months, in time to celebrate the tenth anniversary of the founding of the People's Republic, as Mao had wished.

31. Glenn Beall was a moderate Republican and a real gentleman. We were friends both before and after the 1978 election. *Courtesy of the* Baltimore Sun.

32. My core transition staff in 1978–79 (from left): Paul Farley, Mike Canning, Louise Keelty, Joe Coale, Mike McWilliams and me. *Courtesy of Joseph M. Coale III.*

33. Weather for my first inauguration was dreary, rainy and cold. In my remarks, I said my inauguration was more than tradition and more than transition, but rather "a celebration of real change." *Courtesy of the* Baltimore Sun.

34. Chief Judge Robert Murphy of the Court of Appeals administers the oath of office to me in the Senate chamber. *Courtesy of Governor Hughes's personal collection.*

35. Former Acting Governor Blair Lee III, my primary election opponent, joins Governor J. Millard Tawes and me at my 1978 inauguration. *Courtesy of the* Baltimore Sun.

36. Our inaugural ball was held at the U.S. Naval Academy. That is Sam and Rita Bogley (left) and Pat and me dancing. *Courtesy of the* Baltimore Sun.

37. Johnny Johnson was loyal, competent and a top-notch chief of staff. *Courtesy of the* Baltimore Sun.

38. There is no one more important to an executive than a very competent and loyal secretary and I could not have asked for a better one than Annette Silverman. Annette is on the right and my executive assistant, Sylvia Ramsey, on the left. *Courtesy of Sylvia Ramsey.*

39. Pat and I annually had entertainment at Government House for children from the School for the Deaf and the Maryland School for the Blind. *Courtesy of Maryland State Archives.*

40. Here I greet Deng Xiaoping during my 1979 path-breaking trip to China. Between us is my host, Vice-Premier Wan Li. *Courtesy of Governor Hughes's personal collection.*

41. Wan Li and I got along very well. Here I struggle with chopsticks while Wan Li tries a knife and fork. *Courtesy of Joseph M. Coale III.*

42. I established the National Institute Against Prejudice and Violence and convinced former U.S. Senator Birch Bayh of Indiana to serve as chairman. With him is executive director Joan Weiss, me and Connie Beims, my talented appointments secretary. *Courtesy of Constance R. Beims.*

43. In the "Harry, Harry and Harry" Democratic primary of 1982, my opponents were (left to right) Ocean City Mayor Harry W. Kelley and Baltimore Senator Harry J. McGuirk. *Courtesy of the* Baltimore Sun.

44. My Republican opponent in 1982 was Anne Arundel County Executive Bob Pascal. *Courtesy of the* Baltimore Sun.

45. For my second term, I was fortunate to convince longtime friend, state Senator J. Joseph Curran Jr., to be my running mate. Since his years as lieutenant governor, he went on to become Maryland's longest-serving attorney general. Here we are on election night 1982, his wife Barbara, Joe, me and Pat. *Courtesy of the* Baltimore Sun.

46. The Board of Public Works—the governor, comptroller and state treasurer—must approve all major state contracts in Maryland. I spent many hours at BPW meetings with Comptroller Louis L. Goldstein (left) and Treasurer William S. James. At far right is General Services Secretary Earl Seboda. *Courtesy of the* Baltimore Sun.

47. By the time of my 1983 state of the state address, the Reagan budget cuts combined with a national recession were creating severe budget problems for Maryland and most other states. *Courtesy of Governor Hughes's personal collection.*

48. One of the best programs we ever developed was the Gateway program as a one-stop shop to assist the elderly in obtaining needed government services. *Courtesy of Maryland State Archives.*

49. We had a statewide celebration of Maryland's 350th anniversary, including a visit by the Duke and Duchess of Kent, here pictured in Government House with Pat and me. *Photo from Governor Hughes's personal collection.*

50. Pat in the Billy Baldwin Room, which was named after the mid-twentieth-century interior designer from Baltimore. It featured brown lacquered walls, clear cylindrical lamps with white shades and Baldwin's signature slipper chairs. *Photo from Governor Hughes's personal collection.*

51. Pat and me in the Empire Parlor with its chrome yellow walls (a color copied from Homewood, the 1802 house on the Johns Hopkins University campus). We were disappointed when Governor Schaefer undid all we had done at Government House. *Courtesy of Maryland State Archives.*

52. After signing our regional Chesapeake Bay agreement, the participants took a boat ride on the Chesapeake: (left to right) Virginia Senator John Warner, me, Pennsylvania Lieutenant Governor William Scranton, Maryland Senator Paul Sarbanes, Virginia Governor Chuck Robb, Maryland Senator Charles McC. Mathias Jr. and EPA Administrator William Ruckelshaus. *Photo from Governor Hughes's personal collection.*

53. Pat and I have always loved eating crabs, a Maryland tradition. *Photo from Governor Hughes's personal collection.*

54. I loved going out on the Chesapeake Bay. Here I am with my Natural Resources secretary, Torrey C. Brown (left) and an unidentified angler after a good day fishing for blues. *Courtesy of Maryland State Archives.*

55. During my second term, my State House staff posed with me in the Governor's Reception Room. That's Lieutenant Governor Joe Curran to my right and press secretary Lou Panos to my left. Johnny Johnson and Connie Beims are second and third to Panos's left. Just to Curran's right are Andrew B. Wigglesworth, who handled health issues for me and later was pressed into service as manager of my 1986 U.S. Senate campaign, and Jim Rowland, a former newspaperman who staffed the Board of Public Works for me. My longtime secretary, Annette Silverman, is at the far left of the picture. *Courtesy of Constance R. Beims.*

56. The run on Maryland S&Ls began in May 1985 when depositors demanded their money back from Old Court Savings and Loan in Baltimore. *Courtesy of the* Baltimore Sun.

57. In one day, I flew from Tel Aviv to Cairo, from Cairo back to Tel Aviv, from Tel Aviv to New York and from New York in a little state-owned airplane back to Annapolis. It was evening by the time I got to the State House and I immediately went into a series of meetings with my staff, Sachs, Steinberg, Cardin and federal bank officials. I finally held a news conference about midnight. *Courtesy of the* Baltimore Sun.

58. House Speaker Ben Cardin and Senate President Mickey Steinberg join me for a press conference about S&Ls. *Courtesy of the* Baltimore Sun.

59. Four Maryland governors: Marvin Mandel, William Donald Schaefer, Parris N. Glendening and Harry Roe Hughes. *Courtesy of Maryland State Archives.*

60. Paul Sarbanes and I have been friends for years. Here we testify together before a congressional committee. *Courtesy of Maryland State Archives.*

We were entertained at a banquet everywhere we went. And everywhere we went, the food was, well, like you wouldn't believe! They served us sea cucumber, which was a piece of lettuce and a slug. Ever see a slug? That's a delicacy there. They served us shark's fin soup, which was pretty good, and tree fungus soup, which had a lot of protein. And, of course, duck. They served the whole duck, the head and everything. They also had a favorite drink they used for toasts, a Maotai, which was almost pure liquor, about 150 proof. The only way I could describe it is to say it tasted dirty. But it was powerful. I found out I had to be careful, that they might put mineral water in their glasses while giving us the real thing.

We visited Yellow Mountain, which is a national shrine, a very mystical and spiritual place for the Chinese. When you think of images of the traditional Chinese landscape, you usually are thinking of a place that looks like Yellow Mountain, with craggy, rocky peaks soaring up and into the clouds. There are fifteen hundred steps up the side of this mountain and Johnny Toll and John Deely decided to climb them. But they had a bus to take Pat and me and some of the others up the mountain. It was a rainy, foggy morning and the road up the mountain was a dirt road that had just been carved out of the side of this mountain. It had been raining pretty hard for quite a while and as we started up the mountain, you could see there had been a lot of erosion and parts of the road were washed away. The farther we went, the more frightening it became. Pat and Beth, I thought, were going to go crazy if the bus driver didn't stop. I said, "Stop the bus," but he kept on driving. Then I yelled, "Stop the damned bus!" Finally, he stopped and we got out and walked back down. I suppose that was a disappointment to our hosts, but I wasn't going to run that risk just to see the top of Yellow Mountain.

As we moved from town to town, they drove us in what they called a "Red Flag Limousine." It was a big, Russian-made limousine, with red flags on both bumpers near the headlights. They'd whisk us through the countryside, but in practically every town and village we went through there were people standing out on the street waiting. I'm sure they must have announced our pending arrival over the radio. At one town, I said, "Stop the car, I want to get out." When I stepped out, the people just came from everywhere and were just as friendly as they could be. Wayne Cawley got out and began passing out ballpoint pens, which was about the only thing we had to give away. But after that, the limousine never stopped for me again. I guess the drivers were ordered not to do that again and when they have orders to do something, they do it. Maybe they were afraid some incident might happen, but my recollection is mostly how friendly the people were. Even on the streets of Beijing, little kids would come up and try their English on me: "Hey," or "How are you?"

The real purpose of this trip was to try to make some connections between the Maryland businesspeople and the Chinese. The first day we were in Beijing, Charlie Cole was able to establish a corresponding banking relationship with the Bank of China. For us, that was a big accomplishment because prior to that, Cole's First National Bank had to go through a New York bank in order to conduct any business with China.

Others, like George Bunting at Noxell, were trying to find ways to sell their products in China, which of course was a potentially huge new market. Noxell made Noxema skin cream, but also made Lestoil, a cleaning fluid. At one point I remember saying to one of the Chinese, "From the looks of things, I think you could use some!" I didn't mean to be quite so blunt, but no one seemed to be offended.

In general, I'm not sure that first mission to China resulted in much international trade for Maryland, but it opened the door. Columbia developer Jim Rouse later arranged for a planner from Anhui to come to Maryland to train with his company for a year. Eventually, farmers from Maryland established some poultry business with China and the University of Maryland developed a student exchange program with a university in Anhui. Today, many businesses in Maryland regularly do business in China and many of the students in our state universities are Chinese.

This was an eye-opening exchange for both sides—the first grassroots diplomacy with China. Wan Li and the other Chinese who visited our country and hosted us there seemed genuinely surprised at how friendly Americans were. It was Wan Li's first exposure to how an open society works and it made a lasting impression. In later years, Wan Li became a major force for friendship with the United States and can fairly be credited as one of the two or three top reformers in recent Chinese history.

A Return Visit

I was invited back for a visit in 1997, and to see the changes that have occurred over the intervening two decades was just incredible. When we went there in 1980, there were no private restaurants and no private stores. There was one store they called the Friendship Store, where you could buy different kinds of clothing and articles, but the Chinese were not allowed to go there. We found one hotel that had an American restaurant, but it was the only one we could find. And in the streets, there were no automobiles, just bicycles (someone told me there were three million bicycles just in Beijing) and there was very little grass. I think that was all the result of the Cultural Revolution; they didn't want anything fancy or luxurious.

During that first trip, I remember seeing little stoves in backyards, which, during the Cultural Revolution, peasants would use to melt down iron ore. It was an incredible culture. It was particularly interesting because the Chinese had lost an entire generation of engineers and doctors because they were taken out of their professions and put to work in fields and farms.

When we went back in 1998, it was a different world. There were automobiles everywhere; four-star and five-star hotels; and Kentucky Fried Chicken and McDonalds outlets all over Beijing. In Shanghai, there was an area called Pudong, where they were attempting to create another Hong Kong. To make way, they just moved one hundred thousand people out of the area and started building huge buildings. There were factories and private stores everywhere. There were so many automobiles in Shanghai that drivers were restricted to going into or out of the city only on odd- or even-numbered days. It was unbelievable change in just twenty years and it is still going on. There are businesspeople in China now from all over the world. They say there are more construction cranes in Shanghai than in anywhere else in the world, and I believe it.

When we returned to China, Wan Li was living in the Forbidden City, where old retirees live. He invited us to lunch in the Great Hall. His wife was there. He looked pretty good, but he was old and his wife was not well. I asked, "Are you going to write your memoirs?" He said, "No, if I did my memoirs, I'd say good things about people but I'd also have to say bad things about people and there are still too many around." He indicated that such a book might get him in trouble.

Wan Li had been in the United States when the Tiananmen Square showdown occurred in May 1989 and made a public statement—something like, "the students are really good citizens"—that got him in trouble at home.

The story I heard was that he was smart enough not to go directly back to Beijing, but instead went to Shanghai, where he was admitted into a hospital. That bought him enough time for it to all blow over and give his friend, Deng Xiaoping, time to take care of the problem for him. That apparently worked and Wan Li avoided further trouble.

One postscript: Jing Yi Hong, the interpreter Wan Li brought with him to Maryland in 1979, ended up marrying Chuan Sheng Liu, the physicist from the University of Maryland who helped arrange both the initial Chinese delegation visit to Maryland and my subsequent 1980 and 1998 visits to China. For years, they have lived near College Park, where he has taught at the University of Maryland for more than three decades. Jing Yi received her PhD from the university and does a lot of interpreting for the U.S. State Department.

For a few years, Chuan Sheng Liu served as president of the Central University of Taiwan before returning to the University of Maryland early in 2006.

15

Into a Second Term

PROBABLY THE BIGGEST CHALLENGE I faced in my first term was to overcome the misperception that we weren't accomplishing anything. There were so many stories about how "dull" my style was that it left the impression that we weren't getting things done. And because I had such a good working relationship with Ben Cardin and Jim Clark, there weren't the usual fights between the governor and the legislature that seemed to signal to reporters that something significant was being done, even if that wasn't always the case.

In our quiet way, we really accomplished a lot. We passed significant tax relief and then weathered a deep national recession without harming the so-called "safety net" programs that protected the poor and disabled who needed government support the most. We addressed the long neglected problem of overcrowded prisons; attacked the problem of drunken driving and raised the minimum drinking age from eighteen to twenty-one. Guided by the diligent work and solid recommendations of Louise Keelty and Connie Beims, we set a new standard for the appointment of women, blacks and other minorities not only to boards, commissions and task forces, but to the judicial bench as well.[121] These were men and women of high caliber and professional capabilities.

In 1982, we raised the gas tax because we had to. Transportation revenues were flat and we faced the potential of project needs going unmet. My campaign staff had brought in a consultant named Dick Morris, whom years later gained notoriety as a political adviser to President Bill Clinton. Morris recommended I not propose a gas tax increase in the same year that I was standing for reelection, but I felt we had no choice. He said, "At least let me do a poll [on the issue] over the weekend." I consented and he returned the next week to say that while he was still worried, he no longer strenuously objected.

That boost in the gas tax provided $600 million in new revenue that, over the next six years, allowed us to begin or complete the Fort McHenry Tunnel, the western Maryland highway through Sideling Hill, the Northwest Expressway and expansions of roads throughout the state. The extra revenue also allowed us to initiate construction of Interstate 97 between Baltimore and Annapolis and new bridges across the Choptank, Nanticoke, Sassafras and Bohemia Rivers.

That year we also had to push through the decennial plans for legislative apportionment and congressional redistricting, plus I had more than thirty

---

121. Out of approximately eighteen hundred appointments during my first term, 25 percent of them were women and 28 percent were minorities.

initiatives on my own agenda in addition to the gas tax. It turned out to be the most successful year of my first term.

On the session's final night, O'Brien suggested I go down to the first floor and formally thank the General Assembly for its support—an act I doubt any previous governor had done. We decided to present Rosalie Abrams, the majority leader, with a gavel that Connie had purchased in recognition of Rosalie's help. But at the last moment, we realized we couldn't give Rosalie a gift and not do the same for her House counterpart, Delegate Donald Robertson of Montgomery County.

Frantic, O'Brien began searching through a small office behind the governor's office, looking for something we could give Robertson. Finally, he found a small framed picture of the State House that someone had given me, had it wrapped and took it downstairs to deliver to the House majority leader. I ended up receiving a standing ovation in both houses, which I took as not only acknowledgement of the great session we had just completed together, but on how far my administration had come in four years. It was a nice moment.

Reelection

Once the session was over and the '82 election was in sight, Panos began to rev up my public persona, pushing me out of the office more often to publicize the administration's successes. In a *Baltimore Sun* article that speculated on whether I would run for a second term, Johnny Johnson said, "The people of Maryland knew exactly what they were getting when they elected him—a decent, hard-working, competent guy. We just want to be sure that the people know he really is decent, hard-working and competent."

I felt like we had done a good job in the first term and never considered anything other than running for reelection. In truth, I liked the job. I felt there was a lot more to be done and that the longer I was there, the better I got at the job. As I moved toward a second term, I felt I was better able to focus on the things that were really important and not waste a lot of times on the things that were not.

I didn't get a free ride, of course. I was challenged in the 1982 Democratic Primary by state Senator Harry J. McGuirk of Baltimore—the same senator who four years earlier had famously labeled me a "lost ball in high grass"—and by Ocean City Mayor Harry W. Kelley. I'm not quite sure why either got into the race against me. McGuirk, whose ability to stealthily amend legislation had earned him the nickname, "Soft Shoes," was close to Baltimore Mayor William Donald Schaefer. I had known McGuirk for years. We had served together in the legislature and we had never had any problems, never had any major disagreements that I can recall, which always made me think somebody must have nudged him into the race, and I'm pretty sure it must have been Schaefer.

By that point, I had publicly dropped Sam Bogley from my reelection ticket and picked in his place J. Joseph Curran Jr., a lawyer, veteran state senator from Baltimore and as decent a man as any I knew in politics. Joe and I served together in the Senate for years, we were both committee chairmen at the same time and I still consider him a very close friend. When I told Sam of my decision, I offered to appoint him to the state Workmen's Compensation Commission, but he refused to take the job.

As the end of Sam Bogley's unexpected four years in statewide office drew to a close, members of the General Assembly used to tweak me by giving Sam a particularly loud and raucous ovation whenever he was introduced at one of my state of the state addresses[122] or other joint sessions of the legislature. When McGuirk joined the race, he picked Bogley to be *his* running mate against me.

I knew Harry Kelley, too, though not very well. We had dealings with him regarding the construction of jetties along the Ocean City beaches. He wanted the jetties built in certain places regardless of the advice we were receiving from engineers, even when it became clear that the jetties were not keeping the beach sand from washing away.

During the "Harry, Harry and Harry" primary campaign, we all participated in the customary televised candidate debates, but I never felt threatened. One of the few memorable moments of that primary came when reporters asked Mayor Kelley why his finance reports showed he had used campaign donations to buy himself suits from Brooks Brothers. "Well," the mayor replied without a hint of embarrassment, "my people said, 'Mr. Mayor, if you want to be the governor, you've got to look like the governor.'"

On September 14, 1982, I again won the Democratic gubernatorial nomination, this time by sweeping Baltimore and all twenty-three counties. My 393,244 votes were more than McGuirk's (129,049) and Kelley's (61,271) totals combined.

Robert A. Pascal, the Anne Arundel County executive and another ally of Mayor Schaefer's, won the Republican primary. Pascal had accused me of being soft and indecisive on prison issues, tardy on transportation funding and otherwise ineffective on a host of other topics from higher education reform to handling hazardous waste. But I think his true colors came out when he complained that I had failed "to continue to aid Mayor Donald Schaefer in his successful efforts to revitalize Baltimore City."

I welcomed Pascal into the campaign, but warned that the public should not confuse his complaints with true leadership. Leadership, I said, "is not just bluster. It's not just standing up and yelling loud."

As for my own reelection campaign, I simply pointed out that I did what I promised I would do. "Unchanged is the Hughes emphasis on integrity," reported the *Sun*'s Tom Linthicum in a September 1982 piece. "It is the heart of his campaign, the bedrock of his image."

In the end, Bob Pascal didn't prove to be much of an obstacle, either. I won the general election on November 2 with 705,910 votes to Pascal's 432,826.

---

122. "They cheered, shouted, whistled and banged their desks and stamped their feet for Bogley," the *Sun*'s Matt Seiden reported after my 1982 state of the state address.

"A Stockman Sea of Insensitivity"

I never thought Ronald Reagan was the great president many say he was. I know he is apparently admired by millions, but from my perspective as a governor, he just wasn't a very good president. He said he was going to give states more flexibility, but what he really did was use that as a smokescreen to sharply scale back federal aid to the states to pay for his tax cuts. I didn't believe then in his economic philosophy that the fruits of tax cuts to the wealthy would somehow "trickle down" to everyone else and I don't believe in it now. Instead, I believe it just widened the gap between the haves and have-nots.

In my first state of the state address following my reelection, I reported the state's condition was "basically sound, but gravely threatened." I was angry that the federal government under Reagan's budget director David Stockman had "reversed a half-century tradition of greater federal government compassion and of a greater commitment of the federal purse to ease the apprehension and anguish of our poor, our handicapped, our elderly [and] our mentally ill."

"The least fortunate of our fellow citizens were cast adrift on the Stockman sea of insensitivity,"[123] I said.

Beyond the federal budget cuts and the national economic collapse, the state faced other problems. One of the biggest was a state employee pension program that allowed for unlimited cost of living increases—a plan so generous that actuaries predicted it would eventually bankrupt the state if left unchanged. The cost of living increases, called COLAs, were going up 8, 9 or 10 percent a year and there was no question we had to do something to modify that, but state employee unions and especially the state teachers' union were adamantly, vehemently opposed to any curtailment of benefits. We were undoubtedly in store for a nasty fight over pensions, one that would reverberate in Maryland politics for years to come.

By the winter of 1984, states were still reeling from the downturn of 1981 and '82, the nation's most severe economic recession in nearly a half-century. Rather than propose a tax increase to cover that year's budget deficit, I recommended instead that we balance our slumping budget with $92 million in savings we would receive if we could push through the pension reform bill. When bond rating houses suggested such a plan could threaten the state's coveted triple-A bond rating, that plan immediately became too risky for legislators and I withdrew it. In its place, I substituted a plan for a temporary tax surcharge.

"I am not unmindful of the difficulty associated with the enactment of a tax increase, however short the duration," I acknowledged. "[But] it is a simple, straightforward solution to a complex problem."

123. Governor Harry R. Hughes, state of the state address (January 21, 1983).

For once, I unified the legislature: everyone was against the surtax idea!

Delegate Timothy F. Maloney, a likeable young Democrat from Prince George's County, said, "I think the surcharge proposal was dead from the moment the words left the governor's mouth. The issue is not whether we are going to have a surtax, because we're not. The issue is what kind of cutbacks and revenue measure the legislature can agree on."

For the rest of that legislative session, critics pounded me for not getting my way, but I had no pride of authorship. If Speaker Cardin and the new Senate President, Melvin A. Steinberg of Baltimore County, could find a more politically palatable way to balance the budget and it was one that I could go along with, that was fine with me. I truly believe in the independence of the legislature. I was only interested in the outcome, not the process of getting there.

"Harry will look okay," Prince George's County Delegate Gerard F. Devlin said of me at the end of that legislative session. "It's like a baseball game: when it's over, you don't remember the dropped flies and the missed balls, you just remember the score."

By abandoning the idea of using the savings expected from pension reform to balance the budget, we also inadvertently made it easier to push the reform bill through a reluctant legislature. Until then, it looked as if we were trying to balance the budget on the backs of teachers and state employees. Cardin got the pension bill out of the House Appropriations Committee only by convincing one member to abstain from voting. He then needed two tries before pushing it through the full House of Delegates, finally passing the bill by a single-vote margin.

Once pension reform passed the House, Mickey Steinberg decided he was not going to subject himself or the other members of the Senate to days of intense lobbying by the teachers' and employee unions. He rammed the House bill through the Senate Finance Committee and then, by convincing the Senate to suspend the rules, rammed it through preliminary and final votes on the Senate floor—all in the same day. Accused by the unions of "railroading" the bill through to passage, Steinberg triumphantly left the State House that evening wearing a blue-and-white striped train engineer's cap.

A New Lineup

By early in my second term, half of my original Cabinet secretaries had departed for one reason or another. Tom Schmidt, for example, retired and I brought in Frank A. Hall, who had headed adult corrections in Massachusetts and juvenile corrections in New York. His style was somewhere between Schmidt's "lock 'em up" philosophy and Kamka's bent toward rehabilitation and early release.

In three departments, I simply elevated top deputies: at General Services, Earl Seboda for Max Millstone, whom I had appointed to the Workman's Compensation Commission; at Human Resources, Ruth Massinga for Buzzy Hettleman, who took a job teaching at the University of Maryland; and at Health and Mental Hygiene, Adele Wilzack for Chuck Buck, who had moved to a hospital in Philadelphia.

After Jim Roberson, my Economic Development secretary, took a job with the Louisville Chamber of Commerce, I replaced him with the flamboyant Frank J. DeFrancis. DeFrancis was a successful businessman and international lawyer, but he also was a controversial figure and a surprise choice. But Frank loved the work and did a good job. He was instrumental in helping us convince Citicorp to establish a major credit card processing facility in Hagerstown and in developing plans with the National Security Agency to locate a state-of-the-art computer center at the intersection of U.S. Routes 50 and 301. After eleven months on the job, DeFrancis ended up leaving the administration in December 1984 after he bought Maryland's Laurel Race Course. At the time, several important racing bills were about to come before legislature and we both agreed his continued service would raise ethical and conflict of interest issues.[124]

I replaced Frank with Thomas "Tuck" Maddux, but poor Tuck never had much of a chance to work on Economic Development projects. Almost his entire tenure in state government focused on ways to extricate us from our problems with savings and loan institutions.

One of the most significant changes was at Natural Resources, where Jim Coulter retired after heading the department for a dozen years. In his place, I named Torrey C. Brown, a physician from Baltimore who had been a state delegate and chairman of the House Environmental Matters Committee. I wanted to do more about cleaning up the Chesapeake Bay and Torrey shared my enthusiasm for the task.

Gateway for the Elderly

Throughout my years in elected office, I tried whenever I could to provide assistance for those who needed help from government. This included the poor who depended on state programs just to get by, the disabled and those in our state mental institutions who we thought would benefit by being moved into community settings and children who too often were denied three meals a day, lacked basic health care or access to equitable educational opportunities. Some people, I suppose, would describe this as a liberal agenda, but I would characterize it as a caring agenda—using the resources of a relatively wealthy state as the tide that can lift all ships. I believe one of the fundamental purposes of government is to assure that no one is left behind—that everyone in the community has a fair opportunity to get an education, lead a healthy life, be protected from crime and enjoy the other basic services and functions of a free and civilized society.

124. Scott Duncan and Leslie Walker, "DeFrancis Quits Development Post," *Baltimore Evening Sun*, December 6, 1984.

Toward the end of my first term, it became obvious that the state offered a number of programs to help Maryland's senior citizens, but often the intended recipients of this assistance did not know the programs existed nor had any idea how to access them. Seniors represented the fastest growing segment of our population. To address this shortcoming, we started a program in 1982 we called "Gateway." The idea was to establish an entry point or "one-stop-shop" for programs specifically targeted to the elderly. We went to every senior center in the state and told them, "Here's a program that could help you and here's how you get access to it."

Part of our focus was to provide nutritional assistance, transportation and other resources to elderly residents, many of them frail or suffering from health problems, that would enable them to remain in their own homes and communities as long as possible. In addition, we set up programs to provide shelter for destitute seniors, special transportation services for the elderly who could no longer drive, a program to prevent inappropriate admission to nursing homes and bond financing for the construction, expansion or improvement of senior centers around the state.

This was a really good program, but when Schaefer became Governor, he dumped the name. That was too bad because the phrase "Gateway" symbolized what the program was all about. The Gateway programs were really well received and while, in the larger scheme of things, the programs were relatively modest in size, they remain one of my proudest accomplishments as governor. To me, this is precisely the type of service government should provide.

Fred Malkus and the Choptank River Bridge

Toward the end of my years as governor, Senator Fred Malkus introduced legislation to build a new bridge across the Choptank River at his home city of Cambridge. But Malkus drafted the legislation as part of the Transportation Authority section of the law, which meant the new bridge would have to be a toll facility. I don't think Fred knew what he was doing because when I told him this, he said he didn't want a toll on the new bridge. This was the same year we enacted the new gas tax, which provided enough revenue for me to authorize a number of new transportation projects around the state, including the Cambridge bridge.

Once funds were in place to build the new bridge, Fred's original legislation was repealed. Then, in 1986, as construction of the bridge was underway, the Senate unanimously passed legislation to name the new span after Malkus. I couldn't believe it.

The new four-lane bridge was to replace the original two-lane bridge that had opened with great fanfare in October 1935 with a visit from Franklin Delano Roosevelt, whose presidential yacht, *Sequoia*, was the first vessel to slip beneath the new bridge. That bridge, in turn, had replaced a ferry linking Talbot and Dorchester Counties. That 1935 bridge was named after Governor Emerson C. Harrington, a native of Dorchester County and Maryland's governor from 1916 to 1920. To now name this replacement bridge after Malkus just seemed wrong to me on three counts:

First, I felt the new Choptank River Bridge already had a name—the Emerson C. Harrington Bridge. Not only did I expect the new bridge to carry Governor Harrington's name, but so did Governor Harrington's descendants.

Second, Malkus had voted against the gas tax that provided the revenue to build the new span.

And finally, of course, I had strong feelings about Malkus for other reasons. I could remember only too well the vicious fights we had with him over public accommodations and other civil rights legislation. His hometown of Cambridge was where most of the riots and fires and shootings erupted in those dark days. Here, at the entrance of the city that had been the center of the civil rights unrest that shook Maryland in the mid-1960s was to be a bridge named after one of the state's staunchest segregationists. It just didn't seem right.

When the bill to name the bridge after Malkus got to my desk, I decided to veto it. But no one on my staff informed Malkus and he showed up at the bill signing ceremony expecting the legislation to be signed into law. This mistake on our part became an embarrassment to a veteran legislator that gave the General Assembly one more reason to override my veto. They rallied to the old man's side and soundly overrode my veto, the first time they had done so since 1981. It would have been almost impossible for them to back down with Malkus seated right there on the Senate's front row.

Maryland has a bad habit, I think, of naming buildings after incumbent members of the General Assembly. It puts the members of the legislature in the awkward position of having to vote against one of their colleagues, so they don't do it.

After the new bridge was built, a big portion of the old Harrington Bridge was left jutting into the river to be used as a fishing pier. It still carrier the former governor's name, but it is not the same.

Fred and I were on oppositve sides of many issues over the years and often fought, sometimes bitterly. But in fairness to him, over his long life he often helped further the career of young people. He showed especially great compassion to a young law associate who suffered a brain tumor, keeping the young man employed long after the illness had disabled him. And, for better or worse, I think Fred always genuinely tried to represent what he thought were the views of his constituents.

Marking and Preserving Maryland's Heritage

The state of Maryland marked an important milestone during my second term as governor: its 350th anniversary. The colony of Maryland was founded in 1634 when 140 men and women arrived aboard two small sailing ships, the *Ark* and the *Dove*, at St. Clement's Island in what is now St. Mary's County. There they established a colony that would be a haven for religious toleration in a world that generally had little toleration for religious diversity. I felt this anniversary represented an opportunity for Marylanders to reaffirm our core values and celebrate 350 years of political, social and cultural achievement.

Shortly after I was inaugurated, I appointed the Maryland Heritage Committee to develop and coordinate celebration plans. The committee established 350 committees spread through every county of the state, each charged with the task of planning events to commemorate local heritage and history. The capstone ceremony was to be held in March 1984, on the 350th anniversary of the original landing, on the same island in the Potomac River where the colony of Maryland was established. But the final celebration did not turn out exactly as we had planned.

The day we were all to convene in St. Mary's County, we awoke to find it cold, blustery and pouring rain. The rain came down in sheets—and it never stopped all day. I had put a retired army general named Orwin Talbot in charge of planning the event and a little rain was not going to deter an old soldier. So the day's events went on as planned, despite the weather.

There was a large tent set up on St. Clement's Island and special guests, invited dignitaries, members of the General Assembly and local inhabitants all had to take a short boat ride from the mainland to the island for our luncheon. I can still recall seeing some of the women step off the boat in the pouring rain and sinking their high-heeled shoes into the mud up to their ankles. I guess General Talbot just figured there were too many people invited and too many special events scheduled to call the ceremony off.

At the luncheon, I sat next to the Duchess of Kent, who with her husband, the Duke, were our special guests. They say that members of the British royal family rarely talk about their own families, but I had a very long talk with her, much of it about her family. I really liked her; she was quite a charmer.

The Archives and Government House

I also took action in other ways to preserve Maryland's rich history. First, I helped establish the Maryland State Archives as an independent agency of state government within the Office of the Governor. Until then, management of the state's permanent records was handled within a division of the Department of General Services. I felt that by making the Archives an independent agency, it would enhance its ability to be the central depository for governmental records of permanent value. It is important to preserve the rich political, social and cultural history of the state so that future generations will have access to these records.[125]

125. Among the records on file at the Maryland State Archives are colonial and state executive, legislative and judicial records; county probate, land and court records; church records; business records; state publications and reports; and special collections of private papers, newspapers and maps.

Before leaving office, I proposed and the state constructed and dedicated a new Hall of Records Building in Annapolis as the home of the Maryland State Archives.

My wife, Pat, had another idea how we might preserve Maryland's heritage—and save taxpayers some money at the same time. As long as anyone could remember, one of the first things an incoming governor did was to redecorate Government House, the mansion across the street from the State House that serves as the official home of the governor and his family. Built in 1868 in the Victorian style, it was remodeled in 1935 as a Georgian revival building.

Toward the end of my second term, in January 1985, a very special event was held in Government House: the marriage of my daughter, Ann, to C. Douglas White. Ann and Doug, who passed away in 2006, were the parents of my only grandson, Andrew.

Years before that, however, Pat's idea was to restore each of the seven public rooms on the ground floor of Government House in the style of seven different periods in Maryland history, ranging from the Federalist period to the twentieth century. The work, supervised by the Maryland Historical Society, was to be historically and architecturally accurate and, we hoped, permanent. Pat and I thought that once this museum-quality renovation was completed, it would relieve future governors—or their first ladies—of the task of redoing the public rooms over and over again. It also would relieve taxpayers of the cost of new renovations every four or eight years and, most importantly, it would provide visitors with an authentic glimpse of what the house might have looked like in bygone eras. We thought that future residents of the fifty-four-room mansion would still have plenty of other rooms on the upper floors to occupy their attention if they felt the need to add wallpaper, paint or new furniture.

"We wanted to do something more than simply redecorate," Pat explained. "It's almost a cliché: when first ladies come in, they redecorate. Our thought was precisely the opposite, something completely different to depersonalize the process. It would take me and anybody who came after me out of it."[126]

The project was so meticulous it took seven years to complete. We set up a group called Friends of Government House that collected $1.4 million worth of authentic Maryland antique furnishings and paintings for the mansion, each item specially selected to fit the era of one of the public rooms. Some pieces, such as a set of ten shield-back chairs that had belonged to Revolutionary War-era governor Thomas Johnson, had obvious historic significance as well. Pat brought in Stiles T. Colwill, then chief curator of the Maryland Historical Society, to supervise the project. The nonprofit group, Friends of Government House, was headed by Leonard "Reds" Crewe, who contributed financially, raised thousands of dollars for the project and was instrumental in its completion.

---

126. James Bock, "Critics Fault Costly Redecoration of Governor's Mansion," *Baltimore Sun*, July 25, 1988.

Our desire to be historically accurate was so pervasive that when a donor offered the use of a fine antique Chippendale sofa, it had to be returned when we learned it had been made in Pennsylvania, not Maryland. A Maryland Chippendale sofa was later found to take its place.

"We used to joke that if the Hugheses wanted to put mirrors on the ceiling in the private quarters, they could. But the public rooms need continuity, just as the White House has public rooms that can't be changed. If every four or eight years, the whole White House was redecorated, it would be ridiculous," Colwill explained.[127]

The result was everything we hoped it would be, from the Empire Parlor with its chrome yellow walls (a color copied from Homewood, the 1802 house on the Johns Hopkins University campus) to the Eighteenth-Century Drawing Room (which had gray walls and stone-colored trim, reflecting the colors in the eighteenth-century Chase-Lloyd House in Annapolis) or the Twentieth-Century Billy Baldwin Room. The dramatic Billy Baldwin Room, a conservatory with multiple windows at one end of the house, was named after the mid-twentieth century interior designer from Baltimore and featured brown lacquered walls, clear cylindrical lamps with white shades and Baldwin's signature slipper chairs. The overall effect throughout the seven public rooms was so grand it merited a wildly favorable review in the national publication, *Architectural Digest*.

"There are few pleasures as sweet as that of moving into a house that needs no work, and whoever succeeds Harry Hughes as governor of Maryland this January should at least include a paragraph of thanks to Patricia Hughes in his inaugural speech," *Architectural Digest* wrote in its seven-page, seven-photograph 1986 spread.[128]

But to say that my successor, William Donald Schaefer, and his "first friend," newly installed State House hostess Hilda Mae Snoops, were ungrateful is to engage in understatement. Within six months of taking office, Schaefer and Snoops began to undo everything Pat and the Friends of Government House had done, first by setting up a new governing board to oversee interior décor in what they had begun to call the "Governor's Mansion," and then by stripping away almost everything we had done in the public rooms.

The Maryland Historical Society let Schaefer change the law regarding Government House oversight without a whimper, but I'm sure they, like many others, were scared to buck Schaefer. I know "Reds" Crewe was particularly angry that no one stood up to Schaefer.

When Snoops took reporters on a tour of her redecorated public rooms in September 1988, *Baltimore Sun* art critic John Dorsey viewed the new white-on-white and blue walls, the Chippendale style furniture that had replaced the precisely-selected period pieces and pronounced the whole effort "bland, dull and lack[ing] coherence."[129]

127. Ibid.
128. Christopher Buckley, "Maryland's Government House: Governor and Mrs. Harry Hughes in Annapolis," text by *Architectural Digest: The International Magazine of Fine Interior Design*, November 1986 155–59, 222.
129. John Dorsey, "Blue, Bland and Boring," *Baltimore Sun*, September 28, 1988.

I almost could not believe Schaefer could be so petty, but of course I should have known better.

"What's obviously going on is an extreme effort to change what was done there," I said at the time. "Others can speculate on the motives. I'm disappointed so many people volunteered so much of their time, money, art work and whatever—all done in a professional way. I'm disappointed for them."[130]

To this day, it is hard for me to understand why someone would so cavalierly, so quickly and so thoughtlessly undo so much good work done by so many people. It is just unfathomable and sad.

130. Bock, "Costly Redecoration."

16

The Chesapeake Bay:
"Let's Do Something!"

THE CHESAPEAKE BAY WATERSHED STRETCHES over more than sixty-four thousand square miles in six states and the District of Columbia, includes 150 major rivers and streams and extends as far north as Cooperstown, New York. But the northern half of the Bay is almost entirely within Maryland and its health has become an iconic symbol of the quality of life of the state as a whole.

By the time I became governor, it was obvious to anyone who had grown up around the Bay that something was seriously wrong. For the three-and-a-half centuries since Europeans arrived, the Chesapeake had been one of the most productive estuaries in the world. But by the latter part of the 1970s, the Bay could no longer produce crabs, fish or oysters in the quantities Marylanders and Virginians alike had come to expect. Oyster populations were crashing. For the first time in Bay history, the value of the blue crab catch exceeded that of oysters, a pattern that has only widened. Landings of the most valuable and sought after finfish in the Bay, the rockfish, were also declining. Scientists had begun to document a substantial decline in underwater grasses.

In 1972, Tropical Storm Agnes ravaged the Bay, buried hundreds of acres of underwater Bay grasses in sediment and signaled an alarming decline in the Bay's health. Three years later, U.S. Senator Charles McC. Mathias Jr., a Republican from Maryland, successfully pushed through Congress legislation that directed the U.S. Environmental Protection Agency to conduct an in-depth study of the Bay. Completed in 1983, the $27 million study graphically documented the Bay's declining resources and focused on three principal causes that required immediate attention: an overabundance of the nutrients nitrogen and phosphorus in the water; excess sediment loadings; and toxic chemical pollution. Over-harvesting of fish, crabs and oysters was also listed as an issue that needed to be addressed. Scientists discovered a large "dead area" in the Bay that was starved of life-giving oxygen.

My interest in the Bay began long before the results of this report were known, but it didn't really stem from anything in my childhood. Remember: my home county is the only completely landlocked county on the Eastern Shore. Denton was on the Choptank River and I did a little crabbing from time to time, but I wasn't really in a boating environment and, frankly, my family didn't have the money for a boat. As I got older, though, the importance of the Bay began to sink in—not only as a traditional place of employment for watermen or as a recreational outlet for hundreds of thousands of sailors and power boaters, but as an intrinsic element of the character of the state.

There used to be an advertisement for National Bohemian beer, which was brewed in East Baltimore, which featured a character called "Chester Peake" and images of skipjacks. The ads carried a slogan that referred to the Bay region as "the Land of Pleasant Living." Over a period of time, that sort of imagery has an effect on you. It had once been the "land of pleasant living," but things were going awry.

In 1982, we supported a tough new law to require developers to do a better job of managing storm water runoff from their projects, and another measure that provided direct financial help to farmers who agreed to employ "best management practices" to reduce runoff from their farm fields. These included reducing the amount of fertilizer they used on their fields, better managing animal waste and planting buffers along waterways.

I was also affected by seeing the Bay first-hand. After I became governor, I traveled around the Bay as often as I could, usually on the state yacht, the *Aurora*. I went out whenever I could on weekends. When you do that, you really get a strong feeling for the Bay and realize how unique it is and what we should be doing to protect it. What really made us turn our attention to the Bay was the EPA study. Shortly after I was reelected, I made it clear that cleaning up the Bay would be a top priority of my second term.

As the preliminary scientific findings from the federal study became available in 1982, Virginia Governor Charles Robb came to Annapolis at my invitation for a joint briefing by EPA and a discussion of a cooperative effort to restore the Bay. One of the reasons I think we were able to get Virginia so quickly involved in the Bay effort was that back during my first term, I signed an agreement with Robb's predecessor, Governor John Dalton, that allowed our respective natural resources departments to share information and work together. I think that laid the groundwork for Robb's visit several years later.

In the legislative session of 1983, I asked the General Assembly for $750,000 to transfer the results of the EPA study to the state for implementation.

"Undoubtedly, one of the greatest tests of our stewardship will be our ability to restore the Chesapeake Bay," I told the General Assembly.[131] "As our mountains and barrier islands define our boundaries, the Bay defines our central character."

That spring, DNR Secretary Torrey C. Brown, William Eichbaum, who headed the water quality office in the Department of Health and Mental Hygiene, and several members of my staff, principally John R. Griffin and Verna Harrison, discussed the EPA report with me and we decided, "Let's do something!" There had been tons of reports and studies done about the Bay, but most of them were just put on a shelf and nothing ever happened. Torrey, Bill and other key members of my staff and Cabinet began meeting regularly at a little cabin on state-owned property at Wye Island, intent that Maryland should demonstrate regional leadership on

131. Governor Harry R. Hughes, state of the state address (January 21, 1983).

Bay issues by developing our own Chesapeake Bay program. Wayne Cawley, my agriculture secretary, was deeply involved in these discussions. He did a great job representing the interests of his farmer constituency, but that sometimes conflicted with our broader Bay cleanup efforts.

The Wye Group, as they called themselves, also developed a plan to sell the idea of a Bay restoration program to the public. All of us spent a lot of time educating various organizations about these efforts and the need to begin to implement a Bay cleanup program. Every time I spoke to the Maryland Association of Counties, Maryland Municipal League, Maryland Chamber of Commerce or other groups, I talked about the importance of the Bay to our state. By the time we got to the 1984 legislative session, we wanted our Bay program to be in a posture where we had broad-based public and stakeholder support and where it would be very hard for lawmakers to vote against it. Importantly, the Wye Group also began working with other states and the EPA to frame a regional approach to Bay restoration. For all of this, the EPA Bay study initiated by Mac Mathias was both our stimulus and guide.

Regional Compact

The first step toward a regional compact was a meeting requested by me at which the governors of Virginia and Pennsylvania joined me in pledging to cooperate to restore the Chesapeake. That summer, I invited those two governors, the mayor of the District of Columbia and the EPA's first administrator, William D. Ruckelshaus, for a cruise on the Bay on the state yacht, replete with Maryland crab cakes. The trip was designed to dramatize the Bay's value as well as the scope of its problems. Ruckelshaus, in particular, was very supportive. When we got back, the group signed a one-page agreement that committed them to a federal-interstate cooperative effort for the Bay.

The idea of doing something to protect the Bay really struck a note with people—it really had a lot of support. I can recall attending parades during the summer and fall of 1983 and hearing people shout, "Save the Bay, Save the Bay," a slogan popularized by the nonprofit Chesapeake Bay Foundation.

The Wye Group continued to meet, developing major Bay initiatives and a set of "Bay budget" increases for the 1984 Maryland General Assembly session. Panels of stakeholders from all the Bay states and the District of Columbia were formed to review initiatives and build consensus for Bay restoration plans.

In December 1983, all our efforts culminated in a Chesapeake Bay Summit, held at George Mason University in northern Virginia. Lasting two days and attended by governors, U.S. senators and congressmen, state legislators, key Bay scientists, environmentalists and such notables as the underwater explorer Jacques Cousteau, the conference endorsed the Bay cleanup strategy and produced widespread support for Bay cleanup.

There, we signed an agreement that established a new Chesapeake Executive Council made up of all of the signatories of the agreement: the governors of the three states, the mayor of Washington, D.C., the chair of the Chesapeake Bay Commission and the administrator of the EPA. The agreement also established the Chesapeake Bay Program office under the EPA. Located in Annapolis, that office still manages interstate Bay restoration efforts.[132]

Although the players have changed over the years, this Chesapeake Executive Council continues to this day to oversee the restoration efforts for the Chesapeake Bay. Under its guidance, the various parties have signed major new Chesapeake Bay agreements that have contained specific nutrient and sediment reduction goals and set deadlines for each state to meet them. The first agreement was one page; the latest agreement, "Chesapeake 2000," is thirteen pages.

An important collateral effect of the 1983 regional Bay Conference was that it sparked widespread public support for the set of the Bay initiatives that had been put together by the Wye Group and which I intended to introduce in the General Assembly.

A Comprehensive Approach

As the General Assembly returned to Annapolis in January and still riding the momentum of the regional agreement, my staff and I proclaimed 1984 "the Year of the Bay." We proposed forty-five initiatives designed to save the Chesapeake from every form of pollution, ranging from bayside industry to upstream farm runoff.

"Much has been said about our initiatives to save the Bay," I said in my annual address to the legislature, "but one thought cannot be repeated too often: for three centuries, generation after generation has taken from the Bay; let those who come after us be able to say that ours was the first generation to put something back."[133] I quoted the explorer, Captain John Smith,[134] and told the senators and delegates, "Ladies and gentlemen, the Bay is part of the legacy left in our trust by those who courageously founded our State 350 years ago and by those who have served our State since then. Besides the beauty of the Bay, it is a legacy of freedom and justice. Through our deliberations in these halls over the next few weeks, may we protect that legacy and keep that trust."

That winter, I followed my custom of inviting all the legislators (in groups, of course) to dinner at Government House. To capitalize on these captive audiences, I asked William Warner, author of *Beautiful Swimmers*, the Pulitzer prize-winning book about crabs, watermen and the Chesapeake Bay, to give a little talk to each group about the importance of enacting our Bay program. After dinner, we would

132. In 1984, we were able to obtain a $10 million federal appropriation that funded the Bay program office and grants to the states and D.C. for specific bay clean-up efforts. That funding has exceeded $20 million annually for the last decade and the Bay program office has more than fifty employees.
133. Governor Harry R. Hughes, state of the state address (January 18, 1984).
134. "Heaven and earth never agreed better to frame a place for man's habitation," Smith said of the Chesapeake.

invite everyone to gather in the mansion's large entry hall and Warner would climb about a third of the way up the main staircase and talk to the lawmakers. It had the feel of a minister speaking to his congregation from the pulpit, exhorting them to lead cleaner lives. He was really good. *Beautiful Swimmers* is a wonderful book and Willie had a great sense of humor. He was really helpful on this program.

Our approach was comprehensive. We proposed measures to attack the problem of pollution from single sources, such as factories and sewage treatment plants, as well as from general sources, such as the nutrient runoff from farm fields and suburban lawns. Some of the programs focused on restoration of the resources, such as the Bay's dwindling supply of oysters and bay grasses, and others on resource management, including efforts to reduce the pressure from over-harvesting crabs. Part of the program provided support for controlling stormwater runoff, planting buffers along waterways, for environmental education and for long-term monitoring and research. Before my term was out, we even set up an entity called the Chesapeake Bay Trust to engage citizens and the business community in cooperative Bay restoration efforts by making small grants for worthy projects.

For the first time in state history, we proposed that those who fish in the Chesapeake Bay first obtain a state-issued license—the saltwater sportsfishing license—the proceeds from which would be plowed back into Bay restoration efforts. As you can imagine, that caused howls of protest at first, especially from some of the conservatives from the Eastern Shore. Fishing in the Bay, many thought, was a God-given right; but we thought it was high time to balance the ledger a bit by imposing a user's fee.

That session, seven major legislative initiatives were enacted and almost all the other ideas we proposed were approved, either through legislation or as part of the state budget. In all, $37 million in additional funding was approved for the Bay restoration and 176 new Bay-related jobs were added.

Critical Areas

Clearly, the most important and, naturally, the most controversial part of the package of Bay initiatives was a revolutionary new approach to protecting the land adjacent to the Bay and its tributaries that was under intense development pressure. Anyone who had studied the Bay or, for that matter, anyone who had thought about the Bay's problems, knew there was a direct connection between what we did on the land and the quality of the water in the Bay. Yet every jurisdiction with shoreline on the Bay or its tributaries was permitting forests to be cut and houses to be built right up to the water's edge. As a result, the shorelines were eroding, the Bay was filling with nutrients and sediment and the bay grasses that are so important to the life cycle of the Bay were being destroyed along with other living resources.

To begin to address this problem, we proposed legislation known as the Critical Areas Act, which designated the land adjacent to the water (more precisely, all the land within one thousand feet of tidal waters or tidal wetlands) as a "critical area" subject to special protections from development. For the first time, the state said it intended to place constraints on development within one thousand feet of the entire shoreline of the Maryland portion of the Bay and its tidal tributaries. The net effect of that single piece of legislation was, in essence, to downzone about 10 percent of the landmass of the state. As you can imagine, this created a huge fight in the General Assembly. Yet, Maryland citizens and, eventually, Maryland legislators seemed to understand the purpose and—with exceptions, of course—eventually supported it. I watched through the door of the House balcony as the delegates finally approved the measure, 95–18, and then waited for the Senate to do likewise, 39–6. The measure put the new twenty-five-member Critical Areas Commission in charge of protecting water quality, the habitats of fish, wildlife and plants and the overall health of the environment within the one thousand-foot perimeter.[135]

Criteria later developed by the Commission imposed stringent restrictions on development in much of the existing forest and farmland, marshes and sensitive habitat areas along the shoreline. Perhaps the most significant restriction was a limit of one dwelling unit per twenty acres in over 75 percent of the Critical Areas zone. Without this law, we would have houses lined up along the shoreline of the Bay and its rivers like houses on a Monopoly board. This new state law was so controversial that the General Assembly required that the new criteria be affirmatively approved by both houses of the legislature before adoption. This didn't occur until 1986, which was an election year. But with a groundswell of support from the public and the news media, the Critical Areas criteria were easily approved.

The first two chairmen of the Critical Areas Commission were both retired judges and both did an excellent job. The first was Sol Liss, a city councilman from Baltimore before going on the bench. When I asked the rotund Liss if he would chair the Commission, the longtime city official laughed and said he would be absolutely unbiased because "I've never seen the Chesapeake Bay." But Sol was a quick study and did a fine job. He was ably succeeded by John-Clarence North, a retired judge from Talbot County. North loved being on the water and was an owner, sailor and expert on log canoes, historic sailing craft that are still raced on Eastern Shore rivers.

Over the years, a lot of people have suggested to me that my leadership in starting the regional effort to restore the Bay and forging and gaining adoption of the Chesapeake Bay initiatives in 1983, 1984 and beyond represent my greatest legacy as governor. That may be true, but I didn't consciously think about that at the time. I just felt strongly that we had to do something about the condition of the Bay.

The Bay restoration efforts, of course, didn't stop then and probably will never stop. There is just too much pressure on the Bay to say, "Well, we fixed that." It is all we can do just to keep the Bay from deteriorating further. Maryland can be

135. Karen Hosler, "Legislature Approves Bay Cleanup Bill," *Baltimore Sun*, April 8, 1984.

proud of its leadership in the Bay restoration efforts. In just the last three years I was governor, the state—with the strong and consistent support of the General Assembly—provided more than $150 million in new funding and created more than 270 new Bay-related positions.

Many of our Bay initiatives have had significant success, particularly in removing phosphorous and nitrogen from the effluent of wastewater treatment plants. Many people today may not remember this, but one of the sources of phosphorous in the Bay came from cleaning detergents that contained phosphates. Detergent advertisements claimed that phosphates would rid shirts of that nasty "ring around the collar."

In 1985, we supported, and the Maryland General Assembly passed, legislation introduced by Senator Gerald Winegrad of Annapolis that banned phosphate detergents. The measure was enacted despite a determined fight from detergent manufacturers. Major retailers, such as Giant Food, also fought the proposed phosphate ban, as did the then-mayor of Baltimore, William Donald Schaefer. At least seventeen lobbyists worked against the legislation, but the momentum in favor of the Bay was too strong for them to resist.[136]

In the years since this change, no one has ever complained to me about having "ring around the collar"! This legislation has not only reduced phosphorus loading in the Bay, but it also has saved consumers money by reducing the cost of sewage treatment.

The Rockfish Ban

An obvious indicator of the Bay's decline was the reduction in oysters, crabs, waterfowl and finfish. Striped bass, which are known in Maryland, of course, as rockfish, have for years been touted as the official state fish. Commercial landings in Maryland and Virginia generally increased from the early 1930s, culminating in a record commercial catch in 1973 of 14.7 million pounds. Thereafter the striper harvest fell steadily to a low of 1.7 million pounds by 1983. Sport fishermen reported a similar pattern.

Each year, scientists from the Department of Natural Resources would go to different spots on the Bay to conduct tests to determine how well or poorly rockfish were spawning. But in the late summer of 1984, after another very low "young-of-the-year index," DNR Secretary Torrey Brown and his deputy, John Griffin, met with me and recommended a moratorium. Scientists had been unable to come up with any other answers, so it was the only solution we could think of. I said, "If that's what we've got to do, let's go ahead and do it." It was that simple: one meeting and we did it.

136. Phosphate detergents were subsequently banned in Washington, D.C., in 1986, in Virginia in 1988 and in Pennsylvania in 1990.

In December 1985, I took the unprecedented step of placing a complete ban on fishing or otherwise harvesting rockfish in Maryland waters. Recognizing the impact this would have on the livelihood of Maryland watermen, we simultaneously set up a new Watermen's Compensation Fund. Watermen who were temporarily prohibited from fishing for rockfish could go to work for the Department of Natural Resources collecting data, fixing fish hatcheries or performing other tasks, and would be paid through this new fund. This was a way not only to minimize political opposition to the moratorium, but also to keep the fishermen employed until the striped bass fishery had sufficient time to recover.

We were worried our ban on harvesting rockfish in Maryland would be meaningless if restrictions were not also placed on catching the striped bass when they migrate into the ocean. To address that, I convinced the head of the Maryland Watermen's Association to join me in asking Congress to support a plan by the Atlantic States Marine Fisheries Commission to protect striped bass up and down the mid-Atlantic coast. We thought it would be more diplomatic to work within the Commission rather than have Congress pass a broad and more inflexible ban on harvesting striped bass.

U.S. Senator John Chafee, a moderate Republican from Rhode Island and strong environmentalist, supported our efforts. I testified before Chafee's committee and took him a painting of a rockfish, because I knew he loved rockfish. He was instrumental in getting Congress to hold off on the federal moratorium legislation. Instead, Congress passed the Atlantic Striped Bass Conservation Act in 1984 that gave the Atlantic States Marine Fisheries Commission authority to restrict the fishery. If states did not comply, then a federal moratorium could be imposed. This more flexible approach— and the threat of a moratorium—finally brought in a recalcitrant Virginia and other states to either close or greatly restrict their rockfish harvest.

Meanwhile, I directed our Department of Natural Resources to develop intensive rockfish spawning efforts, including the construction of a new striped bass hatchery. We also began a process of removing dams or highway culverts that blocked spawning stream and installing fish passages to allow rockfish and other spawning fish to get around dams.

It wasn't until 1990, three years after I left office, that the spawning indexes indicated the rockfish were recovering and the moratorium could be lifted. Even then, catching rockfish was still subject to tight fishing quotas put in place by the Fisheries Commission.

Like any restoration effort, it takes years to see if your actions have had any effect. Our ban benefited from similar moratoria in other states and by the federal rockfish law. When the Maryland ban was lifted in 1990, a "white paper" was drafted that devised a management plan that allocated 37.5 percent of the annual quota to recreational fishermen, 37.5 percent to commercial fishermen and 15 percent to charter boats. Once any segment reached its quota, the fishery would be closed for that segment. This successful management regime is still in place.

The moratorium, other fishing restrictions and this tight fishing regime have allowed the species to flourish. Today, rockfish are again plentiful in the Bay. Unfortunately, a new problem (a wasting disease called mycobacteriosis that kills rockfish and can cause skin infections in humans) has spread in recent years to an estimated three-quarters of the Bay's rockfish population and scientists don't know quite what to do about it. By 2006, the disease was threatening anew a $300 million rockfish industry. This new challenge grimly demonstrates how difficult it is to restore and protect the Bay and how stressed it remains from pollution and development pressures along its shores.[137]

Despite these problems, I still believe the proudest achievement of our Bay program—and perhaps its best hope—is something we never could have legislated: a new level of consciousness about the importance of estuaries and the fragility and resilience of coastal ecosystems. We publicized our efforts and brought interest in the Bay to life. We could not have succeeded without the "Save the Bay" ethic, and we could not have gotten our Bay program through without the overwhelming support of the people of Maryland.

137. Elizabeth Williamson, "Chesapeake's Rockfish Overrun by Disease," *Washington Post*, March 11, 2006.

17

The Savings and Loan Crisis

I WAS PRETTY CONTENT BY THE spring of 1985. I had just completed my sixth legislative session as governor, was receiving high marks for our Chesapeake Bay program, and for the first time in three years was not facing a serious budget problem or sharp cutbacks from the federal government. I felt comfortable in the job. I finally had the luxury of turning my attention to a series of new programs that I wanted to push to help children who were poor, abused, hungry, drug-addicted or forgotten. I felt I had steadily built a record of solid achievement and was beginning to think that in 1986, my final year as governor, I might be strong enough politically to run for the seat in the United States Senate that was being vacated by retiring Republican Senator Mathias.

Right after the General Assembly session ended that year, Pat and I took off for a week's vacation at a resort in Fort Lauderdale, Florida. The first Saturday night we were there, April 13, I received a telephone call from an official with the Federal Reserve Bank in Richmond, Virginia. He told me that bank regulators were worried about a spike in "borrowing" at the federal window by savings and loan institutions in Maryland. What that indicated, he said, was that a lot of depositors at Maryland S&Ls were withdrawing their funds and the S&Ls, in turn, were going to the Federal Reserve Bank to get the money needed to pay them.

About a month earlier, I had received a call from Ohio Governor Richard F. Celeste telling me how he had been forced to close seventy-one S&Ls in Ohio following the collapse of Home State Savings and Loan in Cincinnati. Celeste said he called because he knew that S&Ls in Maryland were set up in similar fashion—they were privately insured and not backed by the full faith and credit of either the state or federal government. He said only five states had systems like that and Maryland was one. "I just wanted to let you know," he said, "and also wanted to tell you not to expect any help from the feds." After the call from Celeste, we increased the state's monitoring of S&Ls—but were initially assured everything was okay.

When I received the telephone call that night in Florida, however, I knew we had a serious problem and that we didn't know enough about what was really going on in the industry. After I hung up, I called Johnny Johnson, my chief of staff, told him about the call and directed him to get a group together to assess the situation. Johnson, working in secrecy to avoid any incident that might trigger a bigger or broader run by depositors, convened a meeting at the Annapolis Holiday Inn three days later with several Cabinet secretaries, S&L regulators and officials from the Federal Reserve. What they learned was that five "high-flyer" S&Ls among the 102 Maryland thrifts insured by the privately-run Maryland Savings Share Insurance

Corporation (MSSIC) had borrowed $55 million from the feds since the Ohio crisis became public a month earlier. Still working in secrecy, Johnson and the state and federal regulators met two days later with MSSIC officials, but were again assured that everything was under control. Johnson, who himself was headed out of town for a week's vacation just as I was to return, left me a memo saying he felt the MSSIC officials were being too optimistic and urging me to meet privately with the Federal Reserve officials as soon as I got back.

Still fearful of igniting a run, I said nothing publicly about the brewing S&L problem. The press generally seemed ignorant of it as well, writing instead about whether I would veto legislation to allow slot machines in Eastern Shore fraternal organizations or sign bills to ban phosphate detergents or allow coal mining on sites in western Maryland with particularly steep slopes.

In talks with state regulators on April 28, I learned that a month earlier MSSIC had sent a letter to Jeffrey A. Levitt, the president of Old Court Savings and Loan in Baltimore, detailing a series of Old Court violations of S&L regulations. I later learned, as did the General Assembly and the public, that, despite public assurances to the contrary, MSSIC's executive director, Charles L. Hogg II knew as early as the summer of 1984 that examiners had discovered "some irregularities" at Old Court. In October 1984, Old Court failed to file its required monthly general fiscal report to MSSIC and repeated the violation in November, December and January. In January 1985, MSSIC finally sent a team of auditors to Old Court.

I knew none of this at the time it was happening. MSSIC, the S&L industry's private insurer, shielded its members from outside scrutiny and the state regulators, we later learned, acquiesced. Responsibility for regulating S&Ls within state government was vested with Charles H. Brown Jr., director of the Division of Savings and Loan Associations, a unit within the state Department of Licensing and Regulation, then headed by Secretary Frederick L. Dewberry. MSSIC assured Brown that everything was under control and Brown, white-haired and nearing retirement, either believed it or was afraid to challenge it.

When state Senator Leo E. Green of Prince George's County raised concerns with MSSIC, Hogg sent him a letter on January 16, 1985, saying there was no need to worry about the "financial strength of MSSIC." Hogg said MSSIC's "data processing early warning system, as well as on-site reviews of the operations of members, are tuned to detect conditions in a member association before they can become serious problems." A little more than a month later, unbeknownst to Senator Green, to me or to our state regulators at the time, the MSSIC board voted to send a cease-and-desist order to Old Court that detailed fifteen violations of MSSIC rules.

As the situation worsened by the end of April, we called in Federal Reserve auditors to review Old Court's books. On April 29, I met with Federal Reserve officials, attorneys and staff to map a strategy on how to contain the S&L problem that likely would develop once the mismanagement at Old Court was publicly revealed, as it inevitably would be. Our goal was to avoid a broader, more serious run by depositors that we feared would not only spread to other S&Ls, but possibly to the state's banks as well. Attorney General Stephen H. Sachs, who had been brought into the discussions by Johnson after the Federal Reserve Bank contacted us in early April, directed his office to begin preparing emergency legislation in case we had to summon the General Assembly into special session.

One complicating factor was that I had announced back in March plans to take a two-week economic development trip to Israel and Egypt, beginning in early May. Now the question was: should I go? How would it look if, knowing the seriousness of the smoldering S&L problem, I left the state for an overseas trip? On the other hand, how would it look—and would it spark the depositor run we were trying to avoid—if I suddenly cancelled the trip? How would we truthfully explain such a decision? It was sort of a catch-22.

I met again with the Federal Reserve people, Sachs and others, and we decided the best course was for me to go ahead on the trip as planned in the belief that federal and state regulators could contain the problem. On Thursday, May 2, Jeffrey Levitt was removed as Old Court's chief executive officer. The same day, I authorized Sachs to investigate Old Court. Two days later, I left for Israel.

Over the next week, however, the situation began to unravel. Most of the 102 S&Ls insured by MSSIC were small and not involved in the financially dangerous activities or practices of S&Ls like Old Court, which had been flooded with cash from investors taking advantage of their above-market interest rates and then invested that money in wildly speculative projects all over the country. Often, we later learned, these projects generated excessive fees that were then funneled directly back to the owners, directors and other S&L executives. It was a huge Ponzi scheme with the goal of making the S&L executives rich at the expense of their depositors. We would not understand the full extent of this criminal activity for months to come.

Our people met with officials from the Federal Home Loan Bank Board to begin the process of getting some of the smaller S&Ls that had sufficient capital to qualify to apply for insurance under the Federal Savings & Loan Insurance Corporation, known as FSLIC, an acronym pronounced as "fizz-lick."

On Wednesday, May 8, Levitt's removal was announced and, on Thursday, Sachs's investigation of Old Court became public. Depositors literally began lining up at Old Court's doors to get their money out. At two o'clock the next morning, in a Maryland Circuit Court judge's kitchen, Old Court Savings and Loan was placed under the authority of a court-appointed conservator. Yet the run continued. Another high-flying S&L, Merritt Commercial Savings and Loan went into voluntary conservatorship and was asked to sell its brand-new high-rise headquarters in downtown Baltimore. After that, even more depositors lined up to demand their money back. The run was on.

By the time news of all of this—and photographs of depositors standing in the long lines—hit the newspapers on Thursday, somewhere between $12.8 million and $15 million had been withdrawn from Maryland S&Ls. Johnson, running the show in my absence, briefed House and Senate leaders, but publicly tried to calm depositor fears by maintaining that Old Court was only suffering from day-to-day management problems. He insisted there was no reason to recall me from Israel.

By Friday, however, Johnson acknowledged the problems at Old Court had triggered "a crisis of confidence," but said—hopefully—that there was no reason the crisis should spill over to other thrifts. He said again there were no plans to cut short my trip, which was expected to last until May 17. Several legislative leaders also tried to calm the public.

About halfway through my trip, following a meeting with Prime Minister Shimon Peres in Jerusalem and just as our delegation was about to leave for Egypt, Johnny called me to say the run on the S&Ls had become serious. We decided I had no choice but to come home immediately. We cancelled the rest of the trip and everybody came back. In one day, I flew from Tel Aviv to Cairo, from Cairo back to Tel Aviv, from Tel Aviv to New York and from New York in a little state-owned airplane back to Annapolis. It was evening by the time I got to the State House and I immediately went into a series of meetings with my staff, Sachs, Steinberg, Cardin and federal bank officials. I issued an executive order limiting withdrawals at all 102 institutions to $1,000 in a thirty-day period, which we thought was preferable to closing all of the savings and loans. It was at that meeting we also decided to call the General Assembly back into emergency special session. I held a press conference to announce all of this at about midnight.

That was a rough day.

A Moral Responsibility

One of the obvious problems was that depositors had been led to believe that MSSIC was somehow backed by the full faith and credit of the state. The truth, however, was that MSSIC was a private entity and the state had no legal responsibility to cover deposits in any MSSIC-insured institution. MSSIC had been set up by the legislature in 1962, in fact, after an earlier S&L scandal had erupted. I was in the state Senate when that occurred and I remembered that the state's response had been minimal. Many depositors lost almost all of their savings, receiving only pennies on the dollar and, in some instances, nothing.

I didn't want that to happen again. I felt the state had a moral responsibility to step in and try to save the depositors' money. The advertising by MSSIC could really fool somebody into thinking the state of Maryland was behind it. They used a seal that was almost identical to the state seal. I just felt that the vast majority of these depositors felt their deposits were backed by the state and we therefore had a moral responsibility to do something about it. The General Assembly clearly agreed with me. What else could we have done that wouldn't have caused a real disaster? Those runs would have continued and gotten worse and ruined a lot of very sound institutions and drained away a life's savings from thousands of innocent depositors.

The safest bank in the country cannot withstand a run. They don't have that money sitting in the vault—it's invested somewhere. Everyone said the run would spread like wildfire if we didn't step in. So there was more at stake than just getting rid of the bad apples. There were a lot of very sound institutions at risk. Plus, there was the risk that it might spill over into the banks. The whole system is based on confidence. If there were a run on all the banks, it would have been a disaster.

I called the General Assembly into emergency session on May 18. In my long career in government, I cannot recall another crisis that was so dangerous, so complicated, where it was so unclear how we should respond or where the ultimate outcome was so uncertain. In those most difficult initial hours, the cooperation I received from House Speaker Ben Cardin, Senate President Mickey Steinberg, Attorney General Steve Sachs, officials from the Federal Reserve and members of my own staff and administration was superb.

During a very long day, we worked with legislative leaders to fashion a package of seven emergency bills that I signed into law at a State House ceremony held early Saturday morning, about thirty minutes after midnight. The most important bill established the Maryland Deposit Insurance Fund (MDIF), which became the state-backed replacement for MSSIC and would insure existing S&L deposits up to $100,000 per depositor, although we did permit depositors with multiple accounts to aggregate their deposits up to that amount. We really had no choice: the depositor run drained more than $200 million from the state's twenty largest S&Ls on May 15 alone, more than forty times the amount that had been withdrawn from those same S&Ls a week earlier, on May 8. We had to step in.

In a brief speech to the General Assembly, I said,

> Let me emphasize that it is neither accurate nor helpful toward solution of this crisis to describe any part of this package as a bailout or a break for those few whose ineptitude, mismanagement or greed might have contributed to the current difficulty. It is our aim to hold them accountable for their actions or their lassitude. Instead, this is a lifeline to those hard-working, thrifty depositors who have made possible a savings and loan industry, which is a vital factor in our economy for so many.[138]

The other legislation granted the state broad emergency powers to deal with the crisis, required MSSIC-insured S&Ls to obtain federal deposit insurance, earmarked $1 million from the coming year's anticipated surplus to get MDIF up and running and authorized the sale of $100 million in state general obligation bonds to guarantee the money depositors had entrusted to the S&Ls. This action put the full faith and credit of the state behind those deposits.

---

138. "Text of Governor's Address to General Assembly on State Savings and Loans," Baltimore Sun, May 18, 1985.

The ink was barely dry on the emergency bills, however, when the finger pointing began. While I got high marks for being decisive and taking charge upon my return from the Middle East (the *New York Times* called me "unflappable in a crisis"), my decision to take that overseas trip was immediately second-guessed, as we had expected it would be.

"He leaves for Israel knowing we are sitting on a powder keg," fumed state Senator Thomas V. Mike Miller Jr., a Democrat from Prince George's County. One unnamed senator quoted in the *Baltimore Sun* said, "The public will see that as a vacation—a guy playing the fiddle while Rome is burning. It is easier for the public to personalize [their problems] with the top guy than anything else. I think—right or wrong—the Governor will be blamed."[139]

But I wasn't the only one who was blamed. Some legislators blamed the regulators for failing to know what was going on or, if they knew, failing to sound the alarm. ("It is a lot like the bell that didn't ring or the dog that didn't bark," said Senator Howard Denis, a Republican from Montgomery County.) Some regulators, in turn, blamed the legislature for starving their budgets so severely that many had to work without the updated computers they desperately needed. Attorney General Sachs was even blamed for fanning the flames and exacerbating the depositor run by announcing that he had launched a criminal investigation into the activities at Old Court. Speaker Cardin's cousin, Jerome S. Cardin, was a principal owner of Old Court, a connection that fueled speculation that the legislature had turned a blind eye to the high-flying ways at Old Court and the other big S&Ls.

Fred Dewberry, who as secretary of Licensing and Regulation had oversight responsibility for banks and savings and loans, said he didn't warn me because no one told him there was a problem. He said the first time he found out about the problems at Old Court was in April, the same time I learned about them.

The crisis we faced, however, was so overwhelming, so serious and so complicated that I didn't have the luxury right then to try to figure out who had fallen down on the job. There just wasn't time to dwell on that.

To figure that out, the legislature set up an Office of Special Counsel to investigate the S&L debacle and appropriated a half million dollars to do the job. In June, I selected a Baltimore lawyer named Wilbur D. Preston Jr. to fill the post. Woody Preston, then sixty-three, was managing partner of Whiteford, Taylor, Preston, Trimble and Johnson and had long specialized in large, complex cases that often involved voluminous documents, scores of witnesses and years of litigation. Unlike other Maryland lawyers who might have been considered for the post, Preston was free from any professional relationships with the S&Ls or their principal executives. I called him in and said, "Everything is open. You look at anything you want to." Meanwhile, the state attorney general and the federal U.S. attorney for Maryland launched separate criminal investigations of various S&L owners and executives.

139. John W. Frece, "Banking Crisis Perils Political Reputations," *Baltimore Sun*, May 19, 1985.

As summer ran into fall, we gradually learned more about what was going on; we began to separate the S&Ls into different categories by size, financial health and ability to obtain federal deposit insurance; and we began to identify the 7 to 10 large S&Ls that were at the root of most of the problems. By September, I felt we were making real progress. By then, 77 of the 102 S&Ls had resumed normal operations, 21 of them with newly acquired federal insurance and 20 others with conditional approval. Of the 25 remaining where withdrawals were either restricted or prohibited, 12 had been promised federal insurance or were planning to merge with larger institutions.

By then, my economic development secretary, Thomas "Tuck" Maddux, was spending virtually all of his time trying to find outside buyers for the most troubled of the remaining S&Ls—those with huge portfolios of risky investments that were obviously never going to qualify for federal deposit insurance. It was a hard job because the risks to the outside banks were high and, therefore, so was their price. Plus, there was opposition to letting these huge outside banks into the state from Maryland's homegrown banking industry. This was during the period where states were just beginning to move into the realm of interstate banking and local banks, including those in Maryland, often reacted as isolationists or protectionists. That fall, Maddux thought he had convinced Citicorp to buy First Maryland S&L, which would have freed $300 million in deposits in thirty-four thousand accounts. But just before we could close the deal, Citicorp suddenly backed out.

In mid-October, I again summoned the legislature into emergency session. Maddux had worked out a separate $25 million deal with Chase Manhattan Bank of New York to come in and buy three problem S&Ls: Merritt, Chesapeake S&L of Annapolis and Friendship S&L of Chevy Chase. For the state, such a purchase would relieve taxpayers of any further obligation for the debts at these S&Ls, including an estimated $60 million to $80 million in losses at Merritt alone. For Chase, it was a quick way to enter the lucrative Maryland market in Baltimore, Annapolis and Montgomery County all at once. But as the legislative session approached, I suddenly discovered that Mickey Steinberg, the Senate president, was balking at the deal. We were extremely worried that Chase would get fed up and just back out of the deal, the way Citicorp had done earlier. To this day, I don't know what Mickey's real motivation was to oppose this deal, whether he was representing the interests of the Maryland banking industry, thought the transaction was not in the state's best interests or had some other agenda. But I knew we had no choice but to push through the deal negotiated with Chase.

"In this tragic and frustrating time for thousands of Marylanders, we do not meet as merely legislators or bookkeepers, but as the sole power that can relieve human suffering brought about by evil men,"[140] I told the legislators. "On this day, in this session, we will look our fellow Marylanders square in the eye and say, 'We are here for you. We stand behind you.'"

---

140. C. Fraser Smith, "Assembly Deadlocked on S&L Deal," *Baltimore Sun*, October 18, 1985.

Referring to Steinberg, I added: "In the last twenty-four hours, my friend and one of your esteemed colleagues has sounded retreat. I suggest he review the matter, pick up his trumpet and sound the charge."

I described Merritt as "a sick conglomeration of highly speculative loans, inflated property values, incomplete and in some cases nonexistent records" and said Chase was the only suitor interested in taking those problems off the state's hands. "Ladies and gentlemen of the legislature, this is no game. We need action and we need it now," I warned.

But the wrangling over the Chase deal droned on for five tension-filled days as Steinberg and others in the Senate tried without success to get Chase or me to restructure Chase's deal with the state. Steinberg had personally become such a symbol of opposition that he confided to reporters and colleagues alike that the only way he could save face was "to squeeze some juice" out of one or more of the S&Ls. The senators also said they were particularly worried that Gerald S. Klein, Merritt's disgraced owner (who was then under criminal investigation), might somehow profit from the sale. Because of Klein's intimate knowledge of Merritt's various deals, Chase had refused to complete the transaction without him staying on temporarily as a paid advisor.

Finally, at 4:10 a.m., after an almost all-night legislative session that featured theatrical, almost fire and brimstone speeches by Steinberg and several of his Senate colleagues and the heart-stopping, temporary defeat of the deal when one of our Senate supporters[141] inadvertently voted the wrong way, the Chase Manhattan legislation was finally approved by a one-vote margin.

I finally breathed a sigh of relief, believing the worst of the S&L nightmare was now finally behind me. Boy was I wrong.

The Liebmann Memo

By the time of that October legislative session, five months after the crisis began, angry S&L depositors had become an organized political force. They had banded together to complain that the state should have done a better job protecting their money and should be doing more to free the deposits that were still frozen or restricted. Hundreds of depositors marched on the State House in early October and insisted that I meet with them. I did so for more than two hours, but there was really no immediate relief I could offer them.

In the afterglow of the Chase deal, however, I thought that once thousands of additional depositors began to get their money back, their anger would gradually fade away. We held a ceremony to sign the legislation authorizing the Chase deal into law, which I clearly saw as a victory. When a radio reporter at the ceremony asked

---

141. Senator Arthur Dorman, Democrat from Prince George's County, accidentally cast his vote the wrong way but, upon reconsideration, was permitted to change his vote.

me when I first became aware of the self-dealing within the S&L industry, I said it was at a May 2 meeting with federal and state officials. (I actually was referring to the meeting with regulators held several days earlier, on April 28, but got my dates mixed up.) After the ceremony ended, Tom Kenworthy, then the *Washington Post*'s State House bureau chief, asked to speak with me in my private office. Kenworthy had in his hands a copy of a four-page memo written to me in October 1984—a full year earlier and some seven or eight months before the S&L crisis erupted—warning me about problems within the S&L industry. The memo was written by George W. Liebmann, a Baltimore lawyer and former staff member who by 1984 was working for my administration as a consultant and troubleshooter.

The memo, divided into two sections and intended as advice on both banking and savings and loan issues that were likely to arise in the 1985 legislative session, stated that new recommendations from a legislative committee on S&Ls were likely to be inadequate. It also said that MSSIC was providing "essentially unlimited... insurance coverage" of deposits, and that the state's S&L industry was beset by "very serious problems arising from self-dealing by officers of some of the more high-flying associations."[142] The memo went on to say, with a bit of exaggeration, that most of the associations were "technically insolvent" and the MSSIC Guarantee Fund was threatened by the practice of insuring multiple accounts from the same depositor.

"Although the full faith and credit of the state has not been pledged to the Guarantee Fund, I do not think that anyone seriously doubts the political pressures which would arise in the event of serious defaults," Liebmann wrote. He also said he worried that MSSIC was too industry-friendly because there were too many industry representatives on the MSSIC board. "Put bluntly, the present Guarantee fund, as it functions in this state, is little more than an industry promotion fund and notwithstanding the fine language about no pledge of credit, the state has effectively given the industry a blank check," Liebmann concluded.

A separate part of Liebmann's memo involved banking legislation that might be anticipated for the 1985 session. The reaction of my State House staff to the Liebmann memo was to send it off to Dewberry who, in turn, forwarded it to Margie Muller, the state bank commissioner, and to Brown, head of the S&L Division. In a reply memo to Dewberry on November 21, 1984, Brown acknowledged that he, too, had "reservations about insider loans" at S&Ls and agreed with Liebmann that "the public is generally of the opinion that MSSIC is a state agency and the insurance, is, therefore, backed by the state." But Brown expressed strong confidence in the MSSIC board and, by extension, the financial health of the industry.

"I attend the MSSIC Board meetings and I can say without hesitation that I find the directors to be most interested in the safety and soundness of the industry,

---

142. George W. Liebmann to Governor Harry R. Hughes, "Savings & Loan Insurance and Banking Legislation," October 5, 1984.

and they watch very closely the activities of each association in the state-chartered system," he wrote. In retrospect, this is an incredible statement, little more than a plug for MSSIC. We all know now that neither Brown nor the regulators who worked for him were doing their job.

"That isn't what I would call sounding the alarm," I told the *Post*.[143] I said then— and I still believe now—that Liebmann's memo "was great to look at in hindsight…If I knew what the problems were going to be, obviously, I would have paid a little more attention to it. But everybody was assuring us we didn't have a problem."

As this scandal unfolded, various people suggested that MSSIC should fire Hogg, or that I should fire Brown (who, instead was quickly forced into retirement) or even fire Johnny Johnson for failing to sound the alarm. Firing my chief of staff and making Johnny the scapegoat might have helped me politically. You see that sort of thing all the time at the executive level. But, I didn't believe this was Johnny's fault, I still had confidence in him and I needed his help. I never considered asking Johnny to resign.

If anybody should have resigned, it should have been Dewberry. I always had a high regard for Fred Dewberry and didn't think too much about his role in all of this at that moment. But as time has gone by, the more I've thought about it, the more I realized he was the conduit for information between the S&L industry and me. Yet he made no serious effort and no serious inquiry even when alerted to possible problems. He just sent off the memo to underlings like Brown, got their response back and simply sent it on to Johnny. That really irked Johnny, because, as chief of staff, it put him on the spot. Johnny always said it was what you call a "cover-your-ass" memo and Johnny never recovered from that. Johnny didn't bring the issue to my attention again because it appeared there was nothing to it. I should have called Dewberry on the carpet.

Later, of course, we learned there were some S&L examiners who were concerned about what was going on, but who hid their confidential reports in the trunks of their cars after they alerted their superiors and nothing happened. This undoubtedly happened during the tenure of Dewberry's predecessor at Licensing and Regulation, John Corbley, but Corbley never raised the alarm with me, either. Nor did the examiners tell anybody else or, if they did, it never got beyond the guy who headed the Savings and Loan Division. They didn't blow the whistle—they didn't have the guts to come forth and say, "Look, my superiors aren't doing anything about this and there's a real problem."

But I know only too well that when you're the governor, the buck stops with you. The press ripped me apart. I had publicly maintained that I first learned of specific problems within the S&Ls in the spring of 1985, which as far as I was concerned was true. Nobody involved in regulating the S&L industry came to us with any knowledge of specific wrongdoing, or a specific concern or a specific problem until late April and May.

143. R.H. Melton and Tom Kenworthy, "Memo Warned Hughes about S&Ls; Consultant Had Cautioned About 'Self-Dealing' Thrifts," *Washington Post*, October 26, 1985.

When an aroused group of reporters gathered outside Government House waiting to speak with me about Liebmann's memo, Lou Panos, my press secretary, urged me to go outside and simply tell them what happened. That was the biggest public relations mistake in my career. I regret that. I shouldn't have let Lou talk me into that. A press secretary shouldn't have done it. I did what I have always done throughout my career: I told them the truth, saying I had forgotten about the memo. And why wouldn't I? It raised concerns, was sent through the appropriate channels and the response back to my staff was, essentially, there was nothing to worry about.

"I didn't think that memo sounded enough of an alarm," I said.[144] "You must remember: hindsight's very good. I get hundreds of memos, and I refer them to the departments involved." I also pointed out that even if the General Assembly and I had addressed issues raised in the Liebmann memo during the 1985 session, it was too late. The damage was already done. New legislation would not have become effective until July 1, or about a month and a half after the crisis began.

I do not regret being truthful; I wouldn't have answered any other way. But I might have done a better job putting that answer into context. The way I handled the Liebmann memo is what any normal, prudent executive would have done. Liebmann, in fact, was in my office more than once after this memo was written and I do not recall that he ever mentioned it or the savings and loan issue to me.

The backlash to the Liebmann memo, however, was harsh and unrelenting. S&L depositors became angrier than ever and started to hold demonstrations wherever I went to speak. All of the progress we had made in getting the S&Ls back on their feet and getting depositors their money back was suddenly overshadowed by accusations and recrimination. The implication was that I knew, or should have known, that some of these S&Ls were being run by crooks. Protestors began carrying signs that said things like, "Hughes is Political Deadmeat," or "Annapolisgate" and even one that featured side-by-side photos of me next to Richard Nixon. It was ugly.

On January 9, 1986, Woody Preston delivered his 475-page report. In a fifty-six-minute speech to a hushed, standing-room-only joint session of the General Assembly, he said the S&L crisis was caused "by an industry virtually unregulated by the state, by the criminal greed of S&L executives who stole millions of dollars from their own depositors, and by a hopelessly flawed system that permitted the industry to make and enforce its own rules."[145]

Woody's report placed most of the blame on S&L industry owners and executives and on the private and state regulators who were supposed to monitor the industry. But it also attached some of the blame to me ("for failing to heed early warnings about problems within the S&L industry") and more specifically to Johnny Johnson. It also criticized the assistant attorney general assigned to the S&L Division.

144. Richard H.P. Sia, "Hughes Insists Memo on S&Ls Rang No Alarm," *Baltimore Sun*, October 29, 1985.
145. John W. Frece and Brian Sullam, "S&L Report Cites Greed, System; Violations Spread Like 'Virus,' Prober Says," *Baltimore Sun*, January 10, 1986.

Preston said Brown was "too willing to listen to the pleas and excuses of poorly and criminally managed savings and loan associations" and saw himself "as a protector of the industry and failed to carry out regulatory responsibilities." It said Brown and his deputy, William S. LeCompte Jr., "time and again [were] presented ample evidence of wrongdoing, including criminal misconduct...[and] almost without exception the director took no action, paralyzed by the fear that regulatory sanctions of any major association would result in publicity that would denude the industry he felt bound to protect."[146]

Preston reserved some of his strongest condemnation for the Baltimore law firm of Venable, Baetjer and Howard, which he said was guilty of a conflict of interest because it had represented MSSIC while it simultaneously and unethically also represented Old Court, its subsidiaries and its three owners. Even more problematic, Preston said, was Venable's advice to MSSIC that caused it, in 1976, to begin providing insurance coverage to every account up to $100,000, instead of limiting its coverage to $100,000 for every depositor. That decision allowed depositors to obtain virtually unlimited insurance by simply opening multiple accounts.

I think Preston did a very good job on a very complicated issue in a relatively short time. My only complaint about his report is that he was too easy on the General Assembly. Legislators had the opportunity and the authority to provide stronger oversight to the S&L industry, but failed to do so. Yet Preston, I felt, only gave the legislature a slap on the wrist. I also think he was too easy on the S&L examiners for failing to blow the whistle.

We gradually worked our way out of the S&L problem throughout the remainder of 1986, right up to the end of my term. In fact, the full extent of the problems created by the criminals who ran these S&Ls were not finally put to rest until almost the end of the second term of my successor as governor, William Donald Schaefer.[147]

As we now know, the extent of the problem, the level of criminal self-dealing, greed and sleaze and the flagrant disregard by S&L executives for the money entrusted to their care, was just mind-boggling. S&L executives conspired to enrich themselves through a plethora of "cross-lending" practices, insider loans and fees generated from inflated loans on poor investments. The S&Ls sank depositors' money in anything and everything: in hotels, tomato canneries, a pig farm, a hardware store and all types of speculative residential and commercial developments, including one that was to be built on a contaminated landfill in Glen Cove, New York. S&L executives diverted depositor money into huge salaries, bonuses and fees for themselves, family members and colleagues. Levitt even used

146. Ibid.
147. Alec Matthew Klein, "S&L Meltdown," *Baltimore Sun*, May 7, 1995. As late as May 1995, a full decade after the crisis began, the state was still trying to get rid of the final $20 to $30 million in assets inherited with the demise of Old Court, including the swank Canterbury Hotel in Indianapolis. It wasn't until 1997 that the state was able to unload for $5 million a string of Jiffy Lube outlets once owned by Old Court. Michael Dresser, "Recouping of '85 losses nears end," *Baltimore Sun*, May 3, 1997.

money from Old Court depositors to hire a psychiatrist to help him deal with the tragedy of being a millionaire, Preston reported. It was theft on a grand scale.

Most of the crooks were eventually caught, tried, convicted and sent to jail. Several who were accused, including Merritt's Gerald Klein, were acquitted. Levitt pleaded guilty to twenty-five counts of embezzling and misappropriating $14.6 million of depositor funds and was sentenced to thirty years in prison. He served seven and a half before being paroled. His two partners, Jerome S. Cardin and Allan H. Pearlstein, were also convicted. Cardin was sentenced to fifteen years, although due to failing health, he only served one. Pearlstein was sentenced to eight years and served three.

But they weren't alone. At least thirteen executives at First Maryland S&L and at a number of other corrupt thrifts were convicted as part of this scandal. One of the most audacious was Tom J. Billman, who had been the chairman of Community Savings and Loan of Bethesda and a national real estate empire called EPIC. Community's collapse left twenty-two thousand depositors stranded and the state holding an $88 million problem. Billman spent nearly five years on the run until he was finally arrested in Paris in 1993. Tried and convicted in federal court, he was later sentenced to forty years in prison. The feds, however, were never sure if they had recovered all of the millions of dollars Billman had secretly stashed away in bank accounts in Switzerland and elsewhere.

The law firm of Venable, Baetjer and Howard ultimately settled a legal malpractice suit with the state for $27 million, which at the time was believed to be the second largest legal malpractice settlement in the nation's history.

Of the 102 S&Ls insured by MSSIC when the calamity began, a little more than half stayed in business by obtaining federal insurance. Another 14 or so merged with larger, federally insured thrifts. Of the rest, some became banks or merged with banks or were converted into mortgage companies or credit unions. The 6 worst S&Ls were forced into receivership and about 13 were simply dissolved.[148] The state finally got out of the deposit insurance business when the Maryland Deposit Insurance Fund, which at one point employed 170 people, closed its doors for good on July 1, 1989, a little more than five years after it was created.

It took that long before the last Old Court depositors got all of their money back, but eventually they all got their money back. The state had no legal obligation to do that, but we did it—not just for Old Court depositors, but for all of the depositors who were caught up in this mess.

It is difficult to say precisely what the crisis ultimately cost Maryland taxpayers, but it clearly was nowhere near the original estimates in 1985 of $500 million or more. State analysts estimated in 1998 that the final cost of the crisis to Maryland taxpayers was probably a quarter of that amount, or around $125 million, but it may well have been even less than that.[149]

148. Jon Morgan, "State Almost Out of the Business of Backing Savings Deposits," *Baltimore Evening Sun,* June 22, 1989.
149. Laura Sullivan, "S&L Files from '85 Still Yielding Clues by the Boxloads," *Baltimore Sun*, March 24, 1998.

Insofar as solving the problem, I believe my administration's handling of the S&L crisis was a success—a great success—and in the best interests of both the depositors and the taxpayers. But as a political matter, it was a failure. I don't know if there was any other way I could have handled it to avoid that. I was very pleased with the outcome—while they lost access to their money for a time, in the end the depositors didn't lose a penny, not one penny, other than the interest they might otherwise have accrued.

If I made any mistakes, it was in how I handled the press, particularly over the Liebmann memo. In retrospect, that could have been handled better and it cost me politically.

For a while after I left office, there would be some sensible depositors who would come up to me and thank me—not too many, but every once in a while someone would come up and thank me for saving their money for them.

18

The "Sunshine Kid" Runs Out of Steam

I DON'T KNOW IF YOU CAN stand the heat, but I have good news to report today,"[150] I sarcastically told members of the Maryland General Assembly in my eighth and final state of the state address in January 1986.

Speaking six days after Woody Preston delivered his damning savings and loan report to the legislature, I commented: "The music heard in these halls in recent weeks has had all the uplift of a dirge directed by a funeral director, played by an orchestra of morticians, and sung by a chorus of embalmers."

I was absolutely convinced the eight-month-old savings and loan ordeal had obscured and distorted the true "state of the state," hidden the successes the legislature and my administration had together steadily achieved and left citizens with the false impression that the state was spiraling downward when, in fact, the reverse was true.

"Today, I offer a different tune," I said. "Let me tell you something: the state of the state of Maryland—what we've done together and what we're going to do together in this session—is what Irving Berlin had in mind when he wrote *God Bless America*, and what Jackie Gleason means when he says, 'How sweet it is.'"

Then, in a line that many reporters—and most legislators—later described as uncharacteristic of me, I urged the delegates and senators to "close your eyes to some of the more recent signs of the times…signs that read, 'We're Going to Get You Harry'…and look upon me not as 'Harried Harry,' but as the 'Sunshine Kid.'" The previous seven or eight months had been so awful that my optimism surprised them.

In an unusually brief six-page speech, I went on to detail the many accomplishments we had achieved in my seven years in office, from broad-based tax relief to construction of major transportation projects and the creation of thousands of jobs; from establishing hospital Shock Trauma Centers to efforts to protect the Chesapeake Bay and the creation of an Institute Against Prejudice and Violence.

"If you can see one area of Maryland life that hasn't improved over the past seven years…then you have better eyes than I do," I said emphatically.

Quite intentionally, I never mentioned the three words "savings and loan." Everyone had heard enough about that already. I wanted to talk about everything

---

150. Governor Harry R. Hughes, state of the state message (House-Senate Joint Session, January 15, 1986).

else we had done, and what we still could do in my final year as governor. For two-thirds of a year, I felt like we focused on almost nothing but the savings and loan crisis and I felt we could no longer afford to be so myopic. The S&L problem was gradually, painfully working itself out. I felt we had done an admirable job extricating ourselves from a serious mess. The worst was clearly behind us. It was time to move on. After suffering through a deep national recession and severe budget cuts from the Reagan administration, our economy had finally recovered. For my final year—an election year—the state was blessed with a $118 million budget surplus. I intended to use it.

"Our state is healthy. Our state is sound. Its economy is thriving. Its future is bright. And that permits us to reach out to make life a little better, a little easier, for all of our citizens," I said.[151]

My budget for 1987 included $14 million for public schools and $3.5 million for "magnet schools" that were to be part of a long overdue desegregation plan in Prince George's County. It included more than $1 million to replace some of the federal funds cut from school breakfast and lunch programs for the children of poor families. My final budget expanded programs for battered spouses, displaced homemakers and victims of rape. It also included another $5 million for our Chesapeake Bay cleanup program; another 5 percent increase in welfare grants; and a 10 percent increase in General Public Assistance grants, which went to the most destitute men and women in our state. Again, my budget secretary, Lou Stettler, was one of the biggest proponents for this program, arguing that the need was high and the money well-used. Lou was typical of the quality, competence and compassion of the people I was fortunate to have working for me.

I put special emphasis on programs to provide improved shelter for the poor, piecing together $44 million from various sources to address the problem. It is hard to imagine today, but in 1986 there were still some thirty thousand Maryland homes without indoor plumbing. These funds were to be used for housing rehabilitation, home weatherization, abatement of lead paint that too often led to poisoning and expanded emergency housing.

An additional $2.2 million was appropriated for a program to fight what was then an epidemic of teenage pregnancies, a new approach that I acknowledged had been suggested to me by an unusual coalition of anti-abortion and pro-women's rights legislators.

"Instead of inflaming emotions and resorting to extremism—like those who are distorting and exploiting the issue—these legislators have used reason and logic to shape a sensible and sensitive answer to a difficult issue," I said.[152]

I even had enough money available that year to offer all state employees a 3.5 percent pay raise. And, I noted with some satisfaction, we could fund all of these new programs and initiatives without raising taxes.

151. Ibid.
152. Ibid.

Paying Off Depositors

Despite my best efforts to the contrary, the lingering S&L issue still hung over everyone. Even though most of the S&Ls were back in business, there were still nearly 112,000 depositor accounts frozen in three of the largest, and most corrupt, of the S&Ls: Old Court, Community Savings and Loan and First Maryland Savings and Loan. By January 1986, the depositors at those three institutions were angry, organized and motivated. They wanted their money back and they wanted it back now.

We had been able to get rid of three other troubled thrifts, Merritt, Chesapeake and Friendship, by selling them to Chase Manhattan, but we could not find an outside bank willing to buy Old Court, Community and First Maryland. So that January, we presented to the General Assembly a plan[153] to pay back the depositors their money gradually over the next four years, through December 31, 1989. We figured that would give the state enough time to try to identify and sell most of the assets in which these S&Ls had invested to offset the funds that taxpayers were advancing to pay back the depositors. We took a cautious approach, saying that if we had only moderate success in unloading the assets of these three S&Ls, the total cost to the state would be about $134 million. That figure—far, far below the earliest estimates of what backing the S&L deposits would ultimately cost the state—did not include any monies that might be recovered through a variety of civil suits then pending or contemplated against S&L executives and owners. The more the state recovered from those lawsuits, the lower the cost to taxpayers would be.

The initial reaction, especially among depositors, was that spreading this payout over four years was too long. But the legislature's own budget staff agreed that the more we speeded up the payout, the larger the cost would be to taxpayers. As a result, Speaker Cardin and Senate President Steinberg concurred with our payout plan.

One thing that was very helpful in all of this was the relationship that I encouraged between William S. Ratchford, director of the legislature's Department of Fiscal Services, and Stettler, my budget secretary. This cooperation really began years before the savings and loan crisis. Ratchford and Stettler really worked well together. Lou would give information to Bill in advance so he would have time to work it over and study it. It was a "good government" way of doing business. The importance of this relationship of trust is hard to overstate. I always thought that consensus was the best way to get things done in government, but there aren't too many people who want to do

---

153. We presented nine separate payout scenarios, four separate payout schedules and two different assumptions about the speed with which S&L assets could be sold.

that these days. Ratchford's support was helpful because he was really respected by the legislature. It would have been a mess otherwise.

But even a plan to free up money for the last major group of depositors was not enough to heal the political injuries I had suffered due to the S&L debacle. My careful and prudent handling of the crisis might have been rewarded had it not been for the bad press I received after the Liebmann memo became an issue. To me, that was the turning point—the one incident that really did me in.

In late November 1985, about a month after the Liebmann memo became public and a full year before the 1986 Senate election, a poll showed me trailing Baltimore Congresswoman Barbara A. Mikulski, one of the candidates for the Senate seat, by 20 percentage points. It was pretty obvious to everyone that I was in political trouble.

Yet I thought—naïvely, perhaps—that if we continued to handle the S&L problem well, that if the depositors got their money back and the cost to the state was minimal, that the public would recognize that the problem was not of our doing, but the solution was. Besides, I felt we had managed the state well for seven years and that the public would, in time, recognize that.

Another poll came out in the middle of the '86 legislative session pairing me against my potential Democratic primary opponents: Mikulski, Eighth District Congressman Michael D. Barnes of Montgomery County and Baltimore County Executive Donald P. Hutchinson. Of that group, I was dead last, with only 9 percent of the vote.

All I could do was remind reporters—and supporters—that I had been there before, back in 1978. "As I have said many times, I am living proof that polls are snapshots and I am not too concerned about them at this point," I told *Baltimore Evening Sun* columnist Peter Kumpa.[154]

Privately, I was worried. I felt like my record wasn't getting out to the public. Lou Panos, my press secretary, had served me well and faithfully for years. He was hardworking and understood the Annapolis scene as well as anyone. But I felt I needed someone with a different perspective to help me make my case for the U.S. Senate. So I moved Lou to another state job up in Baltimore and hired in his place a Baltimore public relations executive named M. Hirsh Goldberg. It didn't help.

Whenever I went somewhere to speak, I was greeted by groups of angry S&L depositors, many of them often wearing yellow lapel pins that said, "Victims of Trust" and carrying paper bags, signifying that they were left "holding the bag." My campaign staff, however, became convinced that some of these demonstrations were not really made up of angry depositors but were politically organized to embarrass me. I don't think there is any question about it.

Toward the end of that session we were finally able to announce that Mellon Bank had agreed to buy Community S&L, which freed up the funds for another

154. Peter Kumpa, "Hughes Faces Uphill Fight," *Baltimore Evening Sun*, February 21, 1986.

twenty-two thousand depositors. Senator Leo E. Green tried in vain to get legislation passed to make it a crime to lie to the General Assembly. Failing that, the legislature began the practice of recording all hearing testimony.

By the time the session ended in April, we had enacted a major overhaul of the S&L regulations[155] and set up a czar to oversee the industry; endorsed new Critical Areas' regulations to protect the shoreline of the Chesapeake Bay; enacted Maryland's first mandatory seatbelt law; and enacted the state's first minimum housing code.

Dealing with Irsay

We also created a new state Stadium Authority to plan for construction of a new stadium in Baltimore to keep the Orioles' baseball franchise from moving to another city. This was a real threat. A year earlier, on March 29, 1984, Robert Irsay, owner of the city's beloved football franchise, the Colts, packed the team's trophies and equipment into a fleet of Mayflower moving vans in the dead of night and moved the entire operation to Indianapolis.

Dealing with Irsay was almost impossible. Schaefer and I met with him frequently, but Irsay was invariably drinking or drunk when we met. Each meeting was like we never had the meeting before. It just started all over again. He was really a mess.

One time, Schaefer and I met Irsay at the hotel at Friendship Airport. The press had been hanging around so when we emerged from the meeting, we held an impromptu press conference. Irsay came out and said, "It was a good meeting: no booze or broads!" Boy, when my wife and daughter read that, they were livid.

Another time we met on Irsay's private jet. It was a big jet that had once been used by American Airlines to train their pilots. I think that airplane cost Irsay about $750,000 a year and contributed to his chronic financial problems. He'd often sit on that plane and drink.

The last time I met with Irsay was on a Sunday morning in Skokie, Illinois. Schaefer, Frank DeFrancis, my economic development secretary and I flew out there in a small private jet and met Irsay at a country club. As the meeting began, everyone ordered a drink and Irsay ordered a double martini. When the waiter came back to see if we wanted another round, Irsay's attorney ordered another one for his boss. I had never seen that happen before, certainly not at a business meeting.

We met all of Irsay's demands. DeFrancis had another meeting with him and reported to me afterwards that he was confident Irsay would keep the team in

---

155. The new S&L law contained a controversial provision that required about six thousand state officials, starting with me and including all top elected officials and the entire General Assembly, to disclose any withdrawals they, their spouses or their dependent children made from state-chartered S&Ls in the two months before the crisis began in May 1985. To my knowledge, there had never been any evidence of this occurring, but there had been a persistent rumor that unnamed state officials with insider knowledge had saved themselves by withdrawing their money early.

Baltimore. Three days later, Irsay moved the Colts to Indianapolis in the dead of night.

When the 1986 session finally ended, the *Baltimore Sun* editorialized that even though it was an election year, when customarily little is accomplished, the session "turned out to be surprisingly productive…The 90-day session was workmanlike and productive—terms that could be applied to the entire four-year record of this group of legislators."[156]

The Democratic Primary

As soon as it was over, I turned my full attention to the Senate race. The Democratic primary was about five months away. I had about $250,000 in my campaign treasury, but knew that would not be nearly enough. I immediately held a fundraiser at the Omni International Hotel in Baltimore. Four days later, on April 14, I returned home to Denton to formally announce my bid for the United States Senate.

For years, I had thought that a seat in the U.S. Senate might be the best job in politics. I was fifty-nine years old, had served nearly eight years as governor, six as transportation secretary and sixteen as a state legislator. I was proud of my record. I felt we had restored the reputation of the state. We had helped people who needed government's help: the poor, the elderly, those threatened by prejudice and hate and the mentally ill. We had enacted far-reaching legislation to protect the state's greatest natural resource, the Chesapeake Bay. We had weathered tough economic times and the collapse of the state's savings and loan industry and yet were still able to provide significant tax relief and keep our budget in balance.

On Monday, April 14, I stood on the steps of the Caroline County Courthouse, a couple blocks from the house where I grew up and just steps from both the soda fountain where I worked as a teenager and the building that was my first law office, and formally announced my candidacy for the United States Senate. The North Caroline County High School band played and about one hundred friends and other longtime local residents turned out for the event.

"I wish to offer my 30 years of experience and bring my vision and insight to the halls of Congress," I said. "I believe I have qualifications unmatched for understanding how best the federal and state governments can work together."[157] I noted that I had won eight of my previous nine election campaigns. "That record of eight wins and one loss is a far better percentage than I would have had as a pitcher," I joked.

---

156. Editorial, *Baltimore Sun*, April 8, 1986.
157. Leslie Walker, "Hughes Announces for Senate," *Baltimore Evening Sun*, April 14, 1986.

I knew the S&L crisis would be a problem for my campaign, so I hit the issue squarely: "I will show that what my administration and I have done is save the state of Maryland from the worst financial problem that ever faced us," I said. "The savings and loan industry, with its $8 billion in liabilities, presented the state with a liability larger than its entire budget. And yet today, 92 out of 102 savings and loans are back in full operation. Depositors have or in due course will receive back all insured monies and taxpayers will not see a tax increase."

But even this optimistic assessment was dogged by a group of angry demonstrators, who stood about fifty yards away behind a police line near the soda fountain where I had worked as a teenager chanting, "Harry is a liar. Harry is a liar." As you can imagine, I felt that was unfair, indecent and unappreciative of the steps we had taken to protect depositors' money. Mostly, I just thought it was sad; I felt I deserved better. This sort of attack was personally draining.

A poll released a week later showed Mikulski with 38 percent of the projected vote, Barnes with 17, me with 16 and Hutchinson with 11.

Some politicians seem to have a Teflon coating—nothing sticks to them. For me, the savings and loan scandal stuck like glue; I couldn't shake it. In mid-May, a year after the S&L crisis erupted and seven months after the Liebmann memo surfaced, I was still being interviewed about it. To try to break the cycle, I changed press secretaries and changed campaign managers, but the results didn't change.

Trailing badly, we tried in early June to turn the S&L issue from a negative to a positive with TV ads that cited our S&L successes by featuring gratified depositors who had received their money back. We also got something of a lift when Don Hutchinson dropped out of the race shortly before the official filing deadline for candidates.

"I sat there listening to Harry and I realized we were selling the same thing: fiscal responsibility, executives running large institutions [and] balanced budgets. We've done the same things. And the reality hit: with both of us in the race, we can't separate ourselves from our opponents," Hutchinson explained.

It was now a three-way race and I felt I had a chance of distinguishing myself from the front-runner, Mikulski. The fundamental problem, I realized, was that Barnes and I were vying for essentially the same group of voters who did not want Mikulski. As long as the two of us remained in the race, neither of us had a chance.

In July, I invited Barnes to meet with me in my offices on the fifteenth floor of the state office building in Baltimore. I thought there was a chance I might convince him to withdraw, but he declined, asking instead that I withdraw. I didn't consider it, although I probably should have. The tone of the meeting with Barnes was friendly—and we're still friends—but neither of us would budge.

In late August, with the September primary just a couple weeks away, I received the results of a private poll our campaign had commissioned.[158] It was neither surprising nor encouraging. It showed Mikulski with 45 percent of the vote, me with 23 percent, Barnes with 20 percent and 12 percent undecided.

My campaign team recommended that we try to recast the campaign as a two-person race: Mikulski versus Hughes, almost as if Barnes had dropped out. They advised that if I dropped out, it would benefit Barnes very little, but if he dropped out, it would benefit me a great deal.

On August 21, I was jarred by an editorial in the *Baltimore Evening Sun* endorsing Mikulski.[159] The editorial stated,

> *It goes without saying that the Evening Sun holds special affection for Harry Hughes. Twice we supported him for governor and he has fulfilled our expectations of restoring dignity and integrity to the top elective office in Maryland. But now he seems to suffer from career exhaustion—a perception rooted in large measure, no doubt, in the collapse of Maryland's S&L industry. This calamity was not Hughes's responsibility, and it is hard to see how he could have dealt with it any differently, once it happened, than he did.*

I suspect the perception of me that summer was of an elected official who was tired, worn down and—as the *Evening Sun* suggested—a victim of "career exhaustion." That may be one way to describe it. I probably felt the Senate campaign was a lost cause and I guess it showed.

The only surprise in the primary election results was how badly I finished. Mikulski won seventeen of the state's twenty-four major jurisdictions and finished with 307,876 votes, more than Barnes and I had together. Barnes finished second with 195,086 votes and I was a distant third with 88,908.[160]

Mikulski, of course, went on to win the General Election against Republican Linda Chavez, 663,566 (60 percent) to 433,741 (39 percent). Despite the lopsided margin, Chavez carried thirteen of the state's twenty-four major jurisdictions, including the state's five westernmost counties and eight of the nine counties on the Eastern Shore.

During that campaign, I had no good idea how I could cut into her lead. Every depositor got every cent back, yet the savings and loan issue just killed me. I don't think there was anything I could have done that could have really changed it.

---

158. The poll of 404 registered voters was conducted on August 21–22 by Cambridge Survey Research.

159. Editorial, *Baltimore Evening Sun*, August 21, 1986.

160. Five other candidates received vote totals of 9,350 or less: Debra Hanania Freeman of Baltimore County; A. Robert Kauffman of Baltimore City; Edward M. Olszewski of Baltimore County; Boyd E. Sweatt of Charles County; and Leonard E. Trout Jr. of Baltimore City.

19

Reflections

Wᴴᴇɴ I ʙᴇᴄᴀᴍᴇ Mᴀʀʏʟᴀɴᴅ'ꜱ ꜰɪꜰᴛʏ-ꜱᴇᴠᴇɴᴛʜ governor, I initially had two objectives: one was to reinvigorate the state's then stagnant economy and the other was to restore Maryland's reputation for integrity in government.

I feel we accomplished those goals—and much more.

By the time I left office, all of the numbers that should have been up, such as job growth or per capita income, were up, and all the numbers that should have been down, such as unemployment and the percent of Marylanders living below the poverty level, were down. We kept the state's AAA bond rating despite unprecedented cutbacks in federal aid and the worst economic downturn since the Great Depression. At the same time, we provided Marylanders with $1 billion in various forms of tax relief.

As proud as I am of those accomplishments, I am prouder still of our overall approach to state government. Maryland's reputation was pretty bad nationally. I think we turned that around. In an article I wrote for the *Baltimore Sun*[161] upon leaving office, here's how I described our record:

> I believe we have restored integrity to all phases of state government. I am proud that no scandal, no sense of impropriety and no abuse of power have touched any of my staff or appointments. The result is that in an age when scandals have regularly wracked federal, state and municipal governments, Maryland can once again be proud.

The word "integrity" meant more to me than simply being free of scandal. It meant doing the right thing. That often meant caring for our fellow citizens who were unable to care for themselves. In my 1982 state of the state address, I said with some satisfaction:

> We can assign a single word to what Maryland state government means to people today: integrity. We have restored integrity to government. We are honest people dealing honestly with the people's business…It means doing what is right at any personal cost. It means taking personal risk for public good. It means not taking advantage of public fears, but taking advantage of every opportunity to put

---

161. Hughes, "The Record and the Legacy."

real fears to rest. It means looking not backwards, but ahead. It means not settling for popular remedies, but proper ones. It means displaying courage when it is not absolutely demanded; giving when no giving is asked for; responding when the call to respond is only faintly heard.[162]

So when people ask me what I feel were the important contributions of my years as the state's chief executive, the programs that come first to mind are those that helped our elderly residents, or those who were sick or disabled or who were both without work and without hope. I strove to meet what former Vice President Hubert H. Humphrey properly described as government's "moral test": "caring for those in the dawn, the twilight and the shadows of life."[163]

In eight years, we raised grants to welfare recipients by 55 percent, including the three largest welfare grant increases in state history. We also began a process of getting people off welfare rolls through a new program that offered job training and job opportunities in the private sector. This shift toward a strategy of preparing welfare recipients to help themselves through job training and work became, in later years, the way the entire welfare system in America was refocused and changed.

We doubled Maryland's health care budget, concentrating on new services for mothers and their babies, for the mentally retarded and the disabled. We established the Gateway program, which provided one-stop access to government services for the elderly—aging citizens who prior to this program often did not know what services were available. We worked to deinstitutionalize the mentally ill, but not before we were sure we had programs in place to allow them to live safely and securely in communities. We developed additional measures to protect abused children, prevent teen pregnancies and help battered spouses.

While it is fair to assess the conduct of elected officials by how they prioritized the money or other resources at their disposal, a career should not be judged by dollars and cents alone. For example, we put lots of money into programs to clean up the Chesapeake Bay, but I do not think those expenditures were nearly as important as the "Save the Bay" ethic we instilled in the people of Maryland. That has had a more lasting impact than any specific Bay cleanup program we could have enacted or proposed. I believe we can rightfully claim some credit for making Marylanders more conscious about the need to protect our environment.

162. Governor Harry Hughes, state of the state message (House-Senate Joint Session, January 20, 1982).
163. Hughes, "Record and Legacy."

Emphasis on Appointments

In a more subtle, behind-the-scenes way, I tried to steadily improve Maryland's record of governmental and judicial appointments. I wanted to distance myself from the criticism leveled at my predecessors—and some of my successors, for that matter—that politics rather than performance was too often the criteria for gubernatorial appointments. In my first inaugural address, I promised that my appointments would be "based on professional competence and a common commitment to change. Experience will be valued, but so will vision, initiative and altruism."[164]

Over eight years, I made more than seven thousand appointments. Working first with Appointments Secretary Louise Keelty and later with her highly regarded successor, Connie Beims, we simply looked for the best people available for the jobs.

I tried to reflect this approach in my own Cabinet by appointing more women and blacks. I increased the number of women appointed to various policy, advisory and regulatory boards and commissions from 16 percent under my predecessor to almost 30 percent, and black representation from 13 percent to 23 percent.[165]

These aren't just statistics: they are a reflection of how I believe leaders within the executive and judicial branches of government should be selected.

I was not only determined to appoint more blacks, women and other minorities, but to do so without regard to party affiliation. I started the practice of interviewing every judicial nominee before making a selection—a practice that, to the best of my knowledge, has been followed by each of my successors. During my two terms as governor, I conducted more than 500 interviews with judicial nominees and appointed 108 of the 217 positions then in the state judicial system. By the time I left office, Maryland ranked first in the nation in the appointment of blacks to the judiciary and was among the top ten states in the country in the appointment of women to the bench.[166]

Legislative Legacy

As I reflect back on my overall career, however, it seems that some of the achievements during my sixteen years as a legislator rank right up there with the major initiatives of my years as governor. The Cooper-Hughes-Agnew

164. Governor Harry R. Hughes, inaugural address (January 17, 1979).
165. Ibid.
166. Hughes, "The Record and the Legacy."

tax reform, for example, was a great accomplishment. That single piece of legislation has had long-term effects on the state, including instituting a system of graduated income taxes, authorizing a piggyback tax to keep local governments from over-reliance on property taxes and providing state financial support for local police protection efforts. I imagine it would be difficult, if not impossible, to get any part of this legislation through today, much less all of it in a single bill.

I am also proud of the change in the way funding for education is allocated, which resulted from a commission I chaired back in the 1960s. Rather than continuing to allocate education funds through the practice of the state setting the salaries for teachers, we recommended that state funding be apportioned on a per-pupil basis. Over the years, that change helped equalize state spending on education, allowing poorer counties to provide a quality of education approaching that of richer counties.

General Assembly Change

As an institution, however, the General Assembly has changed in several important respects since I was a young legislator. In my day, we met during the session and then a joint Legislative Council, with ten members from each house, studied more complex issues during the interim. Now, the General Assembly has become more full-time, with standing committees that meet regularly all year long.

The membership of the General Assembly has also changed. It is, of course, much larger than it was when I first arrived a half-century ago, thanks to the one man, one vote ruling of the U.S. Supreme Court, and it is considerably more diverse, with more women and more African Americans and other minorities. Rural regions of the state, such as the Eastern Shore, no longer hold the power they had when I first arrived in 1955.

These days, there are fewer lawyers in the assembly. Some, I am sure, would say that is a good thing, but I disagree. I always thought lawyers really added something to the legislative debate because they had studied and practiced the law and were familiar with the legal code.

More legislators now depend on their legislative jobs as their primary source of income. An increasing number have become career politicians who are often overly concerned about how their votes will affect their political future. When I started, legislators were only paid $1,800 a year and when their legislative duties were done, they went back home to their real full-time jobs. It was much more of a citizen legislature then.

One of the big changes since the years when I was in the legislature is that these days the budget and many other pieces of legislation are routinely sent to conference committees to resolve House-Senate differences. We never let the budget go to a conference committee because we felt that put too much power in the hands of just four people. Remember, when you get a conference committee with three on each side, it only takes four people to decide how the state is going to spend the taxpayers' money.

Moreover, under legislative rules, once the House and Senate receives a conference committee report on the floor, all that legislators can do is accept it or reject it. It is no longer in a legal posture that allows for amendment. These days, they have a lot of conference committees, which is not such a great idea, in my opinion.

The other obvious change is the way the press now covers Annapolis, making it much more difficult for a governor or a legislator—but particularly a governor—to do their job. When everything you do and every sentence you utter is scrutinized by the press, it has an effect. That didn't used to be the case. When I first went to Annapolis, some of the reporters roomed with legislators and they often partied together. I'm not sure I would recommend such a cozy relationship today. But I will say that in my early days there was a lot more off-the-record interaction, a much closer relationship and often even a sense of friendship. Most importantly, there was a degree of mutual understanding. You could be yourself and not be worried that anything you did or said would automatically wind up in the morning newspaper. The reporters had a better sense of who you were, where you came from and why you supported or opposed certain issues.

Today, the size of the press corps has increased and you always have to be on your guard. I don't know that it is necessarily a change for the better, but I can't say it is a change for the worse. It is a change that just makes being in public office more difficult than it used to be and, particularly as governor, you have less of a private life. I think that, in turn, makes it harder to attract good people to public life. A lot of people who might otherwise be interested just say to themselves, "I don't need that."

Separation of Powers

One aspect of my approach to being governor that surprised even some of my oldest colleagues in the legislature was my willingness to share power with the General Assembly. In my first inaugural address, I clearly stated my understanding of and respect for the separation of powers between the executive and legislative branches.

"While I will fulfill my responsibility to provide leadership and introduce programs, I will not undermine the legislative process," I promised. "My influence will rest upon persuasion based on facts, not manipulation by political pressure."[167]

167. Governor Harry R. Hughes, inaugural address (January 17, 1979).

This approach left me open to criticism that I had abdicated power to the legislature, or that I too easily allowed lawmakers to redraft my proposals or that I was simply weak. At first, I may have gone too far in this regard. In time, I restored more balance to this executive-legislative relationship. But even in retrospect, I have no regrets. I had a pretty good working relationship with the legislature, and my staff did as well. I had the view that the legislature always had the final say. They can override your vetoes or they can put bills in that mandate certain expenditures (as long as they attach a tax proposal to it). They really have the final say. I always acknowledged that and tried to work with them.

The way our government was set up, the legislature is supposed to be the policy-making body of the state. It was intentional, in order to get results, which is really what I was interested in. I think it worked for me because I had good working relationships with House Speaker Ben Cardin and, for the most part, with Senate Presidents Mickey Steinberg and Jim Clark and with their respective committee chairs. So, I think it worked. And having the process work was really all I was interested in.

The Rise of Partisanship

I am sad to say I do not believe that approach would work today. The political atmosphere in Annapolis has become too partisan and polarized. It seems to be infected with the same partisan poison that has almost ruined the ability of the U.S. Congress to function efficiently. I find it unfortunate and do not know how we will ever be able to pull ourselves back to become a more collegial, constructive, cooperative government.

Let me give you one example. During my first term, I hired Tom Schmidt to be my budget secretary. I didn't really know him well, but he was intelligent and a really good budget guy. Tom had strong opinions about things, a no-nonsense attitude and was very conservative. But I have no idea what Tom Schmidt's political affiliation was then or is now. In fact, I didn't know the political affiliation of many of my staff. I suppose I assumed most were Democrats, but I never asked them. And I never asked a candidate I was interviewing for a judgeship what his or her party affiliation was. It just didn't matter to me to know. It wasn't important.

When I was in the legislature, I served under two Republican governors, Theodore McKeldin and Spiro Agnew. Both brought in their own staff and department heads, of course, but neither one of them did what Republican Governor Robert L. Ehrlich Jr. has done in terminating many state employees simply because they were Democrats or were considered too close to the previous Democratic administrations. Terminating long-serving and dedicated civil servants is not only ethically wrong, it robs the governor of precisely the kind of experienced help that is necessary for government to function properly.

This rise in partisanship too often leads to governmental paralysis. In such an atmosphere, too much energy is expended by Democrats and Republicans blaming each other for the lack of cooperation and progress. Increasingly in Annapolis, just like in Congress, legislators vote along party lines. In the six years I was floor leader in the Senate, I doubt that I made a "party call" more than five times. This new partisan approach to government often fails to produce results.

One recent example that has touched me personally involved legislation that would have opened the way for scientific research using stem cells—research that many scientists believe could produce cures for some of the most debilitating diseases of our time, such as Parkinson's and diabetes. My wife, Pat, suffers from Parkinson's, as does my former chief of staff, Johnny Johnson, and my grandson, Andrew, suffers from juvenile diabetes. They are tragic diseases, yet efforts to allow this research to continue have been stymied for partisan and religious reasons that have become too intertwined.

A Workmanlike Career

For a guy who simply wanted to play baseball, I sure ended up with a long career in politics and public life. It was an unexpected journey. As I look back on it now, I think it was a successful career. The word the *Sun* used in one of its editorials— "workmanlike"—is how I think of my tenure as Maryland's governor, as secretary of transportation and as a state legislator. I was really interested in the results. That guided me more than anything else. And I was never very much concerned about or aware of the political part of it, for better or worse. I really was never motivated to get publicity or to do something for a political reason. If I had been worried about political fallout, as a legislator representing the Eastern Shore I never would have voted in the 1960s for civil rights bills. If I wanted to go along just to get along, I wouldn't have resigned over Victor Frenkil's efforts to tamper with that subway contract.

I made every effort to have competent, compassionate and freethinking people on my Cabinet and staff. I was never afraid to hear the unvarnished truth or to get an honest opinion, even if critical, from someone who worked for me or whom I had appointed. From my legislative days to my years at the Department of Transportation and through my eight years as governor, I always had the same approach to my assistants, deputies, staff and Cabinet secretaries. They all were encouraged to feel free to voice their opinion to me. And by that I mean they were free to disagree with me. Some executives make it clear they do not want to hear dissenting views, but I really wanted to know what the people I had placed in leadership positions thought. In fact, I used to joke that I did my best to surround myself with people who were smarter than me. When you operate this way, you are not only likely to solicit the best possible advice, but you minimize the amount of political back-biting that occurs on almost any executive staff.

One of the advantages I had throughout my career was that I always knew there was another life for me outside of politics. With that always in the back of my mind, I never was primarily concerned with getting reelected or staying in office.

Even in retirement, I have continued my work on behalf of issues that have always been important to me, such as protecting the Chesapeake Bay and our environment. These days I serve as chairman of the Board of the Eastern Shore Land Conservancy, which, to date, has preserved more than thirty-seven thousand acres of Eastern Shore farm and woodland. I also serve as chairman of the Board of Visitors for the University of Maryland Center for Environmental Studies and helped create and became the first president of the Maryland Center for Agro-Ecology, which is bridging the gap between the farming and environmental communities. From time to time I still get summoned back to public service, such as when Governor Parris Glendening drafted me to chair a special task force to determine the causes of toxic Pfiesteria in Lower Eastern Shore tributaries.

So I like to think of my career as workmanlike, devoted to accomplishing things and caring for people who need government's help. I never felt like I had to work at being known for honesty and integrity—that just went with it. In my entire career, through thousands of votes, I can recall only one occasion that I regretted a vote I cast, and that was my vote against the bill to eliminate the ban on mixed marriages—a vote I reversed the next day. Whether it was fighting for civil rights, or resigning years later over the disputed Baltimore subway contract or making the decision that the state should assume responsibility for saving the money of thousands of savings and loan depositors, it was never hard for me to do what I believed was right.

In my eighth and final state of the state address to the General Assembly and the people of Maryland, I bid an early goodbye to my years in public life.

> Let me tell you how much it has meant to me to serve with you. You've been terrific! And while there have been times we fought, we pretty much always fought by the rules and fought fairly. Most importantly, we made things happen and we made things better.
>
> Every governor has his own style, and mine has always been to respect the legislature, to seek the counsel of your leaders, and then to hold my own counsel: to try to decide on every issue whether it was fair to the people, good for the people, and worthy of the judgment it was in my power to render.
>
> Some say I should have twisted more arms to get my way. Well, I'm not a wrestler—I was a pitcher.
>
> I've always believed, and still believe, that a governor's job is not to play to the crowd, but to do the hard work away from the glare, to do it honestly and objectively, with sensitivity and caring, and then, and only then, stand before the cameras and take the heat.[168]

I still feel that way.

---

168. Governor Harry Hughes, state of the state message (House-Senate Joint Session, January 15, 1986).

About John W. Frece

JOHN W. FRECE HAS SPENT most of his career as a newspaper and wire service reporter and in other jobs associated with government and politics. He became the Maryland State House bureau chief for United Press International in July 1978, starting the same day as the candidate filing deadline for the 1978 primary—the election in which Harry Roe Hughes scored his stunning upset. Frece, who became the *Baltimore Sun*'s State House bureau chief in 1984, covered all eight years of the Hughes administration, all eight of the term of his successor, William Donald Schaefer, and the first year of the administration of Parris N. Glendening.

In a journalism career that began with the *Reston Times* in Northern Virginia and included one year covering the Virginia General Assembly for UPI in Richmond, Frece subsequently reported on seventeen legislative sessions in Annapolis and some or all of the terms of five Maryland governors. He left reporting in 1996 to become communications director for Governor Glendening. For the final six years of Glendening's term, he was the chief spokesman for the governor's signature "Smart Growth" land use program. In 2003, Frece moved to the University of Maryland, where he is associate director of the National Center for Smart Growth Research and Education.

Frece is married to the children's book author Priscilla Cummings. They have two children, William, twenty, and Hannah, seventeen, and live in Annapolis, Maryland.

Index